Jungian Psychology and the Human Sciences

This volume brings together selected papers from the 2021 IAJS conference focusing on Jungian psychology's place within the broader human science field, with contributions providing an interdisciplinary examination of fields such as psychoanalysis, feminism, critical thought, and eco-psychology.

The historical foundations of Jungian thought in phenomenology, hermeneutics, the significance of imagination, and the body's genetics open the book with outstanding essays from both renowned and aspiring new scholars. Chapters highlighting matters of current social, political, and ecological considerations shed light on the intersections between Jungian psychology and much contemporary thought in these fields. The healing process takes center stage in the last part of the book, which will interest readers involved with the broader psychotherapy field.

With rigorous and scholarly contributions from a variety of international figures in analytical psychology, this book will be of great interest to all Jungian and depth psychology scholars, students, and analysts in training, as well as readers in the broader human science psychology field interested in current Jungian psychology and phenomenology.

Roger Brooke, PhD, ABPP, is Professor Emeritus of Psychology at Duquesne University, Pittsburgh and a Board Certified Clinical Psychologist and psychotherapist in private practice. He is author of numerous articles on Jungian psychology, phenomenology, psychoanalysis, and psychotherapy, but is best known for his book *Jung and Phenomenology*, Classic Edition (Routledge 1991/2015).

Camilla Giambonini, PhD, is a lecturer in forensic psychology at the University of Gloucestershire and a member of the Board of Directors of the International Association for Jungian Studies. Her PhD thesis focused on teenage sexting and the psychosocial articulation of Jungian psychology. Currently, she is a psychodynamic psychotherapy trainee at the Society of Analytical Psychology in London.

Brianna Stich, MA, is a fourth-year doctoral student in clinical psychology at Duquesne University. Brianna is currently writing her dissertation on hoarded homes and the phenomenological and psychoanalytic meanings of their spaces, things, and interrelationship with the bodies which dwell there.

Jungian Psychology and the Human Sciences

Edited by Roger Brooke, Camilla Giambonini, and Brianna Stich

Routledge
Taylor & Francis Group

LONDON AND NEW YORK

Designed cover image: Getty Images

First published 2025
by Routledge
4 Park Square, Milton Park, Abingdon, Oxon OX14 4RN

and by Routledge
605 Third Avenue, New York, NY 10158

Routledge is an imprint of the Taylor & Francis Group, an informa business

British Library Cataloguing-in-Publication Data
A catalogue record for this book is available from the British Library

Library of Congress Cataloging-in-Publication Data
Names: Brooke, Roger, 1953- editor. | Giambonini, Camilla, editor. | Stich, Brianna, editor.
Title: Jungian psychology and the human sciences / edited by Roger Brooke, Camilla Giambonini and Brianna Stich.
Description: Abingdon, Oxon ; New York, NY : Routledge, 2025. | Includes bibliographical references and index. |
Identifiers: LCCN 2024030638 (print) | LCCN 2024030639 (ebook) | ISBN 9781032694580 (hardback) | ISBN 9781032694993 (paperback) | ISBN 9781032694603 (ebook)
Subjects: LCSH: Jungian psychology. | Social sciences.
Classification: LCC BF173.J85 J8925 2025 (print) | LCC BF173.J85 (ebook) | DDC 150.19/54--dc23/eng/20241015
LC record available at https://lccn.loc.gov/2024030638
LC ebook record available at https://lccn.loc.gov/2024030639

ISBN: 978-1-032-69458-0 (hbk)
ISBN: 978-1-032-69499-3 (pbk)
ISBN: 978-1-032-69460-3 (ebk)

DOI: 10.4324/9781032694603

Typeset in Times New Roman
by SPi Technologies India Pvt Ltd (Straive)

Contents

About the Authors

Marco Balenci, PhD, studied bio-medical sciences and psychology at the Universities of Florence and Rome. He is an analyst, a member of the Italian Association for Analytical Psychology (AIPA), American Psychological Association (APA), International Association for Analytical Psychology (IAAP), and International Association of Jungian Studies (IAJS). He was a child psychotherapist in foster-care homes for 30 years and an honorary juvenile judge for 25 years. He has taught and researched at the Universities of Pisa and Rome. He is a former secretary of the Centre for Historical Studies of Psychoanalysis and Psychiatry in Florence and is currently in charge of the Tuscan section of AIPA. He is a reviewer for international journals and has a private practice in Florence. Dr Balenci wrote the chapter on The Self for the Italian *Treatise of Analytical Psychology* (ed. Aldo Carotenuto, 1992), co-edited five academic books from the University of Rome, and edited the Italian version of Anna Freud's biography by Elizabeth Young-Bruehl. He published papers in Italian——including about dreams, Jungian typology, realistic anxiety, Freudian technique, psychic breakdown, identification in the analytic relationship. His research interests mainly concern theoretical topics and psychosomatics. Recent publications include "From Jungian Attitude-Types to a Comprehensive Model of Diseases" (2020); "Lay Analyst Elida Evans in the 1920s United States: A Story Never Told" (2021); "Jung's and Groddeck's Analytic Practice: Alternative Methods That Have Prevailed over Freud's Psychoanalysis" (2022); and "The Analytic Methods of Groddeck and Jung in Light of the Philosophy of Nature" (2022).

Fanny Brewster, PhD, is a Jungian analyst and Professor at Pacifica Graduate Institute. She is a writer of nonfiction including *African Americans and Jungian Psychology: Leaving the Shadows* (Routledge, 2017), and *Archetypal Grief: Slavery's Legacy of Intergenerational Child Loss* (Routledge, 2018) and *The Racial Complex: A Jungian Perspective on Culture and Race* (Routledge, 2019) Her poems have recently been published in *Psychological Perspectives Journal* where she was the Featured Poet. Dr. Brewster is a lecturer and workshop presenter on Jungian related topics that address Culture, Diversity and Creativity. She is a faculty member at the New York C. G. Jung Foundation and the Philadelphia Association of Jungian Analysts.

Robin McCoy Brooks is a Jungian Analyst in private practice in Seattle, WA. She is the Co-editor-in-Chief of the *International Journal of Jungian Studies* and serves on the Board of Directors of the International Association for Jungian Studies. Robin is also a founding member of the New School for Analytical Psychology and active analyst member of the Inter-Regional Society of Jungian Analysts. Robin's book entitled *Psychoanalysis, Catastrophe and Social Reform* is currently in production (Routledge, 2021, Philosophy and Psychoanalysis Series, Ed. Jon Mills).

Betsy Cohen, LCSW, PhD, analyst member and faculty at the C. G. Jung Institute of San Francisco, is the author of *The Snow White Syndrome: All about Envy* (Macmillan, 1987). She has been on 120 TV and radio shows, including *Oprah!* She's also published articles in *The Jung Journal* titled "The Intimate Self-Disclosure," "Emmanuel Levinas and Depth Psychotherapy," "Jung's Answer to Jews," "Dr. Jung and His Patients," "The Flexible Frame: Holding the Patient in Mind" and "The Skinless Analyst: Mutual Transparency in Psychoanalysis." Her paper "Tangled Up in Blue: A Revision of Complex Theory" is in *Why and How We (Still) Read Jung* (J. Kirsch and M. Stein, eds., Routledge, 2013). Her current interest is exploring how ancient wisdom, particularly the erotic dialogues of Plato and the Song of Songs, could be incorporated into contemporary relational Jungian psychotherapy.

Gwenda Euvrard, MSocSc (Clin Psych), has practised for over 20 years as a clinical psychologist and Jungian psychotherapist in Makhanda, a vibrant university town and arts and cultural centre in the Eastern Cape of South Africa. Her practice room has views across her large secluded garden to the veld. She is fortunate to spend a great deal of time in various South African wilderness areas, frequently among the African elephants in nearby Addo, and has long had an interest in how our wilderness encounters bring us into deepened and expanded living.

Erik Goodwyn, MD, is an Attending Physician at Eastern State Hospital in Lexington, Kentucky, Clinical Faculty at University of Kentucky, Clinical Associate Professor at the Billings Clinic, part of the WWAMI University of Washington School of Medicine – Billings, Montana, affiliate, Department of Psychiatry, and Adjunct Professor for University of Louisville, Department of Psychiatry. He has authored numerous publications in the field of consciousness studies, Jungian psychology, neuroscience, mythology, philosophy, anthropology, and the psychology of religion. He is co-editor-in-chief of the *International Journal of Jungian Studies*, and his published books include: *The Neurobiology of the Gods: How the Brain Shapes the Recurrent Imagery of Myth and Dreams* (Routledge, 2012), *A Psychological Reading of the Anglo-Saxon Poem* Beowulf: *Understanding Everything as Story* (Mellen, 2014), *Healing Symbols in Psychotherapy: A Ritual Approach* (Routledge, 2016), *Magical Consciousness*, co-authored with anthropologist Susan Greenwood (Routledge, 2017), *Understanding Dreams and Other Spontaneous Images: the Invisible Storyteller* (Routledge, 2018—Finalist in the 2019 International Association for Jungian Studies Book Award), and *Archetypal Ontology*, with philosopher and psychoanalyst Jon Mills (Routledge, 2023). He has delivered more than 60 lectures, workshops, and essays in peer-reviewed journals on the above topics and has presented at conferences on these topics at sites in the United States, Switzerland and Ireland.

David J. Halperin received his BA in Semitic Studies from Cornell University in 1969, his Ph.D. in Near Eastern Studies from the University of California at Berkeley in 1977. From 1976 until his retirement in 2000, he taught Judaic Studies in the Department of Religious Studies, University of North Carolina at Chapel Hill. He is the author of five books on Jewish messianism and mysticism; *Intimate Alien: The Hidden Story of the UFO* (Stanford University Press, 2020); and the coming-of-age novel *Journal of a UFO Investigator* (Viking Press, 2011; translated into Spanish, Italian, and German). He lives in Durham, NC, with his wife Rose, and blogs on UFOs, religion, and related subjects at www.davidhalperin.net.

Lucy Huskinson, PhD, Professor of Psychology, Bangor University, UK. Author of *Nietzsche and Architecture* (Bloomsbury, in press), *Architecture and the Mimetic Self* (Routledge, 2018), *Nietzsche and Jung* (Routledge, 2004).

Stanton Marlan, PhD, ABPP, FABP, is a Jungian analyst and clinical psychologist with a passion for the study of dreams and alchemy. He holds two PhDs from Duquesne University, in Clinical Psychology and Philosophy. He is Board Certified in Psychoanalysis by the American Board and Academy of Psychoanalysis, and past President of that organization. He is a training analyst with the Inter-Regional Society of Jungian Analysts and President of the Pittsburgh Society of Jungian Analysts. He is an adjunct professor of psychology at Duquesne and supervises doctoral candidates in its Psychology Clinic. Dr. Marlan has lectured widely and has been a keynote speaker at several universities and Jungian training programs. He has taught at the C. G. Jung Institute in Zürich and is the author of numerous publications in Jungian psychology, including *The Black Sun: The Alchemy and Art of Darkness*.

Robert D. Romanyshyn, PhD, Duquesne University, Emeritus Professor, Pacifica Graduate Institute. Affiliate Member, The Inter-Regional Society of Jungian Analysts, 2015. Society for Humanistic Psychology, American

Psychological Association, Division 32, Distinguished Lifetime Achievement Award, 2022. Numerous books include *Victor Frankenstein: The Monster and the Shadows of Technology: The Frankenstein Prophecies* (2019) London: Routledge, *The Wounded Researcher* (2007). New Orleans: Spring journal Books, re-published by Routledge in 2021, *Technology as Symptom and Dream* (1989) London, New York: Routledge.

Mark Saban PhD, trained with the Independent Group of Analytical Psychologists, with whom he is a senior analyst, working in London and Oxford. He is also a lecturer in Jungian and post-Jungian studies in the Department of Psychosocial and Psychoanalytic Studies, University of Essex. Mark co-edited (with Emilija Kiehl and Andrew Samuels) *Analysis and Activism: Social and Political Contributions of Jungian Psychology* (Routledge 2016) and wrote *Two Souls Alas: Jung's Two Personalities and the Making of Analytical Psychology* (Chiron 2019), which won the International Association of Jungian Studies' Best Book of 2019.

Andrew Samuels is the first recipient of the C. G. Jung Award of the International Association for Jungian Studies, which he co-founded in 2002. He was described by the editor of American Imago as "perhaps the most celebrated of today's Jungian analysts." Andrew is a Training Analyst of the Society of Analytical Psychology, in private practice in London, and was Professor of Analytical Psychology at the University of Essex. He was Chair of the UK Council for Psychotherapy and the founder of Psychotherapists and Counsellors for Social Responsibility. His many books have been translated into 21 languages, including: *Jung and the Post-Jungians* (1985); *Psychopathology* (1989); and *Politics on the Couch* (2001). His latest books are *A New Therapy for Politics?* (2015) and *Analysis and Activism: Social and Political Contributions of Jungian Analysis* (edited with Emilija Kiehl and Mark Saban, 2016).

Adam J. Schneider, PhD, is a licensed psychologist and mental health counselor in private practice in Washington State. He completed his PhD in clinical psychology at Pacifica Graduate Institute. His research interests include archetypal psychology, Lacanian psychoanalysis, treatment of psychosis, and intersections with Catholicism.

Susan E. Schwartz, PhD, trained in Zurich, Switzerland, as a Jungian analyst. is also a clinical psychologist and member of the International Association of Analytical Psychology. She presents to numerous Jungian conferences and teaching programs in the United Sates and worldwide. Susan has articles in several journals and chapters in books on Jungian analytical psychology. Her current book, published by Routledge, is translated into several languages and into Ukrainian this April. It is entitled *The Absent Father Effect on Daughters, Father Desire, Father Wounds*. Another book will be published by Routledge in 2023, entitled *The Imposter Syndrome and The*

"As-If" Personality in Analytical Psychology: The Fragility of Self. Her Jungian analytical practice is in Paradise Valley, Arizona, US and her website is www.susanschwartzphd.com.

Michael P. Sipiora, PhD, had a 40-year academic career with professorships at Duquesne University and Pacifica Graduate Institute. He studied with James Hillman while a graduate student at the University of Dallas. Dr. Sipiora's publications and teaching have largely been in the areas of archetypal psychology, and Heideggerian phenomenology. He is the author of *Psychological Citizenship and Democracy: The Political Relevance of James Hillman's Archetypal Psychology* (2023). He is currently an independent scholar and psychotherapist in private practice.

John White, PhD, is a Jungian psychoanalyst and licensed professional counselor in private practice in Pittsburgh, PA, as well as Scholar-in-Residence at the Simon Silverman Phenomenology Center in the Gumberg Library, Duquesne University, Pittsburgh, PA. Dr. White was a philosophy professor for 20-plus years prior to becoming a Jungian psychoanalyst, specializing in phenomenology, environmental philosophy, philosophy of history, and ethics. His forthcoming book examines the clinical concept of adaptation in Robert Langs and Carl Jung and is entitled *Adaptation and Psychotherapy: Langs and Analytical Psychology.*

Introduction

Jungian Psychology and the Human Sciences

Roger Brooke

Jung called himself an empiricist, but the facts to which he appealed were evident in the images and rituals emerging from the psyche – the human imagination – rather than from the measurement of scientifically defined facts. He also called himself a phenomenologist, and rightly described his method as hermeneutic, providing descriptions and psychological interpretations of human experience. Even Jung's word-association studies, in which he studied complexes by measuring galvanic skin responses and reaction times to presented words, involved an interpretation of psycho-physiological findings in terms of meaning, language, and personal history. He thus defined complexes as organizations and centers of *meaning*.

The term "human science" originates from the distinction made by Wilhelm Dilthey (1833–1911) between the natural sciences (*naturswissenschaften*) and the human sciences (*geisteswissenschaften*). The natural sciences included physics, chemistry, biology, and so forth. The human sciences would include psychology, at least before it was redefined early in the twentieth century as a natural science. This redefinition of psychology as a natural science gave rise to behaviorism, an insistence on operational definitions in behavioral research, and statistical research methods. Terms such as consciousness, meaning, significance, or experience had no scientific status at all. The result was that psychology as a natural science separated academic psychology in the universities from psychoanalysis, concerned as it was with understanding the complexities of human experience, the meaningfulness and intentionality of symptoms, and the vagaries of self-awareness. With few institutional exceptions, this natural science approach has remained in the "scientific-practitioner" model of accredited training in the United States and in clinical psychology training in the United Kingdom and elsewhere.

On the other hand, psychology as a human science was based on assumptions and methods that are consistent with the ways in which we understand ourselves and each other: living meaningful lives, dealing with love and loss, life transitions, uncertainty, mortality, questions of identity and citizenship, always embodied and situated as we are in our cultural histories and language. This

DOI: 10.4324/9781032694603-1

field was more fertile in continental Europe than in the English language countries. It flourished as philosophical anthropology, existentialism, phenomenology, hermeneutics, in feminist and critical theory, then later in deconstruction, seeding in the United States and the English-language countries in the second half of the twentieth century. Psychoanalysis, most broadly understood, continued to develop and differentiate into its multiple forms, now reaching across the human science field, producing hybrids with feminism, social constructivism, critical theory, and so on. The Jungian field is no different. Significantly, recent links between psychoanalysis and neuroscience should not be understood as attempts to reduce experience to brain processes, but attempts to work toward a genuine, dialectical integration of our genetics and brain processes with an ontology of human being as irreducibly being-in-the-world (Johnston, 2019).

A founding assumption underlying human science psychology, and all the chapters in this volume, is that psychological life can never be understood as taking place in the brain or an encapsulated mind cut off from the world. As Jung said, the psyche is not inside us, but, rather, we are inside it, inside psychological life in the same way as we are inside language and cultural history. To say that a human being is a being-in-the-world means that psychological life is unintelligible apart from this network of relationships we call a world. What we call a world is not what we see when we look outside, an environmental *umwelt*, or a collection of objects to which we as self-contained subjects relate. Nor is the world an external set of "variables" having an effect on us. It is that network of relationships between persons, events, and things, gathered in the myths, images, and narratives of our culture, which form the very stuff of our identities and psychological lives. Even our brains are ultimately inexplicable apart from their functioning in that human and natural ecosystem we call a world. This ontology of being human is especially significant for post-Jungians, since Jung's emphasis on interiority (quoting St. Augustine, "Do not go outside; truth dwells in the inner man" [Jung, 1963, p. 111]) was interpreted in ways that minimized the significance of the social, political, and cultural constitution of psychological life, including its significance for the structuring of archetypal phenomena and the quality of interiority.

Another assumption is that *what* we are seeing or thinking about is never independent of our *way* of seeing and thinking. There is no ultimately independent observer. As Jung would say, there is no Archimedean point outside the psyche from which to observe the psyche. Human science psychologists are radically self-reflective (Scrag, 1980). This is because our understanding of anything always reveals a prethought orientation toward the world (Heidegger, 1927/62). All understanding involves a measure of preunderstanding without which nothing would be intelligible (Gadamer, 1989/2004). To be human is to be hermeneutical.

A further assumption is that the meaning of any experience, whether in everyday life or in psychopathology, is always to be found in the context in which it is constituted. These contextual horizons of a person's experience, the inner horizons of the person's family and personal history, are themselves constituted within the outer horizons of cultural history and sociopolitical and economic conditions (Fischer, Laubscher & Brooke, 2016). We are no more the authors of our own experience than we are of our language and accents. Psychoanalysis and phenomenology might have originated with Freud and Husserl – and let's add Jung here – but our approach to psychology can never be exhausted within their limited terms of reference.

The Department of Psychology at Duquesne University pioneered the development of psychology as an explicitly human science in the early 1960s (Giorgi, 1970, van Kaam, 1966). Bringing Jungian psychology and the wider human science field together in a conference was a celebration of these fields; housing it at Duquesne University could not have been more appropriate. The conference, Jungian Psychology and the Human Sciences, was held jointly between the International Association for Jungian Studies and the Department of Psychology at Duquesne University. Scheduled for March 2020, it was post-poned due to the Covid-19 pandemic to March 2021, when it was held online. It brought together leading psychologists from both traditions, highlighting the rapprochement between them in a variety of contexts.

We have selected papers that represent both integrations of a lifetime's work and recent graduate research. We are aware of wanting more, but we hope this collection will be enjoyed and invite readers to explore these integrative fields further. Papers seemed to fall into three loose categories: philosophically or theoretically foundational; social/political; and clinical or psychoanalytic. These areas structure the three parts of the book – although we are aware this organization is giving mixed messages, since one of the themes of the papers in this book is that such distinctions are less useful than once assumed. In addition to their intrinsic merits, selected papers all make contributions to the Jungian field as well as to adjacent fields in the broader human science tradition, psychoanalysis, feminist, and critical thought, and eco-psychology.

Roger Brooke
Pittsburgh, USA, December 2023

References

Unless otherwise stated, references to C. G. Jung's writings are to *The Collected Works of C. G. Jung*, R. Hull, Trans. Edited by Sir Herbert Read, M. Fordham, G. Adler; executive editor, W. McGuire. Bollingen Series XX, 20 volumes. London: Routledge and Kegan Paul; Princeton: Princeton University Press, 1953–1979.

Fischer, C., Laubscher, L., & Brooke, R. (Eds.). (2016). *The qualitative vision for psychology: Invitation to a human science approach*. Pittsburgh: Duquesne University Press.
Gadamer, H-G. (1989/2004). *Truth and method*. Second ed., revised. J. Weinsheimer & D. Marshall, Trans. London and New York: Bloomsbury.

Giorgi, A. (1970). *Psychology as a human science*. New York: Harper and Row.

Heidegger, M. (1927/62). *Being and time*. J. MacQuarrie & E. Robinson, Trans. Oxford: Basil Blackwell.

Johnston, A. (2019). *Prolegomena to any future materialism, Volume Two: A Weak Nature Alone*. Wilmette: Northwestern University Press.

Jung, C. (1963). *Memories, dreams, reflections*. Recorded and edited Aniela Jaffe R and C. Winston, Trans. London: Random House, Inc., Fontana Library of Theology and Philosophy.

Scrag, C. (1980). *Radical reflection and the origins of the human sciences*. West Lafayette: Purdue University Press.

Van Kaam, A. (1966). *Existential foundations of psychology*. Pittsburgh: Duquesne University Press.

Introduction to "The Role of the Good-Enough All-Rounder in Jungian Studies: 'Clinic and Academy' Revisited"

The field of Jungian studies was brought together at the University of Essex in 2002, when the International Association for Jungian Studies (IAJS) was founded. The relationship between the International Association of Analytical Psychology, which certified the training of Jungian analysts, and the IAJS has been largely cordial, but the cultural tension between academia and practice has remained in the structure of the two organizations, with less than optimal collaboration. Andrew Samuels, IAAP certified analyst and founding member of the IAJS, was the first recipient of the C G Jung Award, given by the IAJS to persons "who have made significant international contributions in scholarship, leadership, service, mentorship, clinical praxis, renovation, and/or lifetime achievement in analytical or depth psychology and/or post-Jungian studies."

Samuels' keynote lecture is polemical and provocative, but, as usual, he is pointing towards something more nuanced, concrete and manageable than an empty, aspirational "integration" might indicate. Ultimately, his lecture is a welcome to all of us to find our place in the Jungian studies field, linked to the broader human science tradition.

Chapter 1

The Role of the Good-Enough All-Rounder in Jungian Studies

"Clinic and Academy" Revisited

Andrew Samuels

Introduction

At the conference that inaugurated the International Association for Jungian Studies (IAJS) at the University of Essex in 2002, I keynoted on the theme of "clinic and academy," and I used the 2020 conference at Duquesne University to return to the theme.

Despite numerous people who are active in both clinic and academy, there continue to be tensions approximating to splits (in the psychoanalytic sense of the word, including mutual projections) between these two broad groupings: clinicians and academics. This has been marked since our Association's foundation. It has had some negative consequences in terms of our goal of bringing Jung into the academy, but, as we shall see during the chapter, there could also be many positive features of the split.

Nevertheless, what we lack is a theorization and mission statement about what it means to be *both* a clinician and an academic. There are many such at all the conferences of the IAJS (and there is a similar pattern in psychoanalytic studies as well). But what does being an all-rounder (or an all-arounder, as some Americans term it) actually involve? What is being an all-rounder like? Where are ideas about this to be found? How do we understand this as a *lived experience in the world?*

The term "all-rounder" is often used in a sporting context. In cricket, for example, it refers to a player who can both bat (that is, hit a ball with a shaped wooden implement) and bowl (that is, hurl a ball in the direction of the one batting). The most famous all-rounder in our times in England was Ian Botham.

In baseball, there is quite a debate about whether or not pitchers (a bit like the cricket bowler) should also hit (like the cricket batsman). One US baseball league made such an all-rounder illegal by adopting a rule against it. They did so because they believe that the pitcher will be a crappy hitter and spoil the game. This gets my point exquisitely. Of course, the pitcher will not be as good a hitter as a real, specialist hitter. On one level it matters in terms of results. But there is another level to hold in mind, a more psychological and even poetic level, perhaps.

DOI: 10.4324/9781032694603-2

But the other league allows the all-rounder, and I was delighted to read of Bartolo Colon, an ace pitcher, who hit his first home run at the age of 42, and showed he could also make it as a hitter. I dare say he brought a different flavor to the game.

Dictionaries and thesauruses are not kind to all-rounders. They are said to be "generalists," "jacks of all trades and masters of none" and so forth. They are vocationally eclectic, and are not much praised for it. We need, in the spirit of the human sciences, seriously to interrogate these networks of prejudices, mining the gold buried in the shit therein. In plain language, we know some people are better at one thing and some are better at another related or connected thing. But that doesn't stop anyone trying to be good-enough at both.

Let's apply this to the field of Jungian Studies. Let's consider people who are both clinicians and academics. Our all-rounders may not be as good at either academic research or at clinical practice as those who devote themselves exclusively to one or the other. Devotion to a trade or vocation does not necessarily bring excellence in its wake. Yet maybe we need people who are distinctly average in either clinic or academy. That is what good-enough means, given its roots in Donald Winnicott's ideas about the necessity and value of parental failure. Via such humility, we will lose something – but may gain a lot. Let's take this thought a bit further (Winnicott, 1963a).

In 1971, the first-generation London Jungian analyst Gerhard Adler published a remarkable paper entitled "Depth Psychology and the Principle of Complementarity" (Adler, 1971). He picked up on the physicist Niels Bohr's observation that something can't be a wave or a particle at the same time. Adler tweaked this idea to engage with what was the main hot issue in Jungian analysis at the time, and maybe it still is. This is the tension between (*a*) those who work with the numinous, classical models of individuation, dreams and active imagination ("mandalas") and (*b*) those who analyse infantile development ("the breast") and subsequent transference-countertransference, and valorize the therapeutic alliance. In *Jung and the Post-Jungians* in 1985, I called these the classical and developmental schools and, allowing for blurring and cross-fertilisation over the decades, the distinction broadly holds (Samuels, 1985).

Holding these two images – mandala and breast – in mind, we are likely to find that some Jungian analysts will be better at the classical tasks of working with numinous dreams and synchronicities. Other analysts will be better at the more developmental approach, engaging with infantile trauma and subsequent transference-countertransference. It was hard in the 1960s, and it is still hard today to be honest, to think of an analyst who was excellent at both, given the history of antagonism between these perspectives. Adler said he didn't mind the absence of overall excellence a bit, and nor do I.

But today I am going beyond Adler and saying that there will be analysts who seek to work both classically and also developmentally – all-rounders within the clinical field. These analysts may well not be able to interpret dreams as well as a fully committed classical analyst, nor will they be able to analyse infancy as well as the devotedly developmental analyst. Something will definitely be lost by trying to be both classical and developmental. I am not here to simplistically valorize and praise hybrids. Moreover, let's pay due deference to the analyst who sticks to one channel. They will know what they are doing, after all.

But something is also gained, notably by the patient or client, who experiences a broader kind of therapy, which may be closer to what they need. A less knowledgeable therapist is going to be a more human one. Inadequacy on the part of the therapist leaves more space for the client to grow. So, that is how the idea of a good-enough all-rounder plays out in the clinic.

Returning to the specific field of Jungian Studies, I next float the idea of the good-enough all-rounder with considerable awareness of what would be missing as well as what would be gained if it became a goal. For what this project or goal implies is that, not only do we need people who engage with academic work as well as clinical work, but that *they might not be excellent at either enterprise*. I don't think typology helps much with these conundrums. In principle, typology might valorize the all-rounder. But, in practice, as we shall see, the opposite seems to pertain.

President Lyndon Johnson famously said of then-congressman Gerald Ford that "he is so dumb he can't walk and chew gum." Meaning he couldn't do these two things at the same time. Actually, LBJ said that Ford couldn't fart and chew gum, but never mind. My claim is that it is indeed possible to walk and chew gum. But it is sometimes, and for some people, doing the all-round routine is sure as hell not easy. That is why it is worth thinking about. Being good-enough is not easy, either, as all parents know.

Now, there may be people out there who are truly excellent at both clinical and research work. I salute them. But these are outliers and the possibility that such paragons exist does not vitiate what I am saying about the deleterious effects of both-ness. The principle of complementarity holds. Freud might be horrified at this valorization of alloy over gold!

Nothing I am saying undermines the idea that it may be very helpful in one's clinical work to be an academic. And vice versa, when academic perspectives illumine clinical phenomena. But that is not how it is in the consulting room, is it? Too much theoretical thinking isn't good news for the therapy process. In fact, as Robert Morley showed in his 2007 book *The Analysand's Tale*, many, many therapeutic ruptures and failures result from the clinicians' slavish adherence to their theoretical position.

People may want to claim that their research makes them better clinicians and vice versa, but we need to see through this self-congratulation. What is being avoided is the necessary destruction to each of research and therapy. What is being denied is the role of the all-rounder. Specifically, when you sit in that clinical chair, having just been engaged in academic research, it makes you even less likely to work without assumptions, memory and desire. Research – even, dare I say it in a low whisper, research in the human sciences – interferes with therapy. *Research interferes with therapy*. It may be a good thing to foster the role of the academy as the very best critic of the clinic, but there are losses that cannot be denied. Jung was simply talking nonsense when he said we should leave our theories at the door of the consulting room. Michael Fordham's metaphor was to leave theories in a locked filing cabinet. That is also out of the question.

One final point: Of course, there are all-rounders, jacks of all trades *within both the clinical and the academic milieus*. But that is a different, though very valuable, angle and I won't take it up today. I did write about pluralism within the clinical field in *The Plural Psyche*, back in 1989, and I have gone on with it (Samuels, 1989).

I am grateful to Roger Brooke, in his feedback to an early draft of the talk that has now become this chapter, for wondering "if the good enough all-rounder might have a special kind of expertise and contribution to make." Roger felt that my defense of my position was possibly too modest (Brooke, personal communication, 2020).

Do these initial thoughts hold up at all? Have I created a false problem here, only to achieve mastery by overcoming it? Well, I concede that the binary – clinic and academy – may seem simplistic. Look around at the many outstanding figures who straddle the boundary between clinic and academy. Is it offensive to say that, by so doing, they will not be as good as those of their colleagues who stick to one thing, whether that is clinical or academic in nature? Of course, as Brooke pointed out, it will stay offensive, unless and until we see why being a good-enough all-rounder rather than excellent specialist is something at which to aim.

Hence, those who work both clinically and academically are now asked to enter a space in which some absurd, overblown, exaggerated generalizations may be explored. Let's not forget Theodor Adorno's aperçu that "[i]n psychoanalysis, nothing is true but the exaggerations" (Adorno, 1974, p. 49). Here is the first exaggeration – and I mean the words "think" and "feel" in their ordinary sense, not in Jung-speak:

Clinicians Can't Think
Academics Can't Feel

From the academics, we often hear that:

i   Analysts can't really think systematically or rationally.
ii Analysts assert things rather than argue them through.
iii Analysts misuse transferential authority in both the treatment and training environments.
iv The analysts' main research tool – the case study – is badly flawed and not scientific.

From the analysts' side, they say that:

i   Academics can't really feel or suffer complex emotions because they suffer from "precocious intellectual development" (Winnicott, 1963b, pp. 17–20).

ii Concepts developed in analytical psychology are clinical in nature and can only be appreciated if one has clinical training and experience.

iii Whether the academics like it or not, analysts have special foundational knowledge – even a kind of Gnosis.

As far as Jungian analysts are concerned, we are helped in the above characterization of the academics by the various things Jung said about intellectuals. For example, "A psychology that satisfies the intellect alone can never be practical, for the totality of the psyche can never be grasped by intellect alone" (Jung, *CW*7, para 201).

Let's complexify these generalisations a little more, probing the prejudices and projections buried within them. Take the experience of an academic seeking clinical training. It can be awful. It is often hard for intellectuals to feel they have been treated justly by admissions committees when applying for clinical training. I have a lot of empirical (though anecdotal) evidence from my patients and clients to prove this point. The end result is that the clinical world has lost the chance to host creative and original thinkers who would challenge it from within. Go to the other end of the spectrum, and the question becomes why do we demand such high academic standards to enter clinical training? Don't we see how this works against the creation of a diverse community, for people of color and those with low incomes are effectively excluded? So, too, may be artists and mystics. I like to pursue this dichotomy – clinic and academy – even whilst seeing through and recognizing its limitations (after all, I and others are in both camps; we are the poor all-rounders).

Speaking for a moment now as a clinician, here's one particular thing I am concerned about within academic Jungian studies. Many academics are very conservative in their understanding of Jungian and also psychoanalytic ideas and approaches, as if nothing had changed since the early part of the twentieth century. I encounter these academic dinosaurs a lot in my work reading several of the proposals as the consultant to the Routledge Jungian list. It's like a broken clock syndrome, where people stay attached to the past. As if it is all Jung, and the post-Jungians might as well have never existed.

What I want to argue is that there is a serious turf war bubbling under in our field of Jungian studies, and the prize is legitimacy – meaning things to do with power, authority and influence. In any struggle over legitimacy, each side will naturally seek to characterize the other side in ways that enhance their own strengths. These mutual projections make for a deeper problem than one that can be solved by the International Association for Analytical Psychology promoting academic conferences. Methinks the analysts doth protest too much when they go all academic on us.

Now, as promised in my opening segment, I turn to the question of what the clinic might offer the academy. Here are some ideas about what clinical and analytical perspectives can contribute to universities:

i   Balance between rationality (especially in the human and social sciences) – and something softer and more open to experience, especially intense or numinous experience.
ii   Participating in an epistemological shift in which information, abstraction and authority as the power bases for knowledge are expanded by the addition of knowledge deriving from experience.
iii   Contributions to research methodology – the irreducible subjectivity of the researcher including regarding countertransference as useful for historical, literary, cultural and social research.

There are already approaches to learning in our field that could go some way to making these points into practical realities. These should perhaps be adopted more widely. For example, the use of learning journals is already widespread. Or following Susan Rowland in encouraging the use of arts-based approaches in the teaching of concepts, especially where this is unexpected (Rowland, 2020). There is a huge field of experiential education and collaborative research that could be further absorbed into the academic teaching of Jungian Studies and psychoanalytic studies.

How do we open universities to people who are not thinking types and work out new pedagogical structures to put them in touch with their thinkings? To do this, we should take seriously how Bion and Jung have expanded what we mean by thinking. As we all recite, Jung said there are two kinds of thinking. What is the academic role of undirected thinking, thinking in images, fantasy thinking, intuitive thinking?

I turn now to consider what the academy might offer the clinic. Here are some ideas about what "the university" as a perspective, a *Weltanschauung*, or even as a metaphor can contribute to clinical psychoanalysis:

i   The capacity of universities to speak truth to power. The realization that knowledge often "follows the money."
ii   Scepticism is a virtue! For example, what is pretty or aesthetically pleasing or well expressed in emotional terms is not always "true." There's seduction in affect, poetic language and imagery.
iii   The human sciences tell us that everything has a history and a context and this is true of ideas and practices in clinical work. Clinical technique is not a natural phenomenon.

I said earlier that the academy is often the best critic of the clinic. We learn from the human sciences that forms of social organization, history and language structure a great deal that we take for granted. The human body is a kind of text.

With this in mind, here is a brief deconstruction of a conventional clinical attitude. I refer to the idea of containment, with the psychoanalyst Wilfred Bion's "container-contained" (Bion, 1970). How does this work when the clinical dyad is that of white therapist and client of colour? The history of colonialism, with its missionary and other "civilising" projects, gives the coloniser a sort of container status. In this analogy, the client is the "primitive," the "savage." In our work, the patient is contained so as to discover their capacity to think and create symbolic meaning. Their civilised selves. So I am drawing a metaphorical parallel between (for example) people called "Africanists" and the intrapsychic processes Bion called "Beta-elements." In support of this analysis, we may recall Celia Brickman's awesome historical work on the key role of what she calls the "aboriginal mind" in the production of foundational psychoanalytic theory. The title of her book is: *Aboriginal Populations in the Mind: Race and Primitivity in Psychoanalysis* (Brickman, 2003).

This is but one of many examples that can be given showing that contributions from academic perspectives such as the human sciences change how clinicians *think* about what they do. Will it change what they *actually do*? I do not know. ...

This next section concerns the future of Jungian and post-Jungian studies and considers both the emergence and value of *exo*tericism.

I write as an all-rounder. I certainly am not as fine an academic as many of my colleagues. Indeed, I do not have a PhD, nor a master's, nor even a bachelor's degree. And my clinical work is definitely weakened by my academic and political activities. There are many finer clinicians around. But, after over 50 years in clinical practice and 25 years in the university, I am content at the age of 75 to be only good-enough. That, as I have been arguing, is both the fate of the all-rounder and also their strength.

So, as merely good enough, I turn my attention now to the elitism and esotericism of Jungian psychology. For many critics, Jung's recipe for individuation is similarly something open only to an elite, even to an elect. Of course, given the sheer quantity of his writings on this matter, some of such weaknesses are occasionally rectified. So, individuation, which is mostly portrayed as an internal process, is sometimes stated to include relationships and the social dimensions of life. But the impression still remains, despite international developments in China and Japan, that the overall idea of individuation is that it is for older European people of scholarly and reflective bent who speak Latin and have a familiarity with the Jungian body of ideas.

That was why it was so important for Adolf Guggenbuhl-Craig to write *Eros on Crutches*, which argued that even sociopaths, or those with special educational needs, could individuate (Guggenbuhl-Craig, 1980). My teacher Fred Plaut made the same point when he wrote in our *Critical Dictionary of Jungian Analysis* that individuation was not the same as "mental health" or even "maturity" (Samuels, Shorter and Plaut, 1986, pp. 76–79). The thing is, these first-generation Jungians were not stupid. They spotted the ongoing problem I am bringing up here.

Maybe these esotericist weaknesses could be countered by a kind of *exoteri-cism*, meaning a conscious, collective reaching out to the cultural collective. But how do we do this? I think that, to do so, Jungian Studies will have to invoke another kind of all-round capacity. In Jung's words, this will mean twin-ning "the spirit of the depths" with "the spirit of the times." In my favourite words, to twin "analysis" and "activism." Or in the fashionable jargon, to go psychosocial. If we plan to do this, first, we need to address a pile of prejudices on Jung's part.

I have a wide range of prejudices to choose from. I could have spoken about Jung's problematic ideas concerning women or his many anti-Semitic com-ments. But I won't because, I am happy to say, these have been energetically engaged with. The reason why my chapter will now focus on what Jung wrote about Africans and persons of African heritage (such as African Americans), and indigenous peoples is that it is a hot topic today and has *not* been ade-quately addressed despite an increase in interest concerning the matter. The international Jungian analytical community is deeply divided over how (and whether) to respond to concern over Jung's writings in this area. The same is true in the Jungian academy, I believe. – By the way, it is noteworthy that the most downloaded paper ever from the *British Journal of Psychotherapy* is still in fact Farhad Dalal's "Jung: A Racist" (Dalal, 1988).

Whatever concrete response emerges, if any, to the disquiet, we have yet to see any significant public distancing of the international Jungian professional community as a whole from what Jung wrote about Africans and indigenous people. True, there was the Open Letter signed by 35 respected Jungian academ-ics and clinicians and, in the end, carried by a dozen journals in four languages. The signatories may be seen as a stellar group of all-rounders (Samuels et al., 2018). But the collective professional silence remains a serious weakness garner-ing criticism, and nowhere is this criticism more marked and well informed than in the Western academy. In passing, I want to say I think it is a major hurdle to the securing of Jungian and Post-Jungian work in the university.

There may be many reasons for the collective professional silence. For example, the blunt suggestion in Dalal's title that Jung was a "racist" is prob-lematic and has led to an understandable but regrettable defensiveness on our part. The main objection to the word "racist" in relation to Jung is that, if Jung was a racist, then so were Freud and many others of that era. Why – people ask – do we have to sort of *apologise* on behalf of Jung?

At the IAJS conference in Cape Town in 2017, I presented evidence from intellectual history that countered to an extent the idea that Jung was merely a "man of his time." It was published in the IAJS's own estimable journal, the *International Journal of Jungian Studies*, in 2018 (Samuels, 2018).

I really and truly understand the knee-jerk defensive reaction to feeling that Jung was unfairly and unreasonably called "a racist." But I cannot avoid add-ing that the protest against calling Jung a "racist" shouldn't be allowed to post-pone responding to the concerns I mentioned. I am not sure that this satisfies our many articulate and influential critics. It doesn't satisfy me. The issue here is not whether this expressed a racist sentiment. The issue is what today's Jungian academics and analysts have to say about it.

I am coming to the end and I want, in my role as an all-rounder, just to raise one last issue from each of the clinical and academic spheres.

In Britain, psychotherapy as a whole is a remarkably "white" profession. This general lack of diversity matters. It matters a lot. But the small numbers of persons of colour, and specifically of African heritage, in our Jungian professional community are significantly more marked than in other clinical traditions. So: I have tried to compare the situations in Brazil and the United States to that in Britain. My conclusion is that we Jungians may well be less diverse than other schools of therapy. Is it possible that what Jung wrote about "Africans" is putting off more persons of colour training as analysts or seeking analysis? There are not "none." But – to give an example – in the United States, where there are several hundreds of Jungians, only four are African Americans.

So much for the clinic and its problems. Here are some relevant problems from the academic side of the clinic and academy divide.

You know, whether we Jungians like it or not, the idea of "the Jung cult." made famous in Richard Noll's book of that title, just won't disappear (Noll, 1994). I don't think either side in the Noll furore covered themselves in glory. It was very poor public relations by the Jung Estate to cause Routledge to destroy the whole print run of a separate collection of Jung's writings edited by Noll, for which they had given full permission, when they read the cult book. There was nothing wrong with the edited collection – except the editor, who had slipped from grace. Yet it was equally poor judgement of Noll's – truly disgusting if very effective – to write a supposedly thoughtful op-ed piece in the New York *Times* comparing Jung as a cult leader to Jimmy Jones, leader of the Jonestown group that went in for a mass suicide. At least, the *Times* published my letter of outrage.

A second example of what can fairly be called an academic scandal in Jungian Studies concerned me personally. In 1988, William McGuire invited me to prepare a special edition of Jung's 1946 volume *Essays on Contemporary Events*. I did so and it remained on sale internationally until 2002, when I received communications from the Scholarly Adviser to the Jung Estate and from the Estate itself to the effect that the edition was to be removed from sale and destroyed. The reason given by the Jung Estate was that I referred to Jung's writings in the 1930s as emanating from his shadow. Now, that is not what I'd say now, but it is what I wrote in 1988. This, the Jung Estate wrote to me, was an outrage. It got worse. The Jung Estate sent a letter by hand of messenger to our IAJS conference in College Station, Texas, in 2005. The letter threatened me with legal action if I mentioned the destruction of the print run of my edition of *Essays on Contemporary Events* in public. It was what we now call being "canceled."

References

Adler, G. (1971). Analytical psychology and the principle of complementarity. In J. Wheelwright (Ed.), *The analytic process*. Putnam.

Adorno, Theodor. (1974). *Minima Moralia*. (E. F. N. Jephcott, Trans.), New Left Books.

Bion, W. R. (1970). *Attention and interpretation*. Tavistock. Reprinted in: *Seven Servants: Four works by Wilfred R. Bion*. Aronson (1977).

Brickman, C. (2003). *Aboriginal populations in the mind: Race and primitivity in psychoanalysis*. Columbia University Press.

Dalal, F. (1988). Jung: A racist. *British Journal of Psychotherapy*, 4(3), 263–279.

Guggenbuhl-Craig, A. (1980) Eros on Crutches: Reflections on Psychopathy and Immorality. Spring.

Noll, R. (1994). *The Jung cult: Origins of a charismatic movement*. Simon and Schuster.

Rowland, S. (2020). *Jungian arts-based research and "the nuclear enchantment of New Mexico"*. Routledge.

Samuels, A. (1985). *Jung and the post-Jungians*. Routledge and Kegan Paul.

Samuels, A. (1989). *The plural psyche: Personality, morality and the father*. Routledge.

Samuels, A. (2018). Open letter on Jung and 'Africans'. *British Journal of Psychotherapy* 34, 673–678.

Samuels, A., Shorter, B. Plaut, A. (1986). *A critical dictionary of jungian analysis*. Routledge.

Winnicott, D. W. (1963a). Dependence in infant-care, in child-care, and in the psychoanalytic setting. In M. Khan (Ed.), *The maturational processes and the facilitating environment* (pp. 249–259). Hogarth (1965).

Winnicott, D. W. (1963b). Regression as therapy illustrated by the case of a boy whose pathological dependence was adequately met by the parents. *British Journal of Medical Psychology*, 36, 27–36.

Part 1

Philosophical Foundations

Introduction to "The Way of the Daimon: From Jung's *Red Book* to the Alchemical Imagination and the Reddening of Psychology"

The beating heart of Jung's work can be felt through Jung's *Red Book* to his alchemical studies, which began in 1928 and continued to the end of his life. It is the therapeutic and cultural significance of this heartbeat that Marlan discusses, integrating Jung's experience of "the depths" and the *numinous* with the necessities of meeting the ethical and practical obligations of everyday life. In a nuanced and careful reading of the Jungian literature, measured by his own decades of experience and study in the field, Marlan moves our appreciation for the polarities of conscious and unconscious, culturally imagined as darkness and light or matter and spirit, *nigredo* and *albedo*, forward, into the reddening (the alchemical *rubedo*) of psychology. For Marlan, individuation is not adequately described as making the unconscious conscious, or bringing the experiential depths into coherent language, nor as an idealizing submission to the *numinous*. Rather, individuation moves through variously imagined alchemical processes to an existentially enlivened and passionate way of being, with *Psyche* kissed by *Eros*. Readers will appreciate Marlan's deep integration of classical, post-Jungian, and phenomenological traditions.

Chapter 2

The Way of the Daimon
From Jung's *Red Book* to the Alchemical
Imagination and the Reddening of Psychology[*]

Stanton Marlan

Introduction

The Red Book has been called the most important document in the corpus of
Jung's work—a book that will revolutionize our understanding of Jung. James
Hillman considered it a poetic text, one that expresses the living soul in our age
of scientific rationalism and is important for the future of our personal development and our understanding of psychology. It is a book that challenges our
modern intellect and imagination, and is impossible to adequately understand
in the context of our modern scientific worldview. For Hillman, Jung's vision
jars even the most knowledgeable readers. It shocks and pushes us into the very
limits of mind and language—and is an encounter with the numinous, a quality of fear and awe in the face of a *tremendum*. It is an experience that requires
a descent and a decentering, a going under that results in a defeat for and rela-
tivization of the ego. Such an experience of the unknown led Jung to the edge
of his sanity, but the strength of his character allowed him to engage with the
primordial depths in a way that resulted in a movement toward a new vision, a
vision I refer to as the reddening of psychology.

Jung saw these experiences as a confrontation with the primal world of the
unconscious, which burst forth and nearly overwhelmed him. In *Memories,
Dreams, Reflections* (*MDR*), he describes it as hitting upon "a stream of lava,
... [an] incandescent matter" (Jung, 1963, p. 199) whose heat compelled him to
come to terms with the daimonic and numinous reality of the psyche. Elsewhere
he describes it as a "fiery, molten basalt, from which the stone crystalized"
(Jung, 2009, p. 88). Jung found it ironic that, as a psychiatrist, the madness and
chaos of his experiences were composed of the same psychic material "which
is the stuff of psychosis and is found in the insane" (Jung, 1963, p. 188).
Interestingly, Hillman notes that for Hegel "[i]nsanity belongs to soul-making"
(Hillman, 2010, p. 125). It "is an essential stage in the development of the soul"

[*] Segments previously published in *C. G. Jung and the Alchemical Imagination: Passages into the
Mysteries of Psyche and Soul*, by Stanton Marlan, Copyright © 2021 by Taylor & Francis
Informa UK Ltd - Books. Reproduced by permission of Taylor & Francis Group.

DOI: 10.4324/9781032694603-4

and its telos strives to restore "inner harmony" (Hillman, 2010). It is a process Hillman links to "alchemical soul-making," leading to what he ultimately describes as a *coniunctio* of "solar brilliance and ... moon-madness," a conjunction he calls "illumined lunacy" (Hillman, 2010). Ultimately, Jung came to see that these experiences were also at the matrix of a mythopoetic imagination that has vanished from our rational age. He noted that "the gods have become diseases [and that] Zeus no longer rules Olympus" (Jung, 1953/1968, para. 54). As overwhelming as these experiences were, Jung continued to open himself to the depths. Quoting Goethe's *Faust*, he proclaimed "Now let me dare to open wide the gate / Past which men's steps have ever flinching trod" (Jung, 1963, pp. 188–9). For Jung, it was a path that was "[u]npopular, ambiguous, and dangerous, ... a voyage of discovery to the other pole of the world" (Jung, 1963, p. 189). It was a journey that required him to venture forth into the deepest recesses of the psyche.

Jung faithfully recorded his experiences in the *Black* and *Red Books* and deeply valued his discoveries. He ultimately felt that they were of the utmost importance and was committed to the idea that "[t]he decisive question for man is: Is he related to something infinite or not?" (Jung, 1963, p. 325). For Jung, "[i]n the final analysis, we count for something only because of the essential we embody, and if we do not embody that, life is wasted" (Jung, 1963). For him, *The Red Book* spoke in the language of the soul, a primordial expression of the spirit of the depths. Its mode of expression was lacking with regard to his intention to communicate understanding and meaning. In a chapter of *Psychology and Alchemy* (Jung, 1944, p. 39), Jung used a quote from Virgil's *Aeneid* as an epigram, and Shamdasani notes that by doing this Jung is "saying in effect that it's not the descent that is difficult but returning to the upper air, that is the real task" (Hillman & Shamdasani, 2013, p. 54). For Jung, simply giving oneself over to the spirit of the depth is easy and can be self-indulgent and even unethical. He notes that anybody can have weird experiences, retreat and live in Nighttown, as James Joyce called it (Hillman & Shamdasani, p. 171). Jung differentiates his intentions from writers and artists like Joyce and Pablo Picasso who, he says, dwell in the depths and revel "in the Walpurgisnacht, the witches' Sabbath, the carnival" (Hillman & Shamdasani, p. 54) For them the "nekyia becomes a bacchanal" (Hillman & Shamdasani, p. 51). Jung was likewise critical of simply entering "into the flora and fauna of Eastern symbolism," which for him would also have been a "cop-out" (Hillman & Shamdasani, p. 55).

Jung's intention to return to the "upper air" meant "a rigorous process of *understanding*," a need for a "firm ground underfoot" and having to "return wholly to reality" (Jung, 1963, p. 188). Jung explains this as having to attain a "scientific comprehension" and "to draw concrete conclusions from the insights the unconscious had given" him (Jung, 1963). For Jung, science was at first the prime way to extricate himself from chaos (Jung, 1963, p. 192) and to incorporate and make his experiences understandable to others. Just what Jung meant by "incorporate" and how he came to terms with the unconscious is instructive for our understanding of both Jung's psychology and psychology in general. He described a number of different ways he struggled with the visions he recorded in the *Black* and *Red Books*, initially documenting and amplifying them by means of what he called an aesthetic elaboration. It was a process he discarded, feeling it was ultimately inadequate and that he "had not yet found the right language" needed "to translate [these experiences] into something else" (Jung, 1963, p. 188).

The problem of how to achieve the task of return from the depths to the spirit of this time is the crux of the problem posed by James Hillman and Sonu Shamdasani in their book *Lament of the Dead: Psychology after Jung's* Red Book (2013). In a series of nuanced conversations, they note the problem for Jung and for a revisioned psychology is to achieve the task of communicating their experiences in a way that does justice to the soul and "the weight of human history," to what Hillman calls "the voices of the dead" (Hillman & Shamdasani, 2013, p. 66). For both Hillman and Shamdasani, rational explanation is not only insufficient, but it deadens the living expression of the soul. Both seek to explore alternative ways of expressing the spirit of the depths. Hillman, more than Shamdasani, is critical of Jung's notion of translation into the cognitive rationalism of the prevailing scientific views of psychology. For Hillman, this move utterly fails to do justice to the soul and to an enriched idea of what psychology can and needs to be. Likewise, Jung was not completely satisfied with traditional scientific explanations.

In the epilogue to *The Red Book*, Jung writes,

> I worked on this book for 16 years. My acquaintance with alchemy … took me away from it. The beginning of the end came in 1928, when [Richard] Wilhelm sent me the [Chinese] text of the [Secret of the] "Golden Flower," an alchemical treatise.
>
> (Jung, 2009, p. 555)

For Jung, it was alchemy that helped him "absorb the overpowering force of [his] original experiences" and "finally arrange them into a whole" (Jung, 2009). In addition to trying to take a scientific view of his visions, it was placing them in the context of history, which gave him a sense of confidence that his experiences were not simply subjective. He felt that Gnosticism and alchemy were historically resonant with his experiences of the archetypal psyche and the process of transformation. Over time, Jung struggled with many ways to come to terms with his experiences. Lance Owens noted that, after the *Liber Novus*, Jung "turned the rest of his life toward molding a hermeneutics for the visions, a method for telling his tale" (Owens, 2015, p. 2). Owens speaks of Jung's project as a "labor of science, a study of nature, and a confrontation with history at the end of an age. In sum, [Jung] called it his *opus psychologicum*" (Owens, 2015).

For some of Jung's readers, any move toward incorporation, assimilation, and the ego's work on this *prima materia* was problematic, a distortion and rationalistic defense against his most profound expression of the unconscious. For Peter Kingsley, the *prima materia* of Jung's visions were also an *ultima materia*, a primary, fundamental, and sacred substance of Jung's contributions. Kingsley's way of reading Jung is that "the unconscious takes care of everything" (Kingsley, 2018a, p. 82). It does not require mediation to come to terms with it. Only through a direct, deep, and unmediated descent into the intense heat and heart of the divine lava does the shape of truth and reality take its form. In this way, Jung entered into "the land of the dead" (Jung, 1963, p. 181) and encountered Elijah, Philemon, Izdubar, the black serpent, and other presences that he transcribed in the *Red Book*. He had the courage to take them as they were, "as though they were real," and he listened to them "attentively" (Jung, 1963). Such figures were the daimonic force that gave deeper meaning to his life and shape to his psychology.

In an interesting and provocative interview with Murray Stein, Kingsley criticizes Jungians for their "apotropaic" defenses against this "spirit of the depths" as an attempt to distance themselves from the overwhelming power of the numinous (Kingsley, 2018b). For Kingsley, the daimonic and autonomous power of the unconscious was misrepresented by Jung's followers, which led to "the progressive domestication of Jung's" (Kingsley, 2018a, p. 21) ideas and a failure to adequately honor the divine madness and sacred chaos at the core of Jung's prophetic revelations. For Kingsley, it is not simply the Jungians who have lost their way, but Western culture that has progressively lost touch with the primordial reality of the soul in the name of rationality.

Kingsley's challenge opens up important questions about the way in which we engage with the so-called sacred chaos and psyche's volcanic numinosity. With Kingsley, I believe the impetus to reach the deepest mysteries of the psyche is a primordial need and reminds me of Jung's letter to P. W. Martin, where he wrote, "You are quite right, the main interest of my work is not concerned with the treatment of neuroses but rather with the approach to the numinous" (Jung, 1973, p. 377). But, interestingly, this approach is also "the real therapy" (Jung, 1973). Jung notes that inasmuch as you "attain to the numinous experiences you are released from the curse of pathology" (Jung, 1973). Statements like this support Kingsley's conviction about the primary importance of the numinous, but it is also true that, for the majority of Jungians and for Jung himself, it is not the whole story. Nevertheless, what I value about Kingsley's challenge is that if he errs, he does so on the side of appreciating the depth and power of the archetypal imagination, its monstrous chaos and volcanic creativity—as well as his recognition that the loss associated with translating this power into a rational idiom can destroy its numinous potentiality.

The dichotomy Kingsley sets up between the archetypal imagination and its rational translation is both problematic and useful for reflecting on the question of our relations to Jung, the *Red Book*, and psychology. On the one hand,

I know that encountering the archetypal world can directly shape our lives and that, at times, our attempt to rationally understand it can serve a defensive purpose. On the other hand, our need to come to terms with the autonomous power of the unconscious calls forth a response and an engagement with the powers of the unknown. We play a role in our destiny, and our response matters in our lives.

In one way, the autonomous psyche is both *prima materia* and *ultima materia*, but nevertheless, for Jung and the alchemists, the *prima materia* requires a way of relating to and working with it, which is essential to the transformation process. For Jung, his study of alchemy was an important resource for learning how to relate to the *prima materia* and this learning was essential for the development of his psychology.

In an interesting article, "On the Importance of Numinous Experience in the Alchemy of Individuation," Murray Stein articulates a more generally accepted view of Jung's ideas, recognizing his receptivity to the profound significance of the experience of the numinous but also noting that "in itself [this] was not of final import; rather, it provided the essential ingredients for further stages of the individuation opus" (Stein, 2023). For Stein, Jung's originary experiences were essential, but still only *prima materia*, important basic stuff that needed to be worked on and transformed, but not yet an *ultima materia*. For Stein and most Jungians,

> the goal of individuation, unlike that of the religious quest, is not union with the divine and salvation but rather integration and wholeness, the forging of the opposites inherent in the Self into an image of unity and integrating this into consciousness.
>
> (Stein, 2023)

Stein gives a number of descriptions of what has to be done with the *prima materia*. He notes that the work requires the psychological project of sublimation, integration, and forging it into something useful and woven into the fabric of personal conscious identity—conscious structure made up of both personal and archetypal elements.

For Stein, such an integration does not amount to a defensive reduction to the personal ego since what is integrated is unknown and not reducible to a psychological level only. While metaphysical reality cannot be established or disconfirmed by scientific method, he notes that transcendental potential "shine[s] through the fabric of everyday life" (Stein, 2023). For Stein, the integration of personal and transpersonal, ego and archetype, is an essential experience of wholeness and individuation. It requires going beyond one-sidedness and points to the importance of linking together what Jung referred to as his no. 1 and no. 2 personalities.

The importance of individuation and the concern about dividedness are also central to the work of Mark Saban in his book *Two Souls Alas: Jung's Two*

Personalities and the Making of Analytical Psychology (2019). A major point of Saban's work is the importance of not getting caught in one-sidedness and, although Jung emphasized this as central to the individuation process, Saban concludes that Jung overemphasizes the mythical and inner realities over the "historical, sociological, economic, and political" ones, seeing these as "super-ficial" in comparison with the inner work (Saban, 2019, p. 234). For Saban, Jung failed to follow the logic of individuation or to engage adequately with the *outer* "other" and relational issues that could advance the trajectory of Jung's psychology.

Saban extends his criticism to James Hillman and Wolfgang Giegerich. Hillman, like Saban, recognizes the importance of the return of the soul to the world, but due to the fact that he makes the imaginal "psyche into a core prin-ciple, [he] also makes it impossible for the 'outside' to function as a genuinely exterior" (Saban, 2019, p. 206). For Saban, Giegerich's psychology is even more "radically untethered … from actual persons in the world" and "the personal is radically differentiated from the archetypal," creating a "scission" and "com-partmentalisation" between them (Saban, 2019).

Both Stein and Saban make the case for the importance of individuation as a central theme in Jung's work and for going beyond any one-sidedness or overvaluing of the internal over the external or the archetypal over the per-sonal. Both stress the importance for a continuing balance and integration of the opposites and, for both analysts, the numinous is essential but not the final or exclusive goal of the Jungian opus.

Jung clearly emphasized the need to come to terms with the unconscious and, as already noted, to "return it to the upper air" to understand it and to carry its meaning into the spirit of the times. But he was also concerned about finding the right language to do so—to find a way that did not allow directed rational thinking and logos to overpower the wonder, awe, and telos that the archetypal world brought in its wake. For Hillman, Jung did not find an ade-quate way to do this, and while Shamdasani is mostly in agreement with Hillman, he is more accepting of Jung's theorizing language, seeing it as a "safety rail" (Hillman & Shamdasani, 2013, p. 69), noting, like Kingsley, that it has an apotropaic function but nevertheless, for Shamdasani, it has a therapeu-tic value and an important contribution to Jung's psychological vision. Hillman, on the other hand, imagines a number of alternative approaches to expressing the spirit of the depths. For him, if psychology is to move forward it has "to speak to the soul … about the soul" (Hillman & Shamdasani, 2013, p. 38). When we talk about psyche, we have to see what is presented phenome-nologically or, at least, phenomenally. The images themselves have in them everything they need. Hillman is not so much concerned with the process of individuation, which he sees as developmental fantasy, but rather with each thing as it is, as it presents itself. For him, psyche speaks in metaphors, in anal-ogies, and in images. That is its primary language. So then, he asks, why speak differently?

Hillman says that we must express ourselves in a way that evokes the poetic basis of mind with a rhetoric that does not disabuse the psyche of its natural way of talking, and that requires a sensitivity to words—a direct result of thinking non-conceptually. It is on this basis that Hillman entertains the significance of what literature can offer psychology. For him, a literary and aesthetic approach is far richer than scientific studies. What Hillman means by literature is very broad – it includes the arts, great drama, including Homer and Shakespeare, as well as great novels (Hillman & Shamdasani, 2013, p. 192). For him, literature is the proper study of the deepest part of human life. There we find living figures and psychic realities from which we can learn how the human psyche works. For Hillman, we get far more from articulate writers than we get from case histories. While case histories focus on the subjectivity and personal history of patients, for Hillman the deepest subjectivity is *not* simply subjective! Rather, it consists in what he calls "opening the mouth of the dead" (Hillman & Shamdasani, 2013, p. 1)—an engaging with the history of the soul's unresolved questions and archetypal conundrums. In addition, doing psychology is not a descent and return, and our deepest experiences do not require a translation from personality no. 2 into personality no. 1.

Hillman has given us examples of dwelling in the depths. In his book *Dreams and the Underworld* (1979), he challenges the traditional idea of what he called the " one-way street ... moving out of the unconscious" into consciousness (Hillman, 1979, p. 1). He has chosen to face "a different one-way movement, ... [a] vesperal into the dark" (Hillman, 1979), as he calls it, and he admits to this one-way move with a singleness of intent and shocking belief that the entire procedure aiming at more consciousness about living is radically wrong! This move challenges what has been a taken-for-granted assumption about making the unconscious conscious and brings into focus the problematics of one-sidedness in all of its complexity, including the failures and limitations of the Cartesian dayworld and the virtues of the mystic night. Can or should these perspectives be brought together or is this idea itself a Cartesian fantasy at best, an *albedo* achievement still far from a revisioned psychology and the *rubedo* and reddening of the soul? Is the movement into the mythic depth a copout or retreat from reality or does it bring a deep reality into lived experience? For Hillman, dwelling in the depths, in what has been referred to as Joyce's Nighttown, is not a cop-out. Rather, he believes there is already a porous link between the upper and lower worlds and already a communication between them. Images in the depths generate an inner light, an *innerlichkeit*, or *lumen natura* that is sufficient unto itself and illuminates without translation, not unlike the transcendental potential that Stein described as "shin[ing] through the fabric of everyday life" (Stein, 2023)—a phenomenon resonant with Gean Gebser's principle of diaphany (Cheak, 2015). This view opens up the complexity of what we ordinarily imagine as one-sidedness and challenges any simple Cartesian view, a view that is implicit in rational discourse.

Hillman's turn to alchemical language is also a response to the conceptual rationalism of our time. The first chapter of his book *Alchemical Psychology* takes up the therapeutic value of alchemical language. Its value lies in its concrete, precise, and imagistic expression that resists being taken literally. No term means only one thing and every alchemical phenomenon is both material and psychological at the same time. Alchemical language has permeated Jungian discourse, but Hillman is not suggesting we simply exchange alchemical words to replace our concepts, which would be to take alchemical language literally. Rather, he proposes that we restore an alchemical mode of imagining that would recognize in all our concepts a metaphoric reality rather than seeing them as referring to psychological expressions like "the ego" and "the unconscious" as literal things. The tendency to do this in Jung's work is magnified by his tendency to think of psychology in terms of understanding human nature rather than as a practice, "a way of living, a way of seeing, a way of hearing, a way of responding, a way of sensing the Gods in the world" (Hillman & Shamdasani, 2013, p. 195), ultimately as the way of the daimon.

In spite of what some think of as Jung's tendency to objectify, I believe that he nonetheless lived his life in response to the daimonic presences that surrounded him. For Jung, the daimon does not emerge from the conscious personality. We do not fully grasp, dominate, or comprehend it. It emerges from the depths, beyond consciousness, and Jung approached the daimon through the practice of active imagination and dreaming the dream onward. Jung describes how such emergences have been referred to as mana or god as well as daimon, and he notes that science has employed the term "the unconscious," admitting we know nothing about it (Jung, 1963, p. 336). We only know that something alien and numinous comes our way. Kingsley links the daimon with Jung's experience of "the stream of lava: it's the power which is non-human and beyond human consciousness, or mastery or control, that takes care of everything" (Kingsley, 2018a, p. 88). It is for him what shapes consciousness. Here Kingsley refers to the primordial power of the archetypal psyche—a power metaphorized by Jung as a volcanic flow of lava, and as we have noted, an "incandescent matter" and "fiery basalt leading to the stone." It is the eruption and the flow of *prima materia* that shapes the soul as we reengage with it. I consider this engagement as carrying on in the spirit of the depths, a speaking to the soul in the soul's language—a phenomenological, mythic, and imaginal entrance into a daimonic relationship with psyche and soul. An example of this process is expressed in a series of active imaginations that took place during a 15-month period in the context of a longer analysis. What follows is a partial reiteration of a number of these active imaginations in edited form, aiming to capture psyche's intentionality and telos—what I have called the way of the daimon.

A patient of mine who had many losses and an extremely difficult early family life was in a marriage that was not working. He is highly intelligent, a person who has worked with his dreams, active imagination, and magical enactments that activated a deep psychic process. His inner life was an intense struggle and one might alchemically characterize his life at the time of this work as being in a state of *nigredo*, of blackness and burnout.

While I will not elaborate all the personal meanings and development of my patient's active imagination, it may be helpful to revisit some of the archetypal images, and the symbolic and mythical unfolding of the process, linking image to image that shapes the movement of transformation from blackened earth to an illuminated and vibrant renewal and expansion of Eros.

Beginning in a condition of lost vitality, hardened rock, and burnt-out ash, the work of analysis opened a confrontation with this *prima materia*. Active imagination catalyzed a libidinal arousal in the shape of a voluptuous woman. Her blackened body surged with the heat of the volcanic redness, pools of lava melting and flowing in circular patterns. An anima figure comes to life, a lava goddess heating up from within, reflecting an emerging desire beneath the surface. A Falcon,[1] considered by some to be a king of birds, spirit guide, and totem animal, appears as an ally of the goddess. In Egypt, many depictions of the gods bear a Falcon's head, most notably like Ra, an animal energy linked to a solar spirit, like the rising sun. The Falcon reflects an intensity of focus. Its spirit is known for looking directly at things. It has a hood covering its eyes. The hood, an Arabic contribution to falconry, served to keep this creature calm and from seeing something that would cause it anxiety. The removal of the hood opens a face-to-face and eye-to-eye engagement (Symbolikon, n.d.). My patient offers a gift to the goddess, a stone that is also a mirror, a reflectivity that is also described like a shining drop of mercury, a *prima materia* that is also a mercurial illumination. In pre-Columbian Mesoamerica,[2] mirrors were fashioned from stone and served a number of uses, including the practice of divination. They served as portals to a mysterious realm and as metaphors for sacred caves and conduits for supernatural forces closely associated with fire and flowers and as a means of connection with otherworldly entities and spirits (Midnight Muse, n.d.). The English alchemist John Dee (Simon, 2015) contacted such spirits with the help of Skryers and an Aztec mirror fashioned from obsidian. The offering of such a gift to the goddess is reflectivity mirroring a face-to-face engagement. As the hood is removed from the Falcon, it grabs this gift and looks directly at my patient as he returns the gaze. This transforms the gift into an illuminated egg—an archetypal image of origins, unhatched potential, and new life at the root of many creation myths worldwide. For Jung, in his *Red Book*, the opening of the egg brought forth Izdubar, associated with sun god and the potential for an intensification of life. For my patient, it was an image of a readiness to look into the unconscious aspects of his soul. His egg was marked with an intricate design of brightly glowing, iridescent triangles reminding him of DNA, a code intrinsic to all life. As he reaches into the egg, something grabs him as he grabs it and pulls it into consciousness. It is a long snake or eel, and, terrified, he shakes it off. It then frightens and electrifies him. The serpent and eel have many associations that generally express powerful and elusive instinctual forces whose movement is often shocking. Reaching down into the egg again brings up a glowing skull, indicating both the danger and seriousness of his endeavor and the illumination that comes with an encounter with death. Hearing the need to gain some control and come to terms with these images, he coats his hands with an orange powder also found within the egg. This seems to afford him a sense of security and agency, and creates some capacity for control and connection to the larger universe. His hands now feel protected and as he reaches out to the cosmos, a glittering light of purple and black illuminates his hands, as if he is wearing gloves. The powder seems to ready him for a deepened engagement in this process. It is interesting that in heraldry the color orange is symbolic of strength and endurance, and yellow and orange were often a favorite color of the alchemists in their search for gold and the Philosophers' Stone. Reaching down again into the depths, out of the egg comes a large pillar of light pointing toward the sky. The energy appears as a phallic illumination pointing up, but, at the same time, something is transforming below on the black earth, green plants and grasses are growing, and the air is humid around the pillar and rain is falling. The phallic upward light is complemented by the moistening of the green earth as the pillar of light is transformed into an illuminated tree with golden branches. Seen from a distance, this tree appears as a large illuminated brain. The tree looks sentient and fleshy. A tree of life with wide-ranging symbolism is often equated in alchemy with the stone and the goal of the work. The last section of Jung's *Alchemical Studies* is dedicated to rich descriptions of the philosophical tree, the various stages of the process of transformation. For my patient, the tree has become a living presence conjoining up and down, heaven and earth, male and female, into a living symbol—all producing and bringing into focus a child, both inner and outer. As my patient engages with the tree, a deep sadness emerges and tears flow, not unlike the gentle moisture that fertilized the tree's growth. Sparks of light have gathered together into an image of his son. Staying deeply connected to his son after his divorce was an important part of his concern and to do so required a movement of soul, both inner and in relationship to his son. In an experience of joy, the inner and outer child connect and flower.

In the final part of this active imagination, my patient felt a passionate desire for deeper intimacy with the lava goddess. This intimacy took a graphic, erotic form and an engagement with the goddess's backside, shaking and slapping her buttocks until there was an orange glow and spiraling lava emerging from her. He wanted to plunge into it, but was worried about getting burnt by the intensity of heat. A process of transformation begins by the goddess covering my patient with dirt. Elsewhere I have written about the importance of filth in the process of alchemical transformation (Marlan, 2019). The erotic transformation that occurs involves an opening and orgasmic flow of lava, an earth-splitting process that transforms the libidinal passion into an expanded sense of eros. Symbolically, the process involves the goddess holding out a blue apple with a golden interior that she squeezes until the golden juices flow into a chalice. The blue apple denotes that this is not a literal red apple, but rather an imaginary one. In *Alchemical Psychology* (2010), Hillman writes about blue in its relationship to the imagination (Hillman, 2010, p. 110) and notes its importance in the transition from black to white (Hillman, 2010, p. 97), from the *nigredo* to the *albedo*, and from burnout to renewal. Following Martin Heidegger and Robert Avens, Hillman amplifies blueness by noting a quote from Heidegger: "Blue is not an image to indicate the sense of the holy. Blueness itself is the holy, in virtue of its gathering depth which shines forth only as it veils itself" (Hillman, 2010, p. 325). Hillman goes on to explain that, according to Avens, this "holiness is not a property of a God … but a name for all entities insofar as they display a numinous aspect; it is an ingredient that wakens, ensouls, and vivifies everything" (Hillman, 2010). In my patient's active imagination, this blue fruit has a golden interior, and a potion is prepared by squeezing it, so that its juices flow into a vessel from which it can be consumed and digested. To this elixir, the goddess adds a mysterious powder that causes a fizzing and change of color. Both the fizz and the pearl color amplify the vivification of blue. To fizz suggests an effervescence, liveliness, excitement, and exuberance. While the color and symbolism of pearl has many meanings, it is associated with luster, luminosity, and pleasure. In ancient myth it was associated with spiritual power and great vitality. Drinking this potion sends my patient into a pleasurable but cooling transformation.

It is well known that the regulation of heat was a fundamental act of the alchemists and essential to alchemical transformation. In Hillman's *Alchemical Psychology*, he explores this regulation of heat, erotic energy, and the importance of fire. Hillman speaks the language of fire and asks the question "What does the soul want?" He concludes that what it wants is a rethinking of it with the body and the world, which produces "a resurrection in beauty and pleasure" (Hillman, 2010, p. 258), a return to the world "[b]eautiful and glad" (Hillman, 2010, p. 261), that heralds the alchemical *rubedo*, a vital reddening of life beyond abstract psychological life. For Hillman, the beauty of the imagination only makes sense if its desirousness is felt as a libidinal and Aphroditic reality, a "touch of Venus," and, like Voluptas, the goddess of sensual pleasure and delight, of which the lava goddess is an expression (Hillman, 2010).

Once one goes beyond the limits of intellect alone, negates it, and turns to a deeper experience, it opens the potential for an abundant vitality which Lacan noted, "[b]egins with a tickle and ends with blaze of petrol" (Lacan, 1991, p. 72). Lacan's passionate metaphor speaks to the heat necessary for the transformation process, but for Hillman even Lacan's idea of *jouissance* falls short of describing the libidinal erotics of fire. For Hillman, "the libido [is] a cosmic erotic dynamic that permeates the world because it loves the world of matter" (Hillman, 2010, p. 257). Hillman's "Aphroditic language" drips with lust from

the metabolic heats of the body that stew and digest and melt the loins. ...
As the fire licks and clings to the logs it burns, so passion clings to the bodies
of life. ... Like the claws of a cat, the paws of a lion, sulfuric fire attaches to
the object of its desire or attaches itself to its desire. Intense internal heat as
the moment of fertility.

(Hillman, 2010, pp. 21–22)

Initially the heat of passion strives to possess life, the anima as soul. But life
cannot be possessed by our grasp—we cannot own the objects of our lust without diminishing them or ourselves. Hillman traces the notion of libido to "a
word cluster ... that includes ... to make liquid, [to] melt ... to love; as well as
... [to] (free)" (Hillman, 2010, p. 259). Releasing and freeing the passion to possess implies a letting go of the self as well. I believe this is what Hillman means
by "the psychotherapeutic cure of 'me'" (Hillman, 2010, p. 255). Oddly, such a
release does not diminish passion, but increases, tinctures, and matures it
through considerable pain and struggle, returning the adept anew to the world
of matter and nature. The return allows one to see in matter a display, an inner
light, which illuminates the independence of the other. The Stone ripens in the
fire and in the glow of the alchemical imagination. At the end of my patient's
engagement with the lava goddess, she teaches him the alchemical secret of the
regulation of heat, of the transformation and broadening of eros—and who
better than the lava goddess to teach this art. Like Jung and Hillman, I would
claim that Eros is an important part of the reddening of psychology.

The issue of Eros is taken up by Laubscher in his book *Introduction to
Psychology as a Human Science*. Laubscher traces the history, development,
and roots of human science from antiquity to postmodern times. His reflections include his personal frustrations with the limits of psychology as a natural science. What originally drew him to psychology were questions about what
it means to be a human being—a question that filled him with awe and wonder.
The mystery faded as he encountered the reductive limits of a natural scientific
approach to the field. For Laubscher, a certain ontological depth of soul was
missing. In the conclusion of his book, he notes that the meaning of the
English word *psyche* and psychology is the breath of life, the vital force of life
itself. Laubscher amplifies this missing and lost spirit of psychology by recalling the Greek myth of Psyche and Eros. For him, this myth serves as "an origin
story for a reimagined psychology, a psychology that animates life like breath
and breathing does," and refers to the kiss of Eros (love) and awakens both
psyche and soul, noting "[f]or there is no place for love to dwell, save the soul,
who animates all things; and there is no meaning for the soul to live and be
awake, save for the sake of love" (Laubscher, 2016, p. 142). Ultimately, for
Jung, Eros exceeds our understanding, and our inability to possess it is an
important recognition of its divine essence. The "range of activity extends
from the endless spaces of the heavens to the darkest abysses of hell" (Jung,
1963, p. 353). Language fails to capture its paradoxical quality. Eros (or Love)

is man's light and darkness and whose ends he cannot see. It is a *complexio oppositorum* and the "creator ... of all higher consciousness" (Jung, 1963). For Jung, if one possesses "a grain of wisdom, he will lay down his arms and name the unknown by the more unknown, *ignotum per ignotius*—that is, by the name of God" (Jung, 1963, p. 354). It is this spirit that Laubscher sees as essential in a reimagined psychology as a human science and, for me, it is the alchemical process of *rubedo* through which Eros reddens psychology.

There is much more to say about the reddening of psychology and the *rubedo* of alchemy, but that is for another time. However, I would like to note that while the importance of love and soul is essential, Eros is only one opening to the mysteries of psyche. From the perspective of Jung, Hillman, and others, in addition to Eros, there are many important archetypal perspectives, including Hermes/Mercurius, Iris, the Furies, Lucifer, as well as Aphrodite—and these are just a few of the daimons of darkness and light that can illuminate the soul—and I should add that both illuminate and darken at the same time in the spirit of the later Heidegger's *lichtung* and meontology. From a Jungian point of view, these archetypal energies are relatively outside of ego consciousness and yet related to it in a creative tension that is another way of imagining which opens our way toward a language resonant with the soul's journey. The way of the daimon opens many languages, and I believe that Human Science must make room for them and open a space for the multiplicity of these archetypal energies and continue to develop ways of metabolizing the spirits of the depths and perhaps even being metabolized by them to expand our understanding of "science."

I would like to conclude by mentioning the work of John Caputo, who approaches the profundity of this mystery as a radical unthinkable ground—linking it to Heidegger's idea of the "open," to both illumination and darkness, a *mysterium tremendum* that he approaches through imagination and moves through and beyond phenomenology per se to a theopolitics in many respects resonant with the work of Archetypal Psychology.

Notes

1 The symbolic meaning of the Falcon was taken from two sources: Falcon Symbol - Animal Symbolism—Sacred Animals (symbolikon.com) and https://whatismyspirit animal.com/spirit-totem-power-animal-meanings/birds/falcon-symbolism-meaning/#Falcon-Symbolism
2 The symbolic meaning of magical mirrors was taken from Mirrors in Mesoamerican culture - Midnight Muse (midnight-muse.com).

References

Cheak, Aaron. (2015). Rendering darkness and light present: Gean Gebser and the principle of piaphany. *Diaphany: A Journal Plus Nocturne*, 1, 21–37.
Hillman, James. (1979). *The dream and the underworld*. Harper and Row.

Hillman, James. (2010). *Alchemical psychology*. Spring Publications.

Hillman, James & Sonu Shamdasani. (2013). *Lament of the dead: Psychology after Jung's Red Book*. W.W. Norton & Co.

Jung, C. G. (1944). *Psychology and alchemy, the collected works of C.G. Jung*, Vol. 12, edited by Gerhard Adler and translated by R. F. C. Hull. Princeton: Princeton University Press.

Jung, C. G. (1953/1968). "Commentary on *the secret of the golden flower.*" In *Alchemical studies. The collected works of C.G. Jung*, Vol. 13, edited by Gerhard Adler and translated by R. F. C. Hull. Princeton: Princeton University Press, pp. 251–349.

Jung, C. G. (1963). *Memories, dreams, reflections*. Recorded and edited by Aniela Jaffé and translated by Richard and Clara Winston. New York: Pantheon.

Jung, C. G. (1973). *C.G. Jung letters*, Vol. I. Edited by Gerhard Adler and Aniela Jaffé, and translated by R.F.C. Hull. Princeton: Princeton University Press.

Jung, C. G. (2009). *The Red Book: Liber Novus: A reader's edition*. 2009. Edited by Sonu Shamdasani and translated by Mark Kyburz, John Peck, and Sonu Shamdasani. New York: W.W. Norton & Co.

Kingsley, Peter (2018a). "A conversation between Peter Kingsley and Murray Stein." *MYSTERY: Murray Stein in conversation with Peter Kingsley about Jung's "Red Book"*. https://www.youtube.com/watch?v=uWaeqeIi82g&t=8s. Accessed August 19, 2024.

Kingsley, Peter (2018b). *Catafalque: Carl Jung and the end of humanity*. London: Catafalque Press.

Lacan, Jacques. (1991). *The other side of psychoanalysis: The seminar of Jacques Lacan, Book XVII*. Translated by Russell Grigg. New York: W.W. Norton & Co.

Laubscher, Leswin. (2016). *Introduction to psychology as a human science*. Cognella Academic Publishing.

Marlan, Stanton. (2019). What's the matter—with alchemical recipes?: Philosophy and filth in the forging of Jung's alchemical psychology. In J. Mills (Ed.), *Jung and philosophy*. London: Routledge.

Midnight Muse. (n.d.). *Mirrors in Mesoamerican culture*. https://www.midnight-muse.com/mirrors-mesoamerican-culture/

Owens, Lance S. (2015). *Jung in love: The mysterium in Liber Novus*. Gnosis Archive Books.

Saban, Mark. (2019). *Two souls alas: Jung's two personalities and the making of analytical psychology*. Asheville: Chiron.

Simon, Ed. (2015). Notes on John Dee's Aztec Mirror. *Journal of the Northern Renaissance*. https://jnr2.hcommons.org/2015/3990/. Accessed August 19, 2024.

Stein, Murray. (2023). On the importance of numinous experience in the alchemy of individuation. In A. Casement and D. Tacey (Eds.), *The idea of the numinous: Contemporary Jungian and psychoanalytic perspectives* (pp. 34–52). London: Routledge. (2006).

Symbolikon. (n.d.). *Falcon Symbol*. https://symbolikon.com/downloads/falcon-symbol/

Introduction to "In the Gap between Phenomenology and Jungian Psychology: Cultivating a 'Poetics' of Psychological Life"

Romanyshyn's professional life of over fifty years has been devoted to the dialogue between depth psychology and phenomenology. That place of contact, which is lived in the intertwining between ourselves and each other and ourselves and the world, has needed to be rethought because thinking in this region requires new terms. It also requires the recovery of an aesthetic sensibility that has been increasingly forgotten and suppressed in the age of technology's literalized and functional definitions of reality and experience. What emerges in this chiasm, which is Merleau-Ponty's apt term, is a poetics of psychological life where depth is reimagined as much laterally as vertically. Romanyshyn's outline here should be intuitively familiar to Jungian readers for whom what Jung called the symbolic life is readily available in the heart of all experience.

Chapter 3

In the Gap between Phenomenology and Jungian Psychology

Cultivating a "Poetics" of Psychological Life

Robert D. Romanyshyn

Between Merleau-Ponty and Jung: A Poetics of Psychological Life

Merleau-Ponty states that phenomenology and psychoanalysis tend toward the same latency of the body. His word for that body where these two traditions encounter each other is *"chair"* (flesh), which he asserts has no name in philosophy and which is the site of a new ontology (Merleau-Ponty, 1973).

Describing flesh as an elemental reality, Merleau-Ponty is working toward a way of being in the world and knowing it that no longer privileges the point of view of consciousness. In his major work, *The Phenomenology of Perception*, the chapter "The Cogito" already anticipates the flesh. The chapter opens with this remark:

> I am thinking of the Cartesian cogito, wanting to finish this work, feeling the coolness of the paper under my hand, and perceiving the trees of the boulevard through the window.
>
> (1945/1958, p. 429)

One might be stopped in one's tracks by this simple sentence. Mind can lose itself in this jungle of gerunds where thinking is wanting, feeling, and perceiving, where desire is an armature of thinking, where there is a chiasm of a body that is sensitive to the sensuous touch of the world's cool breath, and where perception finds its realization in the perceptible.

Was Merleau-Ponty dreaming when he wrote those words as the Cogito was being drawn out of itself into the boulevard? Or, perhaps, had he slipped into a state of reverie for a moment, seduced by the sensuous charms of the day and the desires of a fleshy mind? Were his words already sketching out the need for a different language, which he noted when he said psychoanalysis is also a new ontology, or at least it is that possibility when Freud's psychoanalysis is freed of its Cartesian metaphysical baggage. Already in his first work, *The Structure of Behavior*, Merleau-Ponty questions "whether the conflicts ... of which he [Freud] speaks and the psychological mechanisms which he described really

DOI: 10.4324/9781032694603-5

require the system of causal notions by which he interprets them." In reply he states, "it is easy to see that causal thinking is not indispensable here and that one can use another language" (1963, p. 177).

That other language is the language of the flesh, which cultivates a poetics of psychological life. Recall that passage in the pivotal chapter, *The Cogito*, where that jungle of gerunds entangles a reader and sweeps him/her along in a flow of action where the "I" who is thinking disappears in tides of desire that draw the "I" who thinks into the world. A chiasm entwines the flesh of the "I" with the flesh of the world, a point which Merleau-Ponty develops in rich detail in his last published essay "Eye and Mind" and in the text *The Visible and the Invisible*, which he was working on when he died.

Alphonso Lingis, the translator of *The Visible and the Invisible*, says, "The concept of flesh emerges as the ultimate notion of Merleau-Ponty's thought" (1968, p. liv). As Merleau-Ponty develops this notion, it becomes clear that flesh is not just what phenomenology describes as the lived body distinguished from the objective body. Rather, flesh is an elemental reality, like the elements of air, water, fire, earth, light, and to understand its elemental presence one finally has to surrender any positivist notion of the body as an empirical given, a corporeal piece of the visible world over against a mind, "the seer, which must be an incorporeal and non-sensorial knowing agency, an immaterial spirit, finally a pure clearing, a nothingness" (p. lv).

The other also belongs to this equivalence of sensibility and the sensible, for just as one is a seer for whom the other is seen, that other is also a seer for whom I am seen. In this respect, flesh is the locus of a crossing, the site where the dichotomies of subject and object and self and other are entangled below the level of reflection. The elemental flesh is a chiasm where self and other are dissolved, where the equivalence is an exchange, a transformation in which "I" who look at a thing or at you am also looked at by things and by you, a pivot where one is simultaneously the seer and the seen, a subject and an object. A pivot so subtle that one is not able, for example, to know on a cold morning as one rubs his/her hands together if the right hand is touching or being touched by the left hand and vice versa. Even with the most concentrated effort of consciousness, subject and object slip into each other and change places. The reflexive form of verbs so much more emphasized in French than in English bears witness to this ordinary miracle.

Flesh exists within the field of the visible. "Things," Merleau-Ponty says, "have an internal equivalent in me; they arouse in me a carnal formula of their presence" (Merleau-Ponty, 1964, p. 164). But if things have their internal equivalence in me, how much more seductive is the internal equivalent of the other, whose flesh so much more mirrors one's own, whose form situates self and other in a circuit of reflection, in a field of reciprocity that is unmatched by other forms of being. But in all cases, whether it be with the other who reciprocates my gestures, or with the things of the world, one's body as flesh radiates beyond itself. Looking at the world, for example, one's eyes do not search out the landscape from some outpost, directed in its gaze like a beam from some flashlight by a mind that is outside the visible. On the contrary, one's eyes are drawn out of their anatomical sockets and wander over there toward the world to ogle, gaze, stare, or otherwise engage it. There is more to seeing than what meets the eyeball—voyeurism is not an ophthalmological problem!

Seeing finds its fulfillment in the other or in the things seen, in that thing or other that has impregnated one's flesh and left a carnal imprint of its presence, in that other or thing that has aroused, seduced, and enfolded one within its embrace. For Merleau-Ponty, then, perception is the enactment of a carnal desire that flesh has for the other, an expression of a carnal hunger.

The notion of flesh gives flesh to the form of Being, and, as an element that is the foundation for a new ontology, there is no other word for this circuit of arousal, for this carnal desire and hunger except Eros. What we arrive at with this notion of flesh, therefore, is that place where Merleau-Ponty's phenomenology of the body encounters the body in depth psychology. In this respect it is no accident that in his working notes to his last book, Merleau-Ponty sets for himself the task of describing the "pre-egology" (Merleau-Ponty, 1964, p. 220) of the flesh.

In "Eye and Mind" Merleau-Ponty, quoting Paul Valery, says, "'the painter takes his body with him,'" to which he adds, "Indeed we cannot imagine how a mind could paint" (Merleau-Ponty, 1964, p. 162). The painter, then, who takes his body with him/her is caught up in this circuit of desire. He or she is one who is impregnated by what he/she paints as much as he/she impregnates what he/she paints. Indeed, we cannot imagine how a mind could paint because it would have no place within the visible structure of the world, no place from which to see and be seen, and no flesh by which it is aroused by the carnal formula of things. To illustrate this point, Merleau-Ponty (1964) cites the artist Paul Klee:

> In a forest, I have felt many times over that it was not I who looked at the forest. Some days I felt that the trees were looking at me, were speaking to me ... I was there, listening ... I think that the painter must be penetrated by the universe and not want to penetrate it ... I expect to be inwardly sub-merged, buried. Perhaps I paint to break out.
>
> (p. 167)

Penetrated, impregnated, submerged, even buried, Merleau-Ponty's notion of flesh challenges any notion of mind as the autonomous author of meaning and any notion of language as the sole creation of mind. Like the painter who paints to break out, to give form and color, line, and expression to what has been given and addressed to him/her, the poet also speaks because he/she has heard and listened. Rilke's *Duino Elegies* is a good example.

Situating us between the Angel, who is self-sufficient in its own beauty and who is indifferent to our cries, and the animal, who is content to remain in the womb of nature that has brought it forth, we exist, stand out and lament our fate of being in the between, our fate of being neither Angel nor Beast, neither spirit nor matter, but flesh.

The elegiac songs of lament are, however, also songs of praise that acclaim our place between matter and spirit. In the flesh we, unlike the Angel or the Animal, are here to give voice to what solicits us. Agents more than authors of meaning, we are in Rilke's fine phrase "bees of the invisible," those who gather the blue honey of the world and in the flesh do the work of transformation. For Rilke we speak in that pause between the two moments of breathing, in that alchemical moment when, having breathed in and been in-spired by the carnal form of the visible, we then breathe out a word in the moment of ex-piration, the moment when we die to our inherence in things and take the leap and the risk of saying.

> Are we, perhaps, here just for saying: House,
> Bridge, Fountain, Gate, Jug, Olive tree, Window, –
> possibly: Pillar, Tower? ...
>   (Rilke, 1939, p. 75)[1]

We should not pass over too quickly the slight hesitation regarding this leap. Perhaps we are here just for this saying; and possibly we are called to say this particular word, or that one. In the poet's hands, the philosopher's insights are re-imagined. Merleau-Ponty's field of flesh is a con-spiracy, a breathing together, a resonance in which as Merleau-Ponty notes in his comments on Klee, "There really is inspiration and expiration of Being, action and passion so slightly discernible that it becomes impossible to distinguish between what sees and what is seen, what paints and what is painted" (Merleau-Ponty, 1964, p. 167). Perhaps! Possibly! But neither poet nor philosopher doubts this vocation that is an obligation. And so, a few lines later in the Ninth Elegy Rilke asks, "Earth, isn't this what you want: an invisible/re-arising in us?"[2] (Rilke, 1939, p. 77) It is a question whose answer has already been given in these songs of lament and praise.

With the notion of flesh Merleau-Ponty claims what he says no other philosophy has claimed, namely, the passivity that is at the heart of our activity, that sense of being claimed by the visible even as we lay claim to it and seek to possess it. He notes, "he who sees cannot possess the visible unless he is possessed by it, unless he is of it" (Merleau-Ponty, 1968, p. 134–135).

What Merleau-Ponty works through in the language of the flesh is analogous to what depth psychology works through in its language of consciousness and the unconscious and the transference and counter-transference relations between patient and therapist. As such Merleau-Ponty is going beyond the Freudian unconscious and moving toward Jung. For example, Jung's diagram of the complexities of transference can be viewed as a deepening of Merleau-Ponty's notion of the chiasm. That diagram, which is a quaternity of conscious and unconscious relations, applies as much to the relation between a reader and text as it does to analyst and patient, It moves Merleau-Ponty's philosophy toward Jung's idea of an unconscious reality beyond a diagnosed one.

This move toward Jung is part of how the notion of the unconscious has developed over the course of the 20th century, how the scope and range of the un-reflected has been expanded. (Thus, when Merleau-Ponty claims for philosophy that passivity is at the heart of our activity, he is opening a space where at all levels of the unconscious, consciousness as the author of meaning encounters its other side, where it is the agent of meaning in service to what has been repressed, and as well in service to those ancestors who linger as the weight of history and who wait for us to respond to what has been "unresolved, unredeemed and unanswered" (Jung 1961, p. 191) in their lives. And here, I would underscore that Merleau-Ponty's notion of the flesh, as that field where the world in its existential and temporal totality impregnates one, converges with Jung's work with Wolfgang Pauli regarding the psychoid archetype. For Jung at this level of the unconscious psyche and nature are one, where, we might say, psyche is elemental. For Merleau-Ponty flesh is that elemental reality where the fleshy mind is impregnated by nature, where mind finds itself already founded within the elemental world. There is a place in each of us where one senses he or she is green, or the wind, or the drop of dew on a blade of grass in the early morning sun, a feeling of a kinship with the elemental world of which flesh is a part. In this respect, we are also agents in service to the ecological unconscious, a bit of nature itself with the power to give expression to its in-spirations, the power to give form to its in-dwellings within us.

So, in the gap between phenomenology and depth psychology,
in the darker light of an embodied mind,
in a cogito that already finds itself emmeshed in webs of desire,
in a mind already entangled with the world in the same erotic love affair
that plays itself out between the shadows and the light,
in a mind that sees the world because it is itself seeable:
Is not the allure of the mystery of psychological life an education rooted
in a hunger for and seduction by the opulent, shameless epiphanies of the
world which, like fireflies in the night, cannot be jarred and sealed without
their light going out?
Do not these epiphanies of psychological life, those momentary sparks in
darkness, require a kind of response to what is almost ineffable, a response
that at best alludes to the elusive, an indirect language that attends to the
voices of silence, which, like dreams, symptoms, feelings, fantasies, reveries
leave clues for a grammar of soul making?

Phenomenology as a Poetic Realism

The sheen of the sheer presence of things as they merely are unfolds the meaning of the world as primarily a poetic realism. One can see this in the simple gesture of the pointing finger of the young child who is not yet the master of words. It also lingers in us who, surprised by the too often forgotten wonder of the world, first points to what in the moment is beyond words. The word is the maturation of this gesture, the moment when the word like the painter's brush arises from the flesh, which reveals the seductive, erotic bond between the sensuous charms of the world and the sensual flesh at the core of a poetic realism.

Bachelard's and Van den Berg's phenomenology invite one to encounter the epiphanies of the world's poetic realism with a recovered sense of wonder. Is this not what phenomenology at its best does: Makes one naive enough to wander as a witness to wonder, to learn to look at the world again? Or, as Merleau-Ponty notes, to be "a perpetual beginner."

As John Sallis notes (1973), phenomenology is a return to beginnings, a task marked by the difference and the strife between the origins to which one returns and the origins from which one has departed. And, as he adds, there is no other term for what lies in the gap and mediates the tension of that strife than imagination.

This return to beginnings is a turning again and again toward things and what we know and believe in order to take note of what still shines with neglected possibilities that seduce us to look again with a soft focus as it were. That soft focus is the cultivation of the eye of the imagination, which William Blake's distinction between seeing through and not with the eye describes. Indeed, Blake points to the consequences when we fail to nurture the eye of imagination. He says, "We are led to Believe a Lie/ When we see with not Thro the Eye" (Blake, 1950).

The poetry of Wallace Stevens ripples with the challenges of that lie. It is there, for example, in just these three lines from "An Ordinary Evening in New Haven":

We keep coming back and coming back
To the real: to the hotel instead of the hymns
That fall upon it out of the winds ...[3]

The Poet as phenomenologist dwells in these lines, telling us we come back again and again to the Visible and no longer see or hear or sense or speak in any way to and of the Invisible that companions the Visible.

And then, several lines down as a counterpoint to the above, Stevens says to us what poetry must be if it cultivates the eye of imagination and attends to the Invisible:

The poem is the cry of its occasion,
Part of the res itself and not about it.
The poet speaks the poem as it is
Not as it was: part of the reverberation

Of a windy night as it is, when the marble statues
Are like newspapers blown by the wind.[4]

(Stevens, 2011, pp. 147, 148)

These lines exemplify the duty of the poet. "The task of poetry," Stevens says, "is the writing of a supreme fiction" so that, he adds, and this is a key insight, one might realize, "The supreme fiction is the fiction of the fact"[5] (Critchley, 2005, pp. 48, 60).

Poets like Stevens are a regular part of my continuing education as a psychologist, which, of course, does not suit the demands of the discipline. But it is and has been a task I must take up because the supreme fiction of psychology today is its belief that it is a science, or a philosophy, or even a poetics. Indeed, I would even suggest that the supreme fiction of psychology today is the belief that it is even a discipline. And yet, as Stevens notes, "The final belief is to believe in a fiction, there being nothing else. The exquisite truth is to know it is a fiction and that you believe it willingly."[6]

So, I believe in the fiction of a poetics of psychological life even as I know I am making believe that I believe it. And I do so because it shows the necessity for and is a condition for an ethical epistemology that opens the space for dialogue and provides ground for action when one must choose. Again, Stevens speaks to this point in "Asides on the Oboe":

The prologues are over. It is a question, now,
Of final belief. So say that final belief
Must be in a fiction. It is time to choose[7]
(Stevens, 2011, p. 145)

It is time to choose because the lie that blinds the eye of imagination fuels the crisis of modernity's dream of a technologically created world. The next part of my presentation explores this theme by recovering the technological worldview as a fiction, or a perspective, or myth if one prefers those terms, that forgets and forgets that it forgets it is a fiction. But a few final words here before that.

A poetics of psychological life underscores the intimate nexus between perceiving and speaking. In one of the working notes to *The Visible and the Invisible*, which I read as the pivot where Merleau-Ponty's philosophical phenomenology turns toward a poetic phenomenology, he says, "we speak because/(as) we see, and we see because/(as) we speak."

Attending to the epiphanies of psychological life with that soft gaze through the eye of the imagination, calls for a psychological language, which, aware of the *fiction of the fact*, simply alludes to those sparks of soul that remain elusive. Both words echo their Latin root *ludere*, underscoring a poetics of psychological life as a way of saying that plays with the world (*al-ludere*), while the world playfully eludes (e-ludere) the play, slipping the net, as it were, of our meanings, setting up a rhythm, a flow between embodied mind and world, refusing the lapidary temptation to fix in stone this meaning or that meaning. A poetics of psychological life is a kind of alchemy where the stone *is* and *is not* a stone, an alchemy, which like alchemy itself works via images, which are and are not what they are, images of symbols now coagulating a meaning and then dissolving it. When Jung notes that psyche is image, he is creating a psychology whose style of discourse, whose way of speaking says and unsays what it says, reveals and conceals what is, a style with a metaphoric sensibility.

Such a sensibility situates one in the realm of "as if." Stevens speaks to the power of the "as if" when he says his theory of poetry is the theory of life,

> As it is, in the intricate evasions of as,
> In things seen and unseen, created from nothingness,
> The heavens, the hells, the worlds, the longed-for lands.
> (Critchley, 2005, p. 17)

Or What's a Metaphor?

A metaphoric sensibility is an unveiling of those evasions, a revelation of possibilities where this thing is seen *as if* it were that thing, where one glimpses through an image a thing's dream of being other. The poetry of Wallace Stevens eloquently exemplifies this sensibility. Starting with things as they merely are, the work of the poet is "the incantation of reality under the spell of imagination" (Crtichley, Things Merely Are, 58). In the space "between imagination reducing reality to itself and reality reducing the imagination's power to impotence" (p. 85), Stevens' poetry aligns with a poetics of psychological life crafted in the gap between phenomenology and depth psychology. And like Stevens' take on poetry, a poetics of psychological life "increases our feeling for reality by allowing us to see it, to focus on that which we normally pass over in our everyday activity" (p. 89). His poetics, like the poetics of psychological life even "offers a possible form of redemption ... which saves the sense of the world for us" (p. 59). Saves the world, and finds in the world the vessel for soul making: "Call the world, if you please, the Vale of Soul Making. Then you will find out the use of the world."

A metaphor is the shortest of short stories. It is a fiction that loosens the thick and heavy weight of reality when it is imagined through something else, as, for example, when, uncertain if the bird I see in the garden is a purple finch, Peterson's *Field Guide* convinces me it is when it says a purple finch is a sparrow dripped in raspberry juice. We would believe a lie were we to see this as a fact, or for that matter as an idea. And, we would miss how image is the domain of metaphor and miss how a poetics of psychological life is an attitude, a style of seeing and saying, as Merleau-Ponty describes phenomenology in his Preface to *Phenomenology of Perception*. Phenomenology and a poetics of psychological life *are* inclinations toward the world whose reach exceeds its grasp – , to which I would add – or what's a metaphor!

The Need for a Therapy of Culture

Attesting to the birthright of flesh, a poetics of psychological life reclaims the erotic bond between the sensual flesh of embodiment and the sensuous flesh of the world. Returning to the flesh *re-minds* us of what we have lost, forgotten, or otherwise disregarded, when we no longer notice those epiphanies of imagination that unfold the extraordinary in the ordinary, the miracle in the mundane, the surprise of the unexpected that erupts from the familiar. Those displays recover the web of enchantment between us and the world. That web has been broken or at least dangerously frayed.

The epiphanies of the world's poetic realism sow the seeds for a cultural-historical anamnesis. James Hillman's notion of a therapy of ideas points to this work. Van den Berg's metabletic phenomenology is this work of anamnesis which he originated and brilliantly describes across multiple books and essays.

His metabletics is a return to the origins of specific cultural-historical events whose origins have been forgotten but still live on as a shared collective dream that pervades waking life as a form of amnesia, a condition of collective forgetting, a double amnesia within which we even forget we have forgotten.

In a series of cultural-historical metabletic studies over the years, my focus has been on the origins of the scientific-technological worldview as a collective cultural-historical dream. Returning to these origins, metabletics re-collects those origins as a possibility and opens a space for imagination to question what we have made of that possibility. Here is the question that has animated my own metabletic reflections:

Have we become so ensorcelled by that cultural-historical dream that we cannot even remember that the multiple ecological, social, political, economic, educational, medical, etc. crises we face today are symptoms of the dark shadows spawned by that double amnesia for those origins?

To conclude my presentation, I offer this closing meditation to illustrate the necessity for a cultural-historical therapy and to set the mood to experience the current crises of this way of framing the world, and, perhaps, underline the need for effective psychological ways to respond, to be response-able as concerned citizens, to them.

100 Seconds to Midnight

In 2019 the Doomsday Clock was set at two minutes to midnight. In January of this year, it was re-set to 100 seconds to midnight, the closest we have been to this mark since it was created in 1947.

Midnight is the moment when the annihilation of the human species and the destruction of nature as we know it happens.

Unthinkable? Unimaginable?

When the first atomic bomb was dropped on Hiroshima 75 years ago how many seconds did those living in the city have left in their lives before their annihilation? Whatever the number of seconds they had, they did not know how much time they had left. They could not even imagine that at ground zero the human body would be vaporized or become a shadow on a wall.

But for this example, we would know.

We would know we have 100 seconds to midnight.

What does 100 seconds to live feel like?

Let us take a moment to imagine those 100 seconds and feel into that day as the first atomic bomb was falling, falling, falling in a kind of deathly silence exploding in a blinding flash of light.

Let us listen to the ticking of the Doomsday clock as it approaches midnight!

Can we hear it?

For a moment let us sink into the final second and then

STOP!

Do we still have time? Do we still have time to ask for whom the Doomsday clock ticks, and to realize it ticks for you and me and all of us?

Do we still have time to wake up even in the last second and know that the Doomsday clock is counting down the seconds for you and me and all of us and all the billon animals burned in the Australian fires, for the dying forests and polluted waters, and for all and each of us and those whom we know and love who have ever been and still might be?

The Doomsday Clock is a mirror, which reflects back to us a disturbing image of the so-called new normal that is a measure of our collective insanity.

In the shadow of the bomb we see the nightmare side of technology as symptom and dream. In the shadow of the bomb we are in our nightmares all shadows on the wall.

How have we arrived at this point?

How do we respond when the alarm wakes us from sleep?

Have we been dreaming?

Are we responsible for our dreams?

Dreams speak the language of unconscious dynamics in terms of images, and regarding such images Jung notes, "The images of the unconscious place a great responsibility upon a man" and "insight into them must be converted into an ethical obligation" (Jung 1961, p. 193).

In the bodies of knowledge we create our failure to take into account the presence of unconscious factors makes our epistemologies one-sided, fixed truths and ideological exercises of power. As such they become expressions of epistemological violence in their blatantly visible forms and their more corrosive still invisible subtle forms. One has only to look at the multiple splitting that has plagued the history and development of depth psychology to see how differences with the other, without proper consideration of the other in oneself, lead to animosity toward and the demonizing of the other. In addition, one has only to consider how the ethos of Western science, despite its great achievements, has cast a huge shadow of destruction over human life and the natural world.

We live today not only in the shadow of the bomb, but also in the deepening darkness of environmental collapse as the polar icecaps continue to melt, the western arm of the gulf stream in the North Atlantic ocean is weakening, the seas and oceans become increasingly polluted, the buildup of carbon-based greenhouse gases reaches ever higher levels and raging fires, floods, and other weather catastrophes are increasingly destructive, while animal and human habitats are destroyed and the number of homeless refuges swells almost beyond belief. All the bodies of knowledge we create, like the bodies of those who create them, cast a shadow. To come to terms with the shadow side of our ways of knowing and constructing the world, an ethical epistemology would have to make a place for unconscious dynamics in our ways of knowing the world.

In the gap between phenomenology and depth psychology, technology as a cultural-historical dream is becoming a nightmare. Coming to terms with our part in this increasingly dire situation is the emergency of our age, the single most important task facing humanity today.

> The prologues are over. It is a question, now,
> Of final belief. So say that final belief
> Must be in a fiction. It is time to choose.[8]
>   (Stevens, 2011, p. 145)

Notes

1   "Ninth Elegy," from *Duino Elegies: A New and Complete Translation*, by Rainer Maria Rilke, translated by Alfred Corn. Copyright © 2021 by Alfred Corn. Used by permission of W. W. Norton & Company, Inc.

2   "Ninth Elegy", from *Duino Elegies: A New and Complete Translation*, by Rainer Maria Rilke, translated by Alfred Corn. Copyright © 2021 by Alfred Corn. Used by permission of W. W. Norton &Company, Inc.

3   "Asides on the Oboe," copyright © 1942 by Wallace Stevens; and "An Ordinary Evening in New Haven" from *The Collected Poems of Wallace Stevens*, by Wallace Stevens, copyright © 1954 by Wallace Stevens and copyright renewed 1982 by Holly Stevens. Used by permission of Alfred A. Knopf, an imprint of the Knopf Doubleday Publishing Group, a division of Penguin Random House LLC. All rights reserved.

4   "Asides on the Oboe," copyright © 1942 by Wallace Stevens; and "An Ordinary Evening in New Haven" from *The Collected Poems of Wallace Stevens*, by Wallace Stevens, copyright © 1954 by Wallace Stevens and copyright renewed 1982 by Holly Stevens. Used by permission of Alfred A. Knopf, an imprint of the Knopf Doubleday Publishing Group, a division of Penguin Random House LLC. All rights reserved.

5   "Asides on the Oboe," copyright © 1942 by Wallace Stevens; and "An Ordinary Evening in New Haven" from *The Collected Poems of Wallace Stevens*, by Wallace Stevens, copyright © 1954 by Wallace Stevens and copyright renewed 1982 by Holly Stevens. Used by permission of Alfred A. Knopf, an imprint of the Knopf Doubleday Publishing Group, a division of Penguin Random House LLC. All rights reserved.

6   "Asides on the Oboe," copyright © 1942 by Wallace Stevens; and "An Ordinary Evening in New Haven" from *The Collected Poems of Wallace Stevens* by Wallace Stevens, copyright © 1954 by Wallace Stevens and copyright renewed 1982 by Holly Stevens. Used by permission of Alfred A. Knopf, an imprint of the Knopf Doubleday Publishing Group, a division of Penguin Random House LLC. All rights reserved.

7   "Asides on the Oboe," copyright © 1942 by Wallace Stevens; and "An Ordinary Evening in New Haven" from *The Collected Poems of Wallace Stevens* by Wallace Stevens, copyright © 1954 by Wallace Stevens and copyright renewed 1982 by Holly Stevens. Used by permission of Alfred A. Knopf, an imprint of the Knopf Doubleday Publishing Group, a division of Penguin Random House LLC. All rights reserved.

References

Blake, William. (1950). *Auguries of innocence*. Poetry Foundation. https://www.poetryfoundation.org/poems/43650/auguries-of-innocence

Critchley, S. (2005). *Things merely are: Philosophy in the poetry of Wallace Stevens*. Routledge.

Jung, C. G. (1961). *Memories, dreams, reflections*. (R. Winston & C. Winston), Vintage Books.

Merleau-Ponty, M. (1945/1958). *The phenomenology of perception*. (C. Smith, Trans.), Routledge.

Merleau-Ponty, M. (1963). *The structure of behavior*. (A. Fisher, Trans.), Beacon.

Merleau-Ponty, M. (1964). *Primacy of perception*. (W. Cobb, Trans.), Northwestern University.

Merleau-Ponty, M. (1968). *The visible and the invisible*. (A. Lingis, Trans.), Northwestern University.

Merleau-Ponty, M. (1973). *The prose of the world*. (C. Lefort, (Ed.); J. O'Neill, Trans.), Northwestern University.

Rilke, R. M.. (1939). *Duino elegies*. (A. Corn, Trans.), Norton.

Sallis, J. (1973). *Phenomenology and the return to beginnings*. Duquesne University Press.

Stevens, W. (2011). *Selected poems of Wallace Stevens*. (J. N. Serio, Ed.). Knopf Publishers.

Introduction to "Two Jungs: Two Sciences?"

Mark Saban's chapter starts off gently enough with a discussion of Jung's well known Nos 1 and 2 personalities, the scientific and the soulful. By reading the tension between these two in terms of the dynamic of individuation, Saban calls for us to follow Jung himself in not one-sidedly solving the challenges involved, either by rejecting science or by looking to science to ground Jungian thought through natural scientific methods and assumptions. Rather we should hold these perspectives in their creative tension. Saban then moves this tension forward, nudging along our own intellectual individuation in a sense, through a discussion of Deleuze and Guattari's (and others') flexible, adaptive, epistemologically polygamous, and thoroughly human conception of what it is to be scientific or rigorous. If the result is a kind of "wholeness," it is less comfortable than we might hope for, but it is alive and, we find, thrilling.

Chapter 4

Two Jungs

Two Sciences?

Mark Saban

Introduction

In my 2019 book, *Two Souls Alas: Jung's Two Personalities and the Making of Analytical Psychology*, I develop an understanding of Jung's notion of individuation (which I take to be the central notion within analytical psychology) as the playing out of an internal logic of opposites. I trace this processual dynamic back to his childhood experience of possessing two conflicting personalities (personality No. 1 and personality No. 2) as described in *Memories, Dreams, Reflections* (MDR). This culminates in Jung's crucial realisation that, because he can reside in neither of these personalities alone, the only way he can achieve a life as a whole person is to dwell in the tension between the two, and thus avoid the perils of one-sidedness (Jung, 1989, pp. 88–89; Saban, 2019, pp. 21–24). Out of this insight emerges Jung's later understanding of psychological development as something that arises out of repeated challenging encounters with a hitherto-unknown and hitherto-unseen other – a factor that gets described in general terms as "the unconscious".

This dynamic – the dynamic of individuation – is in effect the red thread that runs throughout Jung's mature psychology, though perhaps most evidently in his writings on the transcendent function and on typology, and in his fascination with alchemy. Even Jung's earliest psychological work on the unconscious complex (which disrupts and problematises the smooth operation of ego consciousness) adumbrates an individuational understanding of psychodynamics.

These transformational moments of individuation invariably involve confrontation with some kind of problematic challenge. Consequently, the ego, which is tirelessly vigilant and inventive in its attempts to maintain the psychological status quo, will always do its best to pre-empt, shortchange or usurp such painful but essential encounters, precisely because from the egoic point of view transformation is always experienced as subversion.

DOI: 10.4324/9781032694603-6

Jung's Scientific Individuation

From Jung's account in MDR, we can see that his developing relationship to science (both as concept and as practice) was intimately bound up with the unfolding of his engagement with his two personalities, and it was therefore also bound up with the nascent concept of individuation. At school and university, Jung tells us, he was, on the one hand,

> powerfully attracted by science, with its truths based on facts; on the other hand I was fascinated by everything to do with comparative religion ... In science I missed the factor of meaning; and in religion, that of empiricism".
> (Jung, 1989, p. 72)

Jung was well aware that this conflict between the meaningful and the factual was bound up with his two personalities: "Science met, to a very large extent, the needs of No. 1 personality, whereas the humane or historical studies provided beneficial instruction for No. 2" (Jung, 1989, p. 70).

This dichotomy becomes a persistent tension within Jung's approach to the natural world. From the perspective of No. 1, nature reveals itself as the object of scientific, empirical study. From the perspective of No. 2, it is experienced as the numinous and ineffable realm described elsewhere in MDR as "God's world" (pp. 77–78). The incompatibility between these different perspectives presents Jung with what he describes as "an insoluble conflict" (p. 75). It was an experience of precisely this kind of tension that Jung would later claim is necessary to the process of individuation.

In Jung's case it was resolved (for now at least) after two dreams. In one he digs up the bones of prehistoric animals and thinks to himself, "I must get to know nature, the world in which we live, and the things around us." In the other he comes upon the awe-inspiring image of a giant radiolarion and awakens with, as he describes it, a "beating heart". "These two dreams," he tells us, "decided me overwhelmingly in favor of science, and removed all my doubts" (p. 85).

The dreams succeeded in resolving Jung's "insoluble conflict" because they unveiled a vision of science which took a newly "binocular" form. On the one hand, they endorsed his eminently intellectual impulse to seek out the objective truth about nature and on the other they highlighted the numinosity conveyed by the image of the mysterious creature hidden deep in the forest. What had hitherto been experienced in the form of a contradiction now achieved resolution as a newly emergent perspective which enabled the simultaneous re-visioning of two hitherto incompatible dimensions – that of subjective meaning and that of empirical fact.

Experiences like this ultimately transformed the nature of Jung's scientific engagement. For example, while pondering his future specialty in medicine and leafing through the preface to a psychiatric textbook by Krafft-Ebing, Jung was suddenly electrified by Krafft-Ebing's emphasis on the necessarily *subjective* dimension of psychiatry: "My heart suddenly began to pound. I had to stand up and draw a deep breath" (p. 108). In psychiatry, Jung realised,

> the two currents of my interest could flow together and in a united stream dig their own bed. Here was the empirical field common to biological and spiritual facts, which I had everywhere sought and nowhere found. Here at last was the place where the collision of nature and spirit became a reality.
>
> (p. 109)

Jung's use of the word "collision" (*Zusammenstoß*) tells us that what he has in mind is not a smooth process of synthesis or fusion but rather a head-on clash between opposites, identified here as biological or natural versus spiritual. Interestingly, in a subsequent passage he focuses on the collision between another oppositional pair: objective and subjective. Jung parses Krafft-Ebing's meaning in this way:

> [T]he textbook is in part the *subjective* confession of the [psychiatrist] ... [who] with his specific prejudice, with the totality of his being ... stands behind the *objectivity* of his experiences and responds to the "disease of the personality" with the whole of his own personality.
>
> (p. 119) (my italics)

This subtle and difficult encounter between the subjective approach and the objective approach was to remain a central preoccupation for Jung not only within his own psychological development but also with regard to his understanding of psychology itself. (Kotsch 2000) Elsewhere I have invoked the scientific methods of Goethe in order to explain Jung's frequent claims to the title "scientist" (Saban 2014). What particularly interested me about the parallel between the two thinkers was Goethe's conviction that he could do justice to the phenomena only by transcending the objective/subjective dichotomy. As Jung puts it at the end of his life, "My life is what I have done, my scientific work; the one is inseparable from the other" (Jung, 1989, p. 222). What Jung seeks to convey is that in his life/science and in his science/life he has inextricably intertwined both subjective and objective dimensions.

In summary, Jung found in psychiatry a specifically *scientific* arena within which the problematic tension between all these conflicting opposites could be allowed to find various creative resolutions. Throughout his life and his work Jung would repeatedly confront similar difficulties. Having established the importance of these highly unstable oppositional energies (rational/irrational, material/spiritual, objective/subjective: personality 1/personality 2), his life-long task became the elaboration of a scientific methodology that could yoke them together.

The Scientific Individuation of Analytical Psychology

As Jung characterises it, the task of individuation is problematic because the correction of one-sidedness cannot be achieved without the *whole* psyche being put into question. When we channel this insight towards the individuation of analytical psychology itself, it is perhaps not entirely surprising that what has been constellated is a strong tendency to avoid any such challenge. We can identify two contrasting and complementary forms of this will-to-avoidance in post-Jungian attempts to tackle the question of Jung and science.

Anti-science

The first (long established in the Jungian tradition) takes the form of a depreciation or outright rejection of the scientific aspect of Jung's psychology. Dennis Merritt, who in the 1960s was training at the Jung Institute while simultaneously working on a PhD in entomology, tells us that the "scientific attitude was … despised and discredited there". (Merritt, 1988, p. 14) Analysts were "condescending toward [the] scientific attitude and … seemed to think their viewpoint was superior" (Merritt, 1988).

In more recent years we can identify a more aggressive version of this approach in the argument that Jung's own claims to be engaged in science were little more than a sham. Sonu Shamdasani, for example, describes Jung's purported engagement with science as "a makeshift." He claims that after the *Red Book* Jung's writings deteriorate and his theories become merely "an attempt to try to translate as much as he felt he could get away with to the medico-scientific audience of his time" (Shamdasani, 2012, p. 375).

According to Wolfgang Giegerich, post-Jungians have a stark choice. They can either "feel committed to, and base their own work on, [Jung's] body of thought" or be taken in by the "hypotheses of the 'scientist' Jung" (Giegerich, 2008, p. 54). Note the characteristic scare quotes around the word scientist!

James Hillman claims to have "been straining for decades to push psychology over into art, to recognize psychology as an art form rather than a science or a medicine or an education, because the soul is inherently imaginative" (Hillman & Ventura, 1993, p. 154). Note here the implication that science and imagination are mutually exclusive.

Where these influential but varied Jungian writers agree is on the necessity to establish a black-and-white binary contrast between, on the one hand, an *authentic* Jung (often aligned with Jung's personality No. 2 or the *Red Book*'s spirit of the depths) and on the other, an ersatz Jung – a shallow, spirit-of-this-time, personality No. 1 Jung who is represented as betraying the purity of the authentic vision by taking on a scientific persona.

To approach Jung and his psychology in this way brings with it two related problems:

The first is that "science" is set up as a straw-man caricature. We are offered a reductive, one-sided notion of what science is and what scientists do. Stripped of complexity, ambiguity or multiplicity, science gets pigeon-holed as fatally monolithic. For Giegerich, for example, science is all about "Certainty. Proof. Reliability. Validity … Science is the gigantic project of slowly trying to bring all reality inside the fence. Its job is to radically undo all wilderness" (Giegerich, 2008, p. 234). What seems inconceivable here is the notion that science itself might involve us in finding new wildernesses to explore.

The second problem is that if you divide up Jung's psychology into discrete conceptual compartments and label some as authentic and some as inauthentic, you do violence to analytical psychology *as a whole* and particularly to its central logic of individuation, which requires that these disparate aspects be brought into tension with each other.

When, for example, Giegerich lauds personality No. 2 as Jung's "intuitive contact with the depth" and dismisses personality No. 1 as merely a "scientistic façade" (Giegerich, 2008, p. 151), he splits these two dimensions and sets them against each other: intuition good, science bad. What is lost is Jung's own realisation that transformation emerges only from the dynamic and creative meeting of the two.

Shamdasani similarly insists that we choose between two mutually exclusive Jungs, one true and one false. He claims that Jung's authentic voice (identified with personality No. 2) is to be found only in the *Red Book* and that Jung's mature psychology as published in the *Collected Works* represents merely a diminished and watered-down version of this original vision: "[W]hen Jung attempts to formulate [the vision] into a scientific psychology," Shamdasani tells us, it simply "gets lost" (Hillman & Shamdasani, 2013, p. 53).

It is easy to see why such an approach might be attractive. After all, it enables one to discard whichever aspects of Jung's psychology one finds annoying or inconvenient and frees one to embrace him as a prophet, or an artist, or a Hegelian or whatever one might want or need him to be.

However, in my view, this polarising approach not only fatally obstructs the very dynamic that powers analytical psychology but it also inevitably brings about a new form of one-sidedness.

Sub-science

A corresponding one-sidedness can be located in a very different strain of post-Jungian thinking which shows up the inverted version of the approach I have outlined above. For example, in his 1988 *Mythos and Logos in the Thought of Carl Jung*, Walter Shelburne tells us:

In order to argue for the scientific credibility of his theory of archetypes, we must show not only that Jung's theory is a naturalistic one, in the most general meaning of that term, but also that the theory is compatible in principle with standard, scientifically informed understandings of nature.

(Shelburne, 1988, p. 2)

In order to understand the problematic assumptions embedded in this superficially innocuous statement we need to look first at the question of "grounding." In a 2004 article in the *Journal of Analytical Psychology*, Margaret Wilkinson invokes "current neuropsychological and neurobiological understanding of early brain development, memory, emotion and consciousness," and goes on to insist that "[Jung] leaves us with a responsibility to *ground* our work ... in the best science of our day".

A similar assumption lies behind the frequent discussions in the *Journal of Analytical Psychology* about whether Jung's archetypes are or are not consistent with the latest research in evolutionary biology or brain science. Here again the goal seems to be that of proving that the archetype is *grounded* in "hard" science.

It seems to me that this kind of enterprise is in direct conflict with the creative and disruptive indeterminism that characterises Jung's psychology of individuation.[1] The notion that post-Jungians should be seeking to *ground* Jung's psychology by showing that it is in alignment with the latest scientific "facts" is plausible only if we derive our approach from Jung's early works which, as Roger Brooke points out, contain

> some of the essential assumptions of natural science: the human being as a self-contained entity inside of which sickness can be located, health and sickness as reflections of energy distribution and availability (to the ego), and the independence of the observer.
>
> (Brooke 1991, p. 3)

If, on the other hand, we want to explore an approach that is true to Jung's mature psychology, we, like Jung, are likely to find these assumptions highly problematic.

In Roger Brooke's words, Jung's "understanding of man and the psychology that speaks of him ... [sees] through the natural-scientific language to the perspective, or vision, which forms it" (Brooke 1991, p. 5). The notion that any psychology expressing such a vision needs to *ground* itself in natural science reveals itself as deeply contradictory. Indeed, what Shelburne describes as the "standard ... understandings" of science are precisely those understandings that Jung's psychology, when it is doing its job, seeks to radically challenge.

Note, however, that to hold this view is not the same as saying that Jung's psychology needs to exist separately from or outside of the scientific conversation.

The Archimedean Point?

The attempt to ground analytical psychology in natural science is also an attempt to employ natural science as an external, Archimedean point for the purposes of measuring or proving its validity. We should note that Jung very specifically states that it is impossible to do any such thing: Psychology, Jung says, "lacks the immense advantage of an Archimedean point such as physics enjoys" (Jung, 1954b, para. 421).

Jung doesn't mean this as a merely *contingent fact*. He is not suggesting that an external point of this kind, against which psychology could be measured, might be out there, waiting to be discovered. Jung is making the stronger argument that an Archimedean point of this kind is *necessarily* impossible: the existence of such a point is obviated by the *very nature of psychology itself*. To think otherwise is to commit a category error.

However, we need to distinguish this argument from the idea that psychology somehow stands apart from all other disciplines or sciences and is therefore by definition unable to engage with them. The idea that psychology can't be grounded in or measured against a "hard" discipline outside of itself is not equivalent to the idea that it cannot therefore be in a dynamic relationship with other disciplines.

In MDR we find this statement:

We always require an outside point to stand on, in order to apply the lever of criticism. This is especially so in psychology, where by the nature of the material we are much more subjectively involved than in any other science.
(Jung, 1989, p. 246)

At first glance, Jung here seems to be contradicting his earlier point about the Archimedean point. However, when Jung refers to standing upon an "outside point" in this passage, he is not thinking about grounding psychology in or measuring psychology against a harder, more solid science. In fact, he is describing a completely different mode of engagement. Jung is telling us that we can deal with psychology's inevitable subjectivity problem (and the narrowness of perspective that tends to result from it) *if* (and only if) we find a way to bring this perspective into play with something outside of itself. Such a meeting is necessary because it is the only way to correct the narrowness and one-sidedness that will otherwise occur.

This then is the logic of individuation, whereby two different perspectives are put into tension and a third is thus enabled to emerge. For example, the discipline of psychology might be brought into tension with an external perspective such as the scientific discipline of biology, or alternatively with a non-scientific discipline, such as alchemy or astrology. In each of these cases, what matters is the way we expose our own familiar perspective (in this case that of analytical psychology) to the alien perspective of the other discipline and vice versa. It is only if we allow our perspective to be thus *challenged* (and thereby create a differential tension between disciplines) that a potential binocularity – and ultimately a new perspective – can be enabled.[2]

A dialogue of this kind between analytical psychology and, say, neuroscience therefore has the capacity to open up a hitherto unexpected insight that can transcend both the original approaches. This process doesn't ground our psychological standpoint in the external solidity of a harder science, but it does nonetheless enable our psychology to gain a certain complexity, depth and breadth that it would not be able to find from within itself. This is how we evade the trap of conceptual solipsism while remaining true to the essential spirit of analytical psychology.

A particularly fruitful example of this kind of process can be seen in the transdisciplinary dialogue between analytical psychology and quantum physics that eventually gave birth to the notion of synchronicity. In this case we can witness the intellectual and relational process of holding together the differences between the two disciplines in the dialogue between Jung and Wolfgang Pauli that was maintained from 1932 to 1958. The European Organization for Nuclear Research (CERN) physicist Maurice Jacob commented, "It is fascinating to follow how these two intellectual giants argue *from different sides* to find mutual enlight[en]ment" (Jacob, 2000, my italics). This difficult argument "from different sides" is the place of tension within which the two disciplines engage, and, according to Jung, this provides "at least a faint idea of a possible Archimedean point for psychology" (Jung, 1924, para. 164).

Jung tells us in MDR how a transdisciplinary process of this kind works in practice: "I am not concerned with proving anything to other disciplines; I am merely attempting to put their knowledge to good use in my own field" (Jung, 1989, p. 349). Such a process works, Jung suggests, "when one transfers the knowledge of one field to another and applies it in practice."

This act of translation is far more than a re-treading of old ground because when it succeeds, "certain new things come to light." He gives an example: "Had X-rays remained the exclusive property of the physicist and not been applied in medicine, we would know far less" (Jung, 1989). In this case, two fields that are in numerous ways alien to each other, physics and medicine, interact, and what emerges is a hitherto unexpected solution to an old problem.

When this kind of interdisciplinary translation occurs it can at first seem like a kind of misreading: "[Ideas] naturally appear in a different light and lead to conclusions other than those to which they lead when restricted to their proper fields, where they serve other purposes" (Jung, 1989). But, for Jung, conceptual miscegenation shouldn't be thought of as a strange or marginal aspect of science. This transdisciplinary methodology, he thinks, is fundamental to *all* scientific activity:

> Science qua science has no boundaries, and there is no speciality whatever that can boast of complete self-sufficiency. Any speciality is bound to spill over its borders and to encroach on adjoining territory if it is to lay serious claim to the status of a science.
>
> (Jung, 1924, par. 212)

It is precisely these difficult but fertile interstices between disciplines that most fascinate Jung, and it is in such unlikely meeting places, he implies, that we find the proper loci for scientific work. This is the real reason why Jung has no interest in being absorbed into the safe ground of the established truth of any single scientific discipline.

A Syzygy? Nomad Science and State Science

However, it is not only *between* scientific disciplines that we find fertile margins and interstices. Such opportunities also turn up within the scientific endeavour itself.

In *A Thousand Plateaus*, Gilles Deleuze and Felix Guattari describe what they see as a fundamental oppositional dynamic within science. They identify two contrasting dimensions of scientific activity to which they give the names Royal or state science and nomad or minor science.

Royal or state science emphasises the stable, the eternal, the identical, the constant, the uniform, the standardised, the solid, the fixed. It defines itself in terms of theorems, rational order, and limits. It produces universal laws, abstract concepts, and transhistorical theories such as Newtonian mechanics. For royal science, the universe is predictable and deterministic. Particularly attuned to the questions and problems presented by individual solid entities with stable boundaries, state science answers questions like: What are the characteristics that make an entity what it is, in contradistinction with what it is not? These are questions of essence. The answers involve strict adherence to the "laws" of nature envisaged as a pre-ordained plan.

Nomad science on the other hand is heterogeneous and varied; experimental and inventive, it asks questions about becoming, metamorphosis, generation and creation. Its prime concerns are the problematic, the affective, the pliable, the malleable. One example of nomad science is evolutionary biology. It doesn't predict the course of evolution or reproduce it under experimental conditions but traces its development post facto. Nomad science thus follows singularities, operating by rule of thumb. It improvises, using whatever resources are to hand. Another example is non-linear complexity science, which offers a vision of spontaneous emergence and self-organisation – the universe as radically open.

Nomad science asks questions like: What is going on in this situation, interaction or milieu? It is interested in the hows and the whys of transformation.

State science requires its experimental operations to be isolated from "on the ground" conditions at a particular time. The experiments of state science produce results that can be *re-produced* independently of circumstances. These are therefore results that appear eternal and universal.

Nomad sciences, on the other hand, are thoroughly pragmatic. Experiments occur in specific concrete circumstances. These are circumstances in which variables cannot be controlled.

Described in this way the two sciences – nomad and royal – inevitably impress one as warring opposites. The demands and conditions of royal science clearly inhibit or even forbid the practice of nomad science. As Deleuze and Guattari put it, "state science ... imposes its form of sovereignty on the inventions of nomad science" (Deleuze & Guattari, 1987, p. 365). By forcing a particular logic of organization, it curtails and tames nomad science's creativity and inventiveness.

But Deleuze also insists that although state science and nomad science may be "two formally different conceptions of science," nonetheless they are "ontologically, a single field of interaction" (Deleuze & Guattari, p. 367). The dynamic of their interaction is that "royal science continually appropriates the contents of ... nomad science ... nomad science continually cuts the contents of royal science loose" (Deleuze & Guattari). Clearly Deleuze wants us to see the two sciences as abstract and opposing poles of the same continuum. This means that to categorize a particular science as either royal or nomad would be to miss the point; what matters is to recognize that *all* scientific practices involve an interplay between both royal and nomadic tendencies. As Brent Atkins puts it,

> It would be naive to assume that there is a single monolithic "scientific practice." It is more likely that there are multiple competing scientific practices, each with a different ratio of the tendencies toward stability and change.
> (Adkins, 2015, p. 13)

As post-Jungians we might want to put Deleuze & Guattari's insights alongside a Jungian syzygy: that of puer/senex.

Despite an abiding temptation to take puer and senex as separate, individual archetypal configurations, there are huge heuristic benefits to be gained if we see them as yoked together (Hillman, 1967). By doing so we also align ourselves with the logic of individuation, whereby when two apparent opposites are brought into contact, the tension between them constellates a transformative event.

James Hillman makes the point that the puer dimension is to be found buried at the heart of the senex, and a senex dimension also resides at the heart of the puer. If we juxtapose this syzygy with the state science/nomad science pairing, we can see a similar dynamic at play.

Similar to the t'ai chi in which the seed of yin develops as yang finds its fullest expression, and vice versa, the puer/senex dynamic posits a senex that requires puer and a puer that requires senex, just as the energetic movement of state science relies upon the disruptions of nomad science and vice versa.

The Red Book: Nomad Science in Action?

The crisis Jung experienced at the time of his "confrontation with the unconscious" took a double form: it was bound up not only with his own personal one-sidedness but also with a nascent awareness of the one-sidedness of the science of his day. In the *Red Book* we witness his reaction against what we might see as the senex character of the scientific approach of that time. He tells us that his soul could be contained within what he calls "a dead system that I had contrived, assembled from so-called experiences and judgments" (Jung, 2009, p. 232, n. 39). He sees that by making the soul an object of science, we subject it to the senex assumptions of royal science, and thus kill it. In MDR Jung tells us,

> The knowledge I was concerned with, or was seeking, still could not be found in the science of those days. I myself had to undergo the original experience, and, moreover, try to plant the results of my experience in the soil of reality; otherwise they would have remained subjective assumptions without validity. It was then that I dedicated myself to service of the psyche.
> (Jung, 1989, p. 192)

Note that in this situation Jung does not abdicate his scientific responsibility. He responds to the problem not by rejecting science tout court and creating a new religion, or becoming an artist, but by asking the question, How can science make room for what it is missing? As French philosopher Armelle Line Peltier has recently argued, the *Red Book* is Jung's first attempt at an answer to this question. Peltier makes a case for the *Liber Novus* as a work of (albeit unconventional) science (Peltier, 2019).

According to Peltier, Jung's attempt to develop a rounded psychological science involved him first in reversing the traditional approach whereby the scientist/doctor observes the object/patient from the outside. Instead, Jung based his new approach on a reflexive observation of his own case. Combining the examples of Freud's self-analysis and Ludwig Staudenmaier's self-experimentation (Jung, 2009, p. 200), Jung seeks to develop a new form, that which we might call scientific autobiography or perhaps deep autoethnography. His goal is to reveal and explore, in an improvisatory way, the emergence of his inner images and in the wake of these images, the messy and chaotic formation of the ideas that grow out of them. In MDR he insists upon the *scientific* character of this process:

> My science was the only way I had of extricating myself from that chaos. Otherwise the material would have trapped me in its thicket, strangled me like jungle creepers. I took great care to try to understand every single image, every item of my psychic inventory, and to classify them scientifically – so far as this was possible – and, above all, to realize them in actual life.
> (Jung, 1989, p. 192)

The *Red Book* in effect represents an experimental clinical study that Jung undertakes, not only on his own behalf but also for his patients. He seeks experimental results that can be generalised and are applicable to other cases.

This involves him moving between three distinct positions:

1 The protagonist who acts within the scene
2 The narrator who describes the scene.
3 The analyst who reflects upon the whole.

We might describe Jung's approach here as that of the "wounded scientist"; what he brings into simultaneous tension are a determination to be true to his wound and an insistence on being true to his science. This involves him in seeking what Peltier calls "the freedom of one who is neither constrained by knowledge, nor dependent on a given scientific paradigm" (Peltier, 2019, p. 160 my translation). He thus

> finds a kind of emancipation not only in his experience, but also in the exploration of the latter in writing – a writing that is in no way determined by the need to validate. The writing of *Liber novus* and the scientific elaboration it contains mark an attempt at a free understanding of experience, and not a will to prove something.
>
> (Peltier, 2019)

The *Red Book* can thus be regarded as a scientific "creation that is free from epistemological constraints." Pelter parallels this approach with that of philosopher of science Paul Feyerabend, whose approach she summarises:

> Scientific progress is only possible when we go beyond the rules commonly prescribed by science itself. Science and reason cannot always work together, because in order to go beyond a scientific theory it is necessary to get outside of it, otherwise all you get is infinite regress. This reversal of reason is synonymous with a certain form of freedom in research.
>
> (p. 165)

Peltier also highlights a dimension of Jung's method we have already touched on – that of transdisciplinarity. In the *Red Book*, this shows up as a promiscuous tendency to bring into play different methods from different disciplines. Peltier compares this pluri-methodology with Feyerabend's so-called "anarchist" approach to science: an exploratory, trial-and-error "anti-method" (Feyerabend, 1993). This approach offers enormous flexibility through the creative use of serendipity. For Jung it provides an eminently suitable means for encountering an elusive psyche that is not only multiple, but always in motion and located squarely in the blind-spot of consciousness.

French philosopher of science Abraham Moles approvingly describes this approach as "experimental disorder" (Moles, 1957). To use such an approach might be to "play with measuring devices in a new way, reuse obsolete instruments, apply instruments relating to a given object of study to another object totally outside the field of study concerned, etc.". The scientist acts "practically without a guide, at random, with almost mechanical reflexes" (Moles, 1957, p. 77). Jung seems to be employing this kind of anti-method when he says, "Since I know nothing at all ... I shall simply do whatever occurs to me" (Jung, 1989, p. 173).

Jung's attention is particularly drawn to bodies of knowledge that might be considered by many to be non- or pseudo-scientific, such as mythology, theology, parapsychology, the occult, astrology, alchemy. As Feyerabend puts it, in the modern world, "neither science, nor rationalism have ... sufficient authority to exclude myth, or 'primitive' thought, or the cosmologies behind the various religious creeds" (Feyerabend, 1993, p. 125).

It is crucial to remember that Jung never privileges any one of these very different ways of articulating our being in the world as *a primary* heuristic key. He is far more interested in what happens when such varied perspectives come into contact with each other. From a traditional (or as Deleuze might call it, a "state") perspective this looks like a methodology of promiscuous eclecticism, or, as Jung himself describes it, as sheer dilettantism.[3] Peltier amplifies this idea by quoting French philosopher Jacques Billard: "If we cannot avoid the use of a system and the use of a single system leads to error, then it appears that the solution consists in claiming from every system whatever it can give" (Billard, 1998, p. 85).

Conclusion

In order to follow Peltier in seeing the *Red Book* as an example of Jung's science, it is necessary to accept that the scientific method itself is animated by contrasting, mutually interactive oppositional dimensions. These are the aspects that Deleuze and Guattari have chosen to name nomad and royal science. In the light of such an articulation, it becomes possible to see Jung's highly pragmatic, highly concrete (or as Jung liked to call it, empirical) science operating as a kind of nomad science which therefore finds its place in conflictual play with the established royal science. By confronting the one-sidedness of Western science through exposure to this critical counterweight, the individuation of science itself is perhaps progressed.

However, we are obliged to remember that even within analytical psychology itself, we operate in the tension between both dimensions, nomad and state, senex and puer. By working in this way – allowing Jung to be the scientist he always claimed he was while simultaneously encouraging the profoundly disruptive and subversive aspects of his psychology to remain fully in force – we are making a contribution to the individuation of Jung's psychology.

Notes

1 When it comes to describing the archetype Jung's scatter-gun approach (conceiving it in either biologistic, evolutionary, phenomenological, or cultural terms depending on context) seems to me to indicate a desire to avoid scientific (or any other kind of) reductiveness. As Jung puts it, "The archetype is really far less a scientific problem than an urgent question of psychic hygiene" (Jung, 1954a, para. 173). Elsewhere he directs us away from discourse of this kind by reminding us that "[p]sychology, like every empirical science, cannot get along without auxiliary concepts, hypotheses, and models ... my concept of the archetype ... is only an auxiliary idea which can be exchanged at any time for a better formula (Jung, 1952/1975, para. 460).
2 I utilise the metaphor of binocularity because it so clearly illustrates the way in which two conflicting perspectives can come together to achieve a three-dimensionality that transcends both the original perspectives.
3 Jung admits to Jaffe in the MDR protocols, "Ich bin der verfluchteste Dilettant" ("I am the damnedest dilettante who ever lived") (quoted in Kingsley, 2018, p. 698).

References

Adkins, B. (2015). *Deleuze and Guattari's A Thousand Plateaus: A critical introduction and guide*. The Athlone Press.
Billard, J. (1998). *L'éclectisme*. Presses Universitaires de France.
Brooke, R. (1991). *Jung and phenomenology*. Routledge.
Deleuze, G. & Guattari, F. (1987). *A Thousand Plateaus: Capitalism and schizophrenia*. University of Minnesota Press.
Feyerabend, P. (1993). *Against method*. Verso.
Giegerich, W. (2008). *The soul's logical life: Towards a rigorous notion of psychology*. Peter Lang Publishing.
Hillman, J. (1967). "Senex and Puer: An aspect of the historical and psychological present" in G. Slater (Ed.) *Senex and Puer, The uniform edition of the writings of James Hillman* Vol. 4. Spring Publications.
Hillman, J. & Shamdasani, S. (2013). *Lament of the Dead: Psychology after Jung's Red Book*. W.W. Norton.
Hillman, J. & Ventura, M. (1993). *We've had a hundred years of psychotherapy—and the world's getting worse*. HarperCollins.
Jacob, M. (2000, August 17). Wolfgang Pauli: never to be excluded. *Cern Courier*. https://cerncourier.com/a/wolfgang-pauli-never-to-be-excluded/
Jung, C. G. (1924). Analytical psychology and education. CW. 17, 127–229.
Jung, C. G. (1952/1975). Foreword to White's "God and the unconscious". CW. 11.
Jung, C. G. (1954a). Psychological aspects of the mother archetype. CW. 9i.
Jung, C. G. (1954b). On the nature of the psyche. CW. 8.
Jung, C. G. (1989). *Memories, dreams, reflections*. (A. Jaffe, Ed., C. Winston & R. Winston, Trans). Vintage Books.
Jung, C. G. (2009). *Liber Novus*. London and New York: W.W. Norton & Co.
Kingsley, P. (2018). *Catafalque, Vol. 2*. Catafalque Press.
Kotsch, W. E. (2000). Jung's mediatory science as a psychology beyond objectivism. *Journal of Analytical Psychology*, 45, 217–244. https://doi.org/10.1111/1465-5922.00153
Merritt, D. (1988). Jungian psychology and science: A strained relationship. In S. Sternback (Ed.), *Analytic life: Personal and professional aspects of being a jungian analyst*. (pp. 11–33). Sigo Press.

Moles, A. (1957). *La Creation Scientifique*. Kister.

Peltier, A. L. (2019). *Une pensée créatrice en science: l'élaboration de la connaissance chez Carl Gustav Jung (1875–1961) à travers l'étude du Livre Rouge (1913–1930)*. [Doctoral dissertation, Université de Strasbourg]. HAL open science. https://tel.archives-ouvertes.fr/tel-02406862/document

Saban, M. (2014). Science friction: Jung, Goethe and scientific objectivity. In R. Jones (Ed.) *Jung and the question of science*. (pp. 30–50). Routledge.

Saban, M. (2019). *Two Souls Alas... Jung's two personalities and the making of analytical psychology*. Chiron Press.

Shamdasani, S. (2012). After Liber Novus. *Journal of Analytical Psychology, 57*(3), 364–77. https://doi.org/10.1111/j.1468-5922.2012.01975.x

Shelburne, W. A. (1988). *Mythos and logos in the thought of Carl Jung*. State University of New York Press.

Introduction to "Archetypes, Embodiment, and Spontaneous Thought"

Cognitive neuroscience and evolutionary biology are highly relevant to psychology, but conceptual confusions have been in the way of integrating the findings in these fields into Jungian psychology without the result being a sort of add-on eclecticism. One of the claims of psychology as a human science has always been that findings from the natural sciences in biology, genetics, and the consequences of trauma such as brain injury, need to be integrated into an ontology of being human. Otherwise experience becomes merely an epiphenomenon of brain processing and psychology disappears as a fundamental discipline.

In the Jungian field, the concept of the archetype is where the rubber hits the road. Jung's use of the term was both ethological/genetic and imaginal, or natural and human, but his integration was muddled and, it must be admitted, not really coherent. Goodwyn's chapter is a systematic attempt to sieve through fundamental conceptual and scientific issues regarding the archetypes and the foundations of Jungian theory. Its hallmarks are that it is scientifically rigorous and genuinely integrated into the human science foundations of Jungian theory.

Chapter 5

Archetypes, Embodiment, and Spontaneous Thought

Erik Goodwyn

Introduction

The concept of the archetype developed from clinical material, with Jung noticing that his patients sometimes had dreams or fantasies which bore a striking resemblance to mythic narratives that they presumably had no knowledge of. That myth and ritual imagery are remarkably similar, but not identical, cross-culturally, in combination with clinical experience led him to propose that each of us has a shared psychological inheritance he termed "the collective unconscious":

> In addition to our immediate personal conscious ... there exists a second psychic system of a collective, universal and impersonal nature which is identical in all individuals and is inherited. It consists of pre-existent forms, the archetypes.
>
> (Jung, 1959, para. 90)

Given that cross-cultural and spontaneous clinical imagery was so similar, but not identical, he proposed that archetypes could not be innate images. Instead he proposed that they were innate *processes* which structure and organize many similar images:

> Archetypes, so far as we can observe and experience them at all, manifest themselves only through their ability to organize images and ideas, and this is always an unconscious process which cannot be detected until afterwards.
>
> (1960, para. 440)

Thus, inherited archetypes were proposed to use elements of one's memories and cultural expressions, break them down, and reorganize them into novel *archetypal images* at crucial moments in one's life.

Jung has faced resistance to his archetype theory ever since. In his nuanced analysis, phenomenologist and psychoanalyst Roger Brooke identifies a large

DOI: 10.4324/9781032694603-7

part of why, by showing how early psychoanalysis and experimental psychology (among other disciplines) struggled with a historical legacy of *unexamined Cartesian assumptions*. This influential, centuries old view of "science" originated from Galileo and assumed that mind and body were not merely distinct conceptually, but distinct *ontologically*. Under this paradigm, the mind is its own substance and hence disembodied, full of "representations" of the inanimate "physical world of matter," part of which is the body itself.

Despite its persistence, Brooke correctly identifies how inadequate this ontology is when compared with rich clinical data (Brooke, 2009). The early psychoanalysts such as Freud, Bion, Jung, Adler, and others learned this early on through their studied examination of patient experiences. The discovery of the *feeling-toned complex* (as exemplified by the now standardized Jung-Rilkin word association test) in particular "confronted [Freud and Jung] with the reality of a consciousness that is *embodied* and a body that has intentions of its own" (Brooke, 1991, p. 507, emphasis added). In other words, the psyche is embodied and the body is intrinsically psychological.

That the body could have "intentions" and influence the supposedly ontologically distinct mind unconsciously rendered the Cartesian dualistic view incoherent, though this was not noticed in the main. Jung seemed to sense this on some level, though he slipped into Cartesian terminology sometimes. Nevertheless, he maintained throughout his career that psyche and soma were somehow *one*:

> Psyche cannot be totally different from matter, for how otherwise could it move matter? And matter cannot be alien to psyche, for how else could matter produce psyche? Psyche and matter exist in one and the same world, and each partakes of the other, otherwise any reciprocal action would be impossible. If research could only advance far enough, therefore, we should arrive at an ultimate agreement between physical and psychological concepts.
>
> (1959, para. 413)

Unfortunately neither he nor any of the other psychoanalysts of the early twentieth century launched a formal discussion of how their work challenged the Cartesian zeitgeist. Instead, they soldiered on and Jung continued to develop archetype theory despite the objections.

Characteristics of the Archetypes

Before we see how that played out, it is important to understand how archetypes are supposed to work. Brooke sifts through Jung's work, seeking "a definition that does not beg theoretical questions" (2015, p. 143) by retaining the most consistent elements of his lifelong, at times diffuse writing on the subject. First and foremost, Jung saw that even though we have free thought, there are still "revelations" from the unconscious that appear to derive from more primordial dimensions of the psyche "triggered" by universally appearing situations in life (Brooke, 2015, pp. 144–145). In other words, archetypal images are *spontaneously emergent* responses to life.

Jung further characterized the archetypes as non-literal *symbolic* expressions, or "categories of the *imagination*" (Jung, CW6, p. 518). Importantly, when Jung mentioned symbols, he had something special in mind, and *not* arbitrary, essentially meaningless signifiers. Instead Jung referred not as "representations" bouncing about in a Cartesian monad, but rather as "the presencing of a mystery in such a way that psychic life is integrated and the person is transformed" (Brooke, 2009, p. 609). Symbols, for Jung, were not allegories or arbitrary signs, but "the best possible expression for an unconscious content whose nature can only be guessed, because it is still unknown" (Jung, 1959, para. 6). And since archetypal images were "triggered" by universally appearing situations in life (Brooke, 2015, pp. 144–145), they were best seen as *innately constrained symbolic expressions of one's current life situation* – the "current state of things" in images and affect, rather than language per se, arising from the psyche outside conscious will, unbidden. More on this symbolic character later.

In any case, archetypal images are not by simply repeats of early experiences but expressions that *reorganize* memories, reflections, and feelings into novel products in accordance to innately constrained structures. Importantly, this process is *embodied*, and the embodiment derives,

> not merely the body studied in anatomy and physiology (the body according to natural science), but [from] the embodiment of meaning, situated in language and cultural history … what we call consciousness is not an empty realm of ideation and "mental representations" but is an embodied and situated consciousness, frequently opaque to itself.
>
> (Brooke, 2018, p. 659)

Jung moreover attempted to link the archetypes to the body as a whole and not just the brain (Brooke, 2015, p. 146). Later in life he considered that structuring and ordering archetypes may underlie the universe itself (Goodwyn, 2022a), but he never quite separated himself from the idea that archetypal images were biologically ordered to a significant degree. Nevertheless the tendency for Jung and his followers to push the envelope on an already challenging concept sometimes led to a muddying of the term, such that some Jungian authors have complained that nearly anything can be thought of as archetypal (Roesler, 2023, pp. 37–70). Here I will focus on the above *clinical* definition.

Brooke identifies a key feature of the archetypal images important to Jung: that they are *spontaneous responses to species-typical situations* ordered by innate constraints. In Brooke's terms, the archetypes "call into consciousness an image that clarifies one's self and world at that time" (2015, p. 158). Archetypes are thus innate *organizational principles of perception and thought*, not "hypothetical entities that produce images" (Brooke, 2015, p. 154). Archetypal images are spontaneously emergent and emotional metaphors that reflect species-typical situations such as parent-offspring (Mother, Child), youth-mentor (Senex/Puer), long-term pair bonding (Anima/us), and so forth. As Jung puts it, the archetype is "a *condensed expression of the psychic situation as a whole*" (Jung, 1921/1971, p. 442, emphasis original).

The Fate of the Archetype

Eventually the disembodied, implicitly Cartesian psychology of behaviorism and classic cognitive science gave way to several independent developments in the 1970s and 1980s. Evolutionary psychology (Buss, 2005) began to clash with the Standard Social Science Model and its disembodied characterization of the mind. Affective neuroscience (Alcaro & Carta, 2019; Panksepp, 2004; Panksepp et al., 2017) slowly built a vast empirical basis for returning to an embodied view of the *emotions* as strongly innate cross-species and evolution-derived organizers of cognition and behavior. Cognitive *neuroscience* endorsed an evolutionary and embodied view with its intense focus on the brain following the results of the new science of neuroimaging (Panksepp et al., 2017). Psychopharmacology exploded, again piercing the mind-body "barrier" within psychiatry.

Philosophy itself began to see a rising interest in panpsychism and other non-dualistic ontologies, attacking the dualistic paradigm directly as well as its cousin, the physicalist paradigm (for more detailed examination, see Goodwyn, 2021). Somatic therapies (e.g., Levine, 2010; Van der Kolk, 2015) recognized that the body had its own kind of intentionality, perception, and mental capacity–just as we saw with the old feeling-toned complex experiments of the early psychoanalysts. Finally, perhaps the most devastating blow to the above disembodied view of mental contents came from the growing literature of *embodied cognition*, starting with Lakoff and Johnson's famous 1980 book, *Metaphors We Live By* – more on this later.

To update archetype theory, we need an emphasis on *embodiment*. In the present chapter, I will show that the classic qualities of archetypal images can be integrated naturally with the findings in a number of newer, independent fields of inquiry with this key ingredient.

Do Archetypes "Exist"?

Thus far, the foregoing analysis reveals that archetypal images, as originally developed by Jung and his close adherents, are defined as:

1 spontaneously emergent expressions of the imagination
2 emergent in response to or in anticipation of important species-typical environmental situations

3 affectively charged *symbolic expressions* that have an *ineffable core* of meaning (more on these later)
4 quintessentially *embodied* expressions with innate, universal structures, from which *archetypal images* are constructed.

Asking the question of whether archetypes "exist" risks a reification error that already assumes dualism of mind and body. Found where? "Out there" (beyond the mind) in the physical world of the brain? Or perhaps they are organizational structures "in the mind." When formulated with these Cartesian assumptions, archetypes are defined out of existence, but that is the fault of the ontological assumptions, *not* the concept itself.

Once the Cartesian assumptions are discarded for a more holistic and embodied paradigm, however, it becomes evident from the foregoing analysis that an archetypal image is not a something which can be "found," but rather a phenomenological *description* of a particular sort of lived *experience*. Thus, the question is not a reifying "does it exist," but rather, are there any experiences that meet the above criteria? Do at least *some* of our spontaneous thoughts qualify as innately constrained symbolic embodiments of species-typical situations?

Spontaneous Thought, Including Dream Content

Since archetypal images are defined not as willfully directed, free creations of the ego, but as contents emerging spontaneously from the unconscious, we must start our journey by exploring the burgeoning literature on *spontaneous thought* – the study of mental contents that emerge unbidden into our awareness. Such contents would psychoanalytically be seen as originating from the unconscious. Supporting this analogy is the fact that researchers on spontaneous thought differentiate between willfully directed or volitional thought and spontaneous thought in a manner similar to Colman (2006) and Jung (see above).

It has long been held in analytical psychology that such content is not random but reveals depths of intentionality. Empirical backing for this supposition, however, can be found in the experimental psychology of spontaneous thought, which incorporates neuroscience, phenomenology, and many other disciplines. This literature finds spontaneous thought to be non-random, purposeful, organized, and often highly functional. Moreover, it appears to have,

> considerable benefit for our day-to-day functioning and general contentment–affording sense-making and the ordering of recent events, anticipations of and projections into the future, and a starting point for some of our creative ideas.
>
> (Stan & Christoff, 2018, p. 487; see also Klinger & Cox, 1987, 2011)

Research on this subject has expanded tremendously in the past decade. In fact, some researchers have labeled the modern era of neuroscience the "era of the wandering mind" (Callard et al., 2013). Roughly one-third to one-half of thought is spontaneous (Klinger & Cox, 1987), and this doesn't include the particular kind of spontaneous thought represented by dream content. Unsurprisingly, dreaming has been classified as a *type* of spontaneous thought (Fox & Christoff, 2018) that overlaps with waking spontaneous thought. According to experimental psychologists studying dreams, dreaming is actually an *intensified form of spontaneous thought* with many overlapping features. Like waking spontaneous thought, dreams are biased toward personal, affectively salient concerns, and the process comes "online" by around age seven to ten (Domhoff, 2018). The overlap can also be observed in neuroscience data, for the same regions involved in spontaneous thought are recruited (albeit more intensely) during REM dreaming (Fox et al., 2013; see also Christoff et al., 2016).

Analyzing dreams is traditional in psychoanalysis; however, there has been disagreement about whether or not such content is largely occupied with *disguising* deeper thoughts (Freud, 1900/2010), or largely *revelatory* of deeper processes. Jung proposed the latter, describing dream contents as a "spontaneous self-portrayal, in symbolic form, of the actual situation in the unconscious" (Jung, CW8, para 505). Similarly, Bion proposed that dreams transform unprocessed primary experiences into workable thoughts, memories, and mental growth (Bion, 1962). Both of these early psychoanalysts proposed that this process occurs in both waking and sleeping states. By contrast, Freud (1900/2010) argued that dreams *disguised* inner realities rather than revealing them.

In a recent review article by Roesler (2023), however, a large body of empirical literature on dreaming is reviewed and found Freud's idea that dreams disguise meaning has not aged well. Rather, the balance of empirical literature on dreams shows that they have a strong tendency for *meaning creation*, which can be observed in the manifest dream content, providing one recognizes the *symbolic* nature of such content.

Spontaneous Thought Is Organized by Affect and Is Embodied

Affective states influence the amount and direction of spontaneous thought content (D'Argembeau, 2018), and spontaneous thoughts are affectively centered and sensitive to current goals (Fox & Christoff, 2018). Much of the above has been found for dream-state spontaneous thought as well. That is, dreaming has been identified as serving several functions, including mood regulation, problem solving, adaptation, furthering of mastery, fostering insight, and anxiety reduction (reviewed in Roesler, 2023). Psychoanalysts Kramer and Glucksman (2015) showed how multiple dreams in a single person can be observed to be continually working and reworking major *emotional* themes, even to the point that independent evaluators could identify immediate and long-term emotional issues just from dream content. Notably, Roesler states in his review (2023, p. 314):

> This reworking of memory contents in the dream is therefore a highly struc-
> tured, rule-governed and goal-directed reworking process that operates
> largely unconsciously, extensively coordinates various domains of mental
> functioning, but can also only take place while there is no new mental input
> of the kind that occurs in the waking state.
>
> (Roesler, 2023, p. 314)

Spontaneous thoughts, then, appear to arise all the time, and are focused on taking life experiences and re-organizing them into either affectively directed autobiographical narratives (i.e., "memory"), or into symbolic expressions of one's current or upcoming life situation (dreams and fantasies). Importantly, vast literature in affective neuroscience finds that affective states *themselves* correlate with the activity of highly invariant subcortical brain structures that are universal in humans and have strong analogues in other animals (Alcaro & Carta, 2019; Panksepp, 2004; Panksepp et al., 2017). Spontaneous thoughts in general, then, are strongly influenced by deeply embodied processes.

Spontaneous Thoughts Seek Meaning

So what is the ultimate purpose behind these highly constructive processes of spontaneous thought? Toward what end is the psyche taking the raw data of experience and processing it so extensively? The construction of a stable, effectively calibrated self-narrative (memory consolidation, mood regulation/contextualization) appears to be one of the functions, along with creative problem solving and future planning.

A growing number of dream researchers propose that dreaming processes experiences by attempting to connect them with *other* experiences in memory – effectively meaning-making via context construction (reviewed in Roesler, 2023, pp. 303–308). Dreaming functions are identified as the development, preservation, and reintegration of the psychic organization (Fosshage, 1997), which was strongly presaged by Jung's description of dreaming having a meaning-making and integrating function (1969), visible in dream symbols.

Stan and Christoff (2018) argue that the numerous meaning-making bene-fits of spontaneous thought might justify changing the term "mind-wandering" to "mind-ordering," given its functions. Moreover, growing evidence points to spontaneous thoughts being critical in the construction of *personal identity and meaning*, suggesting a role in "reflecting on the broader meaning and implications of personal experiences, thereby contributing to the construction, maintenance, and update of an individual's life story" (D'Argembeau, 2018, p. 187). Still other experimental psychologists identify the *identity-consolidating function* of dreaming (Fiss, 1995; Kohut, 1977; Stolorow, 1978). Kliner et al. (2018) in their review conclude that spontaneous thoughts are involved with goal tracking, planning, creative problem solving, reviewing past experience, memory consolidation, and aligning oneself with goal-attainment, but when in excess can lead to rumination, excessive daydreaming, and dissociation.

The above research, therefore, strongly suggests that the psyche has a continuously active function aiming toward meaning-making, much as Jung and other psychoanalysts hypothesized and clinical experience confirms. In particular, it appears that the psyche works tirelessly "in the background" on the construction of the affectively guided meaning of one's personal identity and narrative. It is therefore evident that spontaneous, affect-charged symbolic expressions of one's current or near-future life situation are actually abundant. Hence we are almost ready to see if any of them qualify as *archetypal*. The final criterion requires that archetypal images should be only those spontaneous affective life-symbols that have been organized in accordance with *universal biological principles of organization*. They should be expressions anyone from any culture could experience, given the right generic species-typical situation. They should not depend on cultural observation, mimicry, or verbal instruction, if they are to qualify.

Embodied Cognition

This final, biological dimension can be found in many newer fields (particularly affective neuroscience and evolutionary psychology – see Goodwyn, 2022b), but most relevant here is the study of *embodied cognition*. Recall that the Cartesian paradigm began to erode in the mid-1970s. Rather than view all cognition as disembodied sign manipulations emerging solely in response to verbal instruction or cultural observation, cognitive linguists challenged the classic paradigm using a number of crucial observations of real-world, everyday language (reviewed in Lakoff, 2012, see also Lakoff & Johnson, 1980, 1999, and Khatin-Zadeh et al., 2023). For example, terms such as color names do not exist in the external world independent of bodies, and so cannot "represent" anything. Another example is that basic level categories and spatial relations across many languages require universal primitives that reference the human body (Langacker, 2008).

I have discussed this embodiment and its relation to archetypes elsewhere (Goodwyn, 2012), but it is worth updating here. The literature of embodied cognition and cognitive linguistics shows that much of our thought can be described not in meaningless signs but in terms of *embodied metaphors*, which are:

> frame-to-frame mappings across conceptual domains … linguistic metaphors are surface reflections of those conceptual mappings … from correlations between co-occurring embodied experiences; for example, Happy Is Up, Sad Is Down; More Is Up, Less Is Down; Affection Is Warmth.
>
> (Lakoff, 2012, p. 776)

These metaphors map abstract or difficult to describe/comprehend domains onto embodied visuospatial domains that are easy to comprehend, like the LOVE IS A JOURNEY mapping (Lakoff & Johnson, 1999, capitalization by convention). Complex conceptual metaphors are composed of primary metaphors, which do not further decompose. Most relevant for our purposes, a subset of these primary metaphors is deeply embodied, occurs cross-culturally, and arises from *physical correlates* of emotion, like when anger is described as a hot liquid ("boiling over with anger," "letting off steam," etc.). In other words, some primary metaphors are reliably and cross-culturally emergent due to universalities in human physiology. More examples of these kind of primary metaphors are:

UNDERSTANDING IS SEEING: "I can't understand his *point of view*," "that argument is *murky*," "his thought is very *clear*."

HAPPY IS UP: "flying *high* with good feelings," "on *cloud nine*."

SAD IS DOWN: "feeling *down* in the dumps," "I'm *depressed* today."

CONCEPTUAL HARMONY IS PHYSICAL BALANCE: "These ideas don't work because they are *unbalanced*."

ATTACHMENT LOSS IS COLD: "he gave me the *cold* shoulder," "she left me out in the *cold*."

In contrast to the classic disembodied-meaningless-symbol theory, cognitive linguists argue that

> conceptual knowledge is embodied, that is, it is mapped within our sensory-motor system [which] characterises the semantic content of concepts in terms of the way that we function with our bodies in the world … Abstract reasoning in general *exploits* the sensory-motor system.
>
> (Gallese & Lakoff, 2005, pp. 456–473)

There is significant empirical support for embodied metaphor theory, coming from action-sentence compatibility studies, eye-tracking studies, hand-prime studies, gesture-in-learning studies, and neuroimaging studies on sensorimotor activation during metaphor processing and mental imagery processing (Khatin-Zadeh et al., 2023). As mentioned, this literature supports the idea that even abstract, complex metaphors are compositions of simpler metaphors that are mappings of ideas onto embodied visuo-spatial and kinesthetic body-movements. Take the ANGER IS HEAT metaphor, for example. The source of this concept is the human body itself and its physiological responses to the emotion of anger (Khatin-Zadeh et al., 2023, p. 8). Other primary metaphors use kinesthetic sense (UNDERSTANDING IS GRASPING, i.e., "I can't *grasp* what he is talking about," or CONTROLLING IS GRASPING "you need to get a *grip* on this situation"), which is naturally embodied. Such a metaphor would make no sense to a whale or a rhinoceros but makes perfect sense for a handy primate like *Homo sapiens*.

The Symbolic Dimension of the Archetypal Image and Embodied Cognition

Recall that archetypal images are supposed to be *symbolic*, and in the synthetic way Jung imagined, *not* the outdated, disembodied way found in classic cognitive science. I think this dimension in particular has caused a great deal of difficulty for theorists. Note how Jung and other commenters claim that archetypes defy "final analysis" – that is, such as when Hillman identifies archetypal images as operationally unknowable, containing limitless mystery, power, and capability for being endlessly articulated verbally (Hillman, 1977) or when Jung says:

> Not for a moment dare we succumb to the illusion that an archetype can be finally explained and disposed of. Even the best attempts at explanation are only more or less successful translations into another metaphorical language.
>
> (Jung, 1940/1969, para. 160)

Elsewhere Brooke reflects that "Archetypes seem mysterious, deep, remote, frightening, and enchanting, and thinking about them remains equally murky and ambivalent" (Brooke, 2015, p. 161).

Such florid descriptions risk making the archetype a difficult and arcane concept, only for the initiated to comprehend. One can see why Jung was accused of "mysticism." But this need not be so. After all, archetypal images seek to *represent* ineffable feelings or perceptions, but the map is not the territory. The archetypal image itself should not be equally murky and impenetrable! No matter how mysterious is the moon, I can still point at it with a humble finger.

Conceptual metaphor theory is helpful here. Consider that a key feature of conceptual embodied metaphor theory is that all metaphors have an *ineffable core of meaning* which cannot be expressed except via other metaphors (Kövecses, 2016; Lakoff & Johnson, 1999; Minervino et al., 2018). This applies not just to fancy expressions of deep mystery (such as poetry, or the Mandala) but also to more prosaic ones like DANGER IS DARKNESS as is seen in the evocative imagery of "the dark forest" found in so many fairy tales. "Danger," after all, cannot ever literally be "darkness," and yet the metaphor is powerful and viscerally resonant for poor humans with lousy night vision. This metaphor, however, would not make much sense to owls, who thrive in darkness.

Hence archetypal images are best seen as *special sorts of spontaneous metaphors*, an idea phenomenology agrees with (Brooke, 2015, p. 148). Therefore the above mystery of the archetypal image is more due to their status as *metaphors* in general, rather than any obscure, impenetrable or unknowable features in themselves.

The Biological Dimension

Now for our final criterion – the innate and biological dimension of the archetypal image. As we have seen, the psyche is continually producing spontaneous thoughts. Some of these will be affectively charged symbolic expressions of our life situation (especially when we are dreaming). But only some of these will qualify as *archetypal images*. The final criteria requires that a given symbolic image/narrative have a primarily *innate* origin, if we are to argue that it comes from "the collective unconscious." Combining the foregoing, then, we can say that an archetypal image is a complex, affect-charged metaphor of one's current life situation that is mainly composed of primary metaphors derived from universal human biology.

In the disembodied Cartesian paradigm, however, *none* of such contents could ever qualify as archetypal images, because all mental contents can only come from verbal instruction and/or cultural observation. Disembodied minds cannot acquire any useful structure or contents from the mindless mechanisms of the body, after all. I believe this confusion persists into contemporary scholarship, as evidenced by Brooke's quote:

> A still-unresolved problem, however, is how Jung can refer on one hand to the archetypes as the cores of meaning within an image or cluster of images, and on the other hand as the species-specific potentialities that structure behaviour and experience.
>
> (Brooke, 2015, p. 152)

Given the trouble caused by Cartesian assumptions, is it any wonder that Jung's concept has received so much resistance during the century since he introduced the term?

Nevertheless, the archetype *absolutely requires* a biological dimension or it becomes a superfluous concept, disposable via Ockham's Razor. In Brooke's terms, "The cultural-historical dimensions of the archetype require a theoretical anchor" (Brooke, 2015, p. 149), by which he means a link to our concrete embodiedness as human beings:

> Child, mother, father, eternal youth, hero, marriage, and sacrifice are fundamental human occurrences that would not be possible for a being born with the genetics of a shark.
>
> (Brooke, 2015, p. 151)

Given that multiple disciplines are pointing to an inherently *embodiedness* of cognition, we can proceed. What follows will attempt to provide a non-reductive biological anchor that not only explains a great deal about the characteristics of the archetypal image but has other advantages.

The Archetype Integrated with Modern Embodied Theory

The recognition that cognition is deeply embodied means that any of the *spontaneous, affectively charged complex metaphors of our life situation that are composed predominantly from innate primary metaphors* will qualify as archetypal images. That's it. All that remains is to determine which primary metaphors are derived solely from our embodiedness as human beings-in-the-world, and which are derived from cultural elaborations, as everyone will naturally acquire both. If no primary metaphors qualify in the former sense, then archetypal images do not exist. In previous work, I have proposed a number of innate primary metaphors I will call *innate mappings.*[1] These include (borrowing and elaborating from Lakoff & Johnson, 1999; see also Goodwyn, 2012, 2022b):

1 KNOWLEDGE/SAFETY/HAPPINESS IS LIGHT (which also implies UNMANIFEST/DANGER/SADNESS IS DARKNESS)
2 POWER/HAPPINESS IS UP (which implies WEAKNESS/SADNESS IS DOWN)
3 CONCEPTUAL HARMONY IS SYMMETRY/BALANCE
4 AFFECTION/ENJOYMENT/LIFE IS WARMTH
5 ANGER/PASSION/LUST IS HEAT/HOT LIQUID
6 COMPLEX PROCESS IS A CONSCIOUS BEING (i.e. personification)
7 EMOTIONS ARE FACIAL EXPRESSIONS
8 UNDERSTANDING IS GRASPING
9 WILLING IS MANIPULATING WITH THE HANDS
10 EMOTIONAL SEPARATION IS COLD

This is not an exhaustive list, but hopefully the gist of the idea is evident. These mappings arise not from cultural observation or verbal instruction but by virtue of having human bodies operating in species-typical, but non-specific environments (i.e., planet Earth in general).[2] But are these so-called innate mappings actually innate? Do I *need* to propose a biological contribution to their existence? Might they all simply be acquired solely via verbal instruction or cultural observation?

Notably, the above *visuospatial* metaphors arise even in the congenitally blind (Minervino et al., 2018), and they can be found in spontaneous gestures and signs in signed languages as well (Cienki & Müller, 2008). Nevertheless, one might argue they were acquired via *verbal instruction*, at least. To rule that out, persons born blind were presented with *novel* visuospatial metaphors (i.e., "he ascribes to a photoshopped version of reality"). They still had no trouble understanding them. This and other data led researchers to conclude: "to a great extent, conceptual metaphors are universal knowledge structures that are associated to the structure of our body and of our exchanges with the world. As such, they impose strong constraints on the space of possible innovations in metaphoric production"(Minervino et al., 2018, p. 7). Such results demonstrate that observation and instruction do not seem necessary to acquire visuospatial metaphors.

To use another example, let's consider ANGER IS HEAT, a mapping I claim is innate. In English, there are many common sayings that utilize this primary mapping, such as "*hot* under the collar," "a real *hot*head," "*boiling* over with anger," and so forth. I argue that this mapping is innate because when we feel anger, our temperature increases along with rising blood pressure. Skin flushing from anger gives the sensation of hotness by virtue of our human physiology. I propose that these conditions are both necessary and sufficient to bring ANGER IS HEAT into our cognitive repertoire regardless of culture or verbal instruction, which implies it should arise cross-culturally. If I am wrong, however, and all that is required is verbal instruction or cultural observation to produce it, then the mapping should *not* be found cross-culturally, and its *opposite* might be found.

When examining unrelated languages, however, the former prediction holds for ANGER IS HEAT. This mapping occurs cross-culturally in English, Chinese, Japanese, Hungarian, Tahitian, Chickasaw, and Wolof – an African language spoken in Senegal (Kövecses, 2007, pp. 156–163). Kövecses reviews many other cross-cultural examples like this and concludes that

> My view is that, given the universal real physiology, members of different cultures cannot conceptualize their emotions in a way that *contradicts* universal physiology … [though] they can choose to conceptualize their emotions in many different ways *within the constraints* imposed on them by universal physiology.
>
> (2007, p. 165, emphasis original)

Elsewhere he states that "Feeling states have an irreducible and probably universal psychobiological basis that accounts for many similarities in the conceptualization of emotions" (Kövecses, 2007, p. 187).

None of this discounts the importance of culture, which may not vary *infinitely* or *arbitrarily*, but it *does* vary a lot nonetheless. Here, we can see that cultural variation can emphasize some innate mappings over others. For example Zulu utilizes ANGER IS HUNGER (both universal situations) to frame many sayings, whereas this metaphor is not commonly found in English. This means some mappings may only exist in potential, as most languages may not use *all* possible innate mappings. Furthermore, many primary mappings are *not innate* at all. Chinese uses HAPPINESS IS FLOWERS IN THE HEART and Zulu uses ANGER IS GRINDING CORN (Kövecses, 2007, pp. 167–9) to organize many sayings in those languages. These are *non-innate*, unique cultural mappings, since flowers and corn do not derive from the human body or its typical species-specific interactions in the generic environment, but both derive from unique cultural traditions.

Conclusion

I think the only way to make sense of the archetypes and the archetypal images is to relieve archetype theory from the disembodied Cartesian assumptions that have held it back. I have situated archetypal images in terms of a number of modern embodied disciplines, including cognitive and affective neuroscience, embodied cognition, spontaneous thought, and dream science. With the conceptual precision offered by phenomenology, we can now formulate archetypes with clarity.

My conclusion is that the archetypal image can be identified easily and clearly as *a spontaneous, affect-charged, complex metaphor for one's current, species-typical life situation that is mainly composed of innate mappings*. One can even make the case that the archetypes themselves (not the images), as constraining organizing principles, are the innate mappings. Note this definition departs from Jung a bit. I do not follow Jung's somewhat tangled application of Kant's noumenon/phenomenon distinction for the archetype and archetypal image. Moreover, I do not see the archetype as the hypothetical core of a cluster of images, and I do not see there being a one-to-one relationship between archetype-as-such and archetypal image. Instead we inherit an "alphabet" of innate mappings that we can use to compose a huge number of archetypal images. Our experience and imagination does the rest, but even this process may evince some level of innate guidance, given the remarkable similarity of some cross-cultural complexes such as ritual structures. In future work I will explore that possibility in more depth. In any case, expressions that utilize mainly culturally invented primary metaphors should *not* be considered archetypal, though they can still carry a great deal of meaning.

This formulation provides an explanation for Classic Jungian archetypal images such as the Mother, the Father, the Senex, the Hero, the Persona, the Shadow, the Puer, the Anima/us, the Child, and so forth: they are complex metaphors of universal situations that use mostly innate mappings in their composition. They will embody and symbolize all the intense emotions that go along with these species-universal situations that will defy easy verbalization. Because they use mostly innate mappings, their source is the human body itself, which naturally has only one source: the genome (see Goodwyn, 2022b). Innate mappings are therefore a biologically transmitted "alphabet," which the unconscious can use to compose all kinds of archetypal images. We do not need to acquire such symbols from cultural material or verbal instruction to have the capacity, indeed *tendency* for such symbols to occur to us spontaneously. In a very real sense, the *body itself* can be considered the collective unconscious.

This formulation has many advantages:

1 It provides easy-to-use criteria to judge spontaneous clinical material to assess its level of archetypality.
2 It is easily falsifiable. Each of my proposed innate mappings can be tested cross-culturally to see if they are contradicted, or if they are instead highly stable like ANGER IS HEAT.

3 It helps us *interpret* the images themselves, since knowledge of the origin of innate mappings means we will have a kind of "Rosetta stone" with which to analyze clinical material of all kinds. Note that each archetypal image should be considered a whole greater than its parts, however, rather than "nothing but X." I do *not* advocate for bioreductionism.
4 It explains *why* archetypal images can appear so mysterious and full of meaning despite their ineffable quality: because as symbols, they are complex metaphors embodying powerful but difficult to verbalize human feelings, perceptions, and expressions of meaning.
5 It explains how archetypal images, despite their biological origins, are not rigid and can respond to large-scale cultural shifts – new compositions of the innate "alphabet" are always possible, though truly novel creations will likely be rare.
6 It explains why mythic narratives can often look so similar but not identical worldwide, and it provides clues as to why: cultural emphasis on some mappings over others.

Hopefully, this integration of archetype theory with the study of spontaneous thought and embodied sciences resolves some of the controversies that have dogged the theory for so long. With it, perhaps we can forge ahead with new studies and developments.

Notes

1 In previous work I called these "archetypal elements," but to avoid confusion I am updating my terminology to the above "innate mappings."
2 I think it is likely that many of these would arise in humans raised in space or other planets. Nevertheless, since no human has been raised off Earth, this hypothesis must remain speculative.

References

Alcaro, A. & Carta, S. (2019). The "instinct" of imagination. A neuro-ethological approach to the evolution of the reflective mind and its application to psychotherapy. *Frontiers in Human Neuroscience* 12: 522.

Bion, W. R. (1962). A theory of thinking. *International Journal of Psychoanalysis*, 43: 306–310.

Brooke, R. (1991). Psychic complexity and human existence: A phenomenological approach. *Journal of Analytical Psychology*, 36, 505–518.

Brooke, R. (2009). The self, the psyche and the world: A phenomenological interpretation. *Journal of Analytical Psychology*, 54, 601–618.

Brooke, R. (2015). *Jung and phenomenology*. Routledge.

Brooke, R. (2018). Descartes dualism and the phenomenological tradition: A response to Elizabeth Urban's 'On matters of mind and body: Regarding Descartes'. *Journal of Analytical Psychology*, 63(5), 656–660.

Buss, D. (Ed.). (2005). *The handbook of evolutionary psychology*. Wiley.

Callard, F., Smallwood, J., Golchert, J., & Margulies, D. S. (2013). The era of the wandering mind? Twenty-first century research on self-generated mental activity. *Frontiers in Psychology*, 4, (891).

Christoff, K., Irving, Z. C., Fox, K. C. R., Spreng, R. N., & Andrews-Hanna, J. R. (2016). Mind-wandering as spontaneous thought: A dynamic framework. *Nature Reviews Neuroscience*, 17(11), 718–731.

Cienki, A. & Müller, C. (2008). *Metaphor and gesture*. John Benjamins.

Colman, W. (2006). Imagination and the imaginary. *Journal of Analytical Psychology* 51, 21–41.

D'Argembeau, A. (2018). Mind-wandering and self-referential thought. In K. C. R. Fox & K. Christoff. (Eds.), *The Oxford handbook of spontaneous thought* (pp. 181–191). Oxford University Press.

Domhoff, G. W. (2018). Dreaming is an intensified form of mind-wandering, based in an augmented portion of the default network. In K. C. R. Fox & K. Christoff. (Eds.), *The Oxford handbook of spontaneous thought* (pp. 355–370). Oxford University Press.

Fosshage, J. L. (1997). The organizing functions of dream mentation. *Contemporary Psychoanalysis*, 33(3), 429–458.

Fiss, H. (1995). "The Post-Freudian Dream. A Reconsideration of Dream Theory Based on Recent Sleep Laboratory Findings." In Traum und Gedächtnis, *Materialien aus dem Sigmund-Freud-Institut*, vol. 15, edited by H. Bareuther, K. Brde, M. Evert-Saleh, and N. Spangenberg, 11–35. Münster: Lit.

Fox K. C. R., & Christoff, K. (2018). Introduction: Toward an interdisciplinary science of spontaneous thought. In K. C. R. Fox & K. Christoff. (Eds.), *The Oxford handbook of spontaneous thought*. (pp. 3–8). Oxford University Press.

Fox K. C. R., Nijeboer, S., Solomonova, E., Domhoff, G. W., & Christoff, K. (2013). Dreaming as mind wandering: Evidence from functional neuroimaging and first-person content reports. *Frontiers in Human Neuroscience*, 7, 412.

Freud, S. (1900/2010). *The interpretation of dreams*. Basic Books.

Gallese, V. & Lakoff, G. (2005). The brain's concepts: The role of the sensory-motor system in conceptual knowledge. *Cognitive Neruopsychology*, 22(3–4), 455–479.

Goodwyn, E. (2012). *The neurobiology of the gods*. Routledge.

Goodwyn, E. (2021). Bodies and minds, heaps and syllables. *Synthese* 1999, 8831.

Goodwyn, E. (2022a). Developing a metaphysical foundation for analytical psychology. In J. Mills (Ed.), *Psychoanalysis and the mind body problem* (pp. 88–118). Routledge.

Goodwyn, E. (2022b). Archetype and clinical application: How the genome responds to experience. *Journal of Analytical Psychology*, 67(3), 838–859.

Hillman, J. (1977). *Revisioning psychology*. William Morrow Publishing.

Jung, C. G. (1921/1971). *CW6*. Routledge.

Jung, C. G. (1940/1969). The psychology of the child archetype. *C.W.9.i.*, 149–81.

Jung, C. G. (1959). *CW9i*. Routledge.

Khatin-Zadeh, O., Farsani, D., Hu, J., Eskandari, Z., Zhu, Y., & Banaruee, H. (2023). A review of studies supporting metapohrical embodiment. *Behavioral Science*, 13, (585).

Kliner, E., Marchetti, I., & Koster, E. H. W. (2018). Spontaneous thought and goal pursuit: From functions such as planning to dysfunctions such as rumination. In K. C. R. Fox & K. Christoff. (Eds.), *The Oxford handbook of spontaneous thought* (pp. 215–232). Oxford University Press.

Klinger, E. & Cox, W. M. (1987). Dimensions of thought flow in everyday life. *Imagination, Cognition and Personality*, 7, 105–128.

Klinger, E. & Cox, W. M. (2011). Motivation and the goal theory of current concerns. In W. M. Cox & E. Klinger (Eds.), *Handbook of motivated counseling* (2nd ed., pp. 3–47). John Wiley & Sons.

Kohut, H. (1977). *The Restoration of the Self.* New York: International Universities Press.

Kövecses, Z. (2007). *Metaphor and emotion.* Cambridge University Press.

Kövecses, Z. (2016). A view of mixed metaphor within a conceptual metaphor theory framework. In G. J. Steen (Ed.), *Metaphor in language, cognition and communication,* Vol. 6. John Benjamins.

Kramer, M., and M. Glucksman. (2015). *Dream Research. Contributions to Clinical Practice.* London: Routledge.

Lakoff, G. (2012). Explaining embodied cognition results. *Topics in Cognitive Science,* 4, 773–785.

Lakoff G., & Johnson, M. (1980). Metaphors we live by. Chicago: University of Chicago Press.

Lakoff, G. & Johnson, M. (1999). *Philosophy in the flesh.* Basic Books.

Langacker, R. W. (2008). *Cognitive grammar: A basic introduction.* Oxford: Oxford University Press.

Levine, P. A. (2010). *In an unspoken voice.* North Atlantic Books.

Minervino, R. A., Martin, A., Tavernini, L. M., & Trench, M. (2018). The understanding of visual metaphors by the congenitally blind. *Frontiers in Psychology,* 9, 1242.

Panksepp, J. (2004). *Affective neuroscience.* Oxford University Press.

Panksepp, J., Lane, R. D., Solms, M., & Smith, R. (2017). Reconciling cognitive and affective neuroscience perspectives on the brain basis of emotional experience. *Neuroscience and Biobehavioral Reviews* 76, 187–215.

Roesler, C. (2023). Dream interpretation and empirical dream research - an overview of research findings and their connections with psychoanalytic dream theories. *The International Journal of Psychoanalysis,* 104(2), 301–330.

Stan, D., & Christoff K. (2018). The mind wanders with ease: Low motivational intensity is an essential quality of mind-wandering. In K. C. R. Fox & K. Christoff. (Eds.), *The Oxford handbook of spontaneous thought.* (pp. 47–53). Oxford University Press.

Stolorow, R. (1978). "Themes in Dreams. A Brief Contribution to Therapeutique Technique." *International Journal of Psycho-Analysis* 59: 473–475.

Van der Kolk, B. (2015). *The body keeps the score.* Penguin.

Part 2

The Social and Political Horizons

Introduction to "Healing Is Political"

From a human science perspective, one of Jung's central difficulties was not that his approach was introverted, but that his introversion tended to be cut off from the sociopolitical and cultural world in which we all, introverts and extroverts alike, live, dream, and understand ourselves. For several decades, especially since the publication of Andrew Samuels's book *The Political Psyche*, there has been a growing appreciation among (post-)Jungians that we need to include these outer horizons in our theory of individuation and wholeness and in our work. What Brooks's chapter does is to sketch the ontological and epistemological issues involved: how we organize our knowledge (epistemology) of what it is (ontology) to be human. Drawing from a number of recent and contemporary thinkers, she persuasively argues for integrating conceptually sociopolitical and socioeconomic realities into our approach to the work of healing. This chapter is a very condensed version of the Introductory Chapter of *Psychoanalysis, Catastrophe and Social Change* (Routledge, 2022, with permission).

Chapter 6

Healing Is Political*

Robin McCoy Brooks

It is apparent that we are living in a state of sustained emergency. The accelerating effects of global warming, the pandemic, essentialist racism, xenophobia, wars, a widening gap between rich and poor and other atrocities leave us bewildered about what is happening or what we can do about it. Stunned by the unfathomable, we may slip into the experience of massive indifference in an ever shape-shifting collective temporality of "anxious waiting." Almost 20 years ago, Julia Kristeva described the modern person as one who had lost their capacity to apperceive or represent their experience in imaginatively empowered ways (Kristeva, 1995). This "malady" of the contemporary psyche, she claimed, was aggravated by the uncoupling of language from the body, that which makes it impossible to feel passionately about life in ways that one can sensibly manifest. Bernard Stiegler describes the emotional and mentally fatiguing effects of chronic catastrophe as "entropic collapse" (2019, p. 8). Entropic collapse can be characterized by the inability to hold on to one's mind, leading to *dis*individuation and a

> loss of the feeling of existing, the loss of the possibility of expressing one's will, the correlative loss of all reason for living and the subsequent loss of reason as such, a loss [that which] strikes entire groups and entire countries.
> (Stiegler, 2019, pp. 8, 75–84)

Indeed, the existential crises at hand arise from a carelessness of thought in the first place and the withdrawal of thought from the body.

How do any of us find the courage to break from the banality of mindlessness and *open* ourselves to others – to a horizon of being where we are able to remake something out of nothing for the sake of someone else in the face of its impossibility? (Kristeva, 1987). Carl Jung proclaimed in 1927 that there exists a state of mind which allows the individual to become co-effected by the shared plight of a differentiated humanity – where one may break through one's

DOI: 10.4324/9781032694603-9

psychic fortressing, thus revealing a truth of what is and the memory of thought and care in times of collective emergency. He writes from the rubble heap of a shattered Europe:

> In this reality we are no longer differentiated persons but are conscious of our common human bonds. Here I strip off the distinctiveness of my own personality, social or otherwise, and reach down to the problems of the present day, problems which do not arise out of myself-or at least I like to imagine. Here I can no longer deny them; I feel and know myself to be one for the many, and what moves the many moves me … for here it is not the individual will that counts but the will of the species.
>
> (Jung, 1927/1970, para. 261)

Jung is making an important distinction, which recognizes that the individuation of one is not detached from the public sphere or the concrete events of history but is situated within the deep conflicts and emerging truths of the age. Our question is, how does this opening lead to political possibility and creative movement toward social reform within psychoanalytic practice, the academy, our institutes, or anywhere?

The need to care for others and to be cared for is at least partially encoded in our genes and fundamental to building what evolutionary sociologist Nicholas Christakis has described as a *good* society (Christakis, 2019). Christakis's extensive research on the biology of social behavior allows him to boldly claim that we are innately equipped as a species to band together, live cooperatively with each other, befriend each other, recognize uniqueness, show kindness, love, and reciprocity in our relationships and learn socially while teaching what we know (Christakis, 2019; see also Plomin, 2018).

I am interested in the conditions that allow an individual and/or community of people to access and optimize these innate and psychological capabilities by engaging the disastrous effects of the emergencies which threaten our lives daily. What is it that allows us to surrender to the *burden of Being* even though we are overwhelmed by the utter realness of our shared corporeal vulnerability and psychological dependency we have on each other as little animals? How do we engage with Judith Butler's (2006) argument that our shared corporeal vulnerability and inter-relationality are the basis making political responsiveness possible? I am interested in how the individual is co-constituted in the center of collective life in ways that individuate both in response to catastrophe; how, in other words, care for others is awakened in the clinic, the academy, our training institutes, and in general? How can the psychoanalyst rebuild a sublimatory knowledge basis to meet creatively the emerging needs of our patients in our era of sustained emergency? How do we find the courage, to as Keven Lu (2020) recently stated it, to "decolonize" our institutions, theories, methods, and practices so that we may meet the needs of our era? (November 2020, IAJS seminar).

These are the central questions engaged through a notion of trans-subjectivity. *The trans-subjective is posited as the nodal point through which the subject may move from personal concern to political responsiveness. Trans-subjectivity is conceptualized as a crucial extra-psychical dimension of sublimation and a psyche-social dynamic that is the precursor to political action* – akin to what Lacan obliquely referred to as "collective logic" (Lacan, 2006; Hook, 2018).

My engagement with the question of trans-subjectivity is also a critique of psychoanalysis whose privileging of the subject has generally disavowed the socio/political dimensions of reality through which we enact our relationship to it. A psychoanalytic understanding of trans-subjectivity will allow us to expand, not only how we think about psychical/social change, but also how to become a part of the social reform we desire within our own discipline in the clinic and beyond.

The Political

What do I mean by *the political?* To answer this question, I first turn to an introductory reading of Heidegger's existential analytic of care (*Sorge*) illuminated by Stiegler's critique (on which I lean) because for Stiegler, *care and the political are inextricably bound.*[1] I begin with Heidegger and Stiegler in order to set out the ontological ground for the necessary connections between the personal, ethical, and political we need to endorse.

Heidegger began to work out his notion of care through factical life experience within community life (Heidegger, 2010). *Dasein* can be roughly translated as *existence* (to stand out beyond one's self). Existence, or being-in-the-world, is always and irreducibly with others along-side things (Heidegger, 2001/1927). Later, Heidegger would emphasize that *Dasein* is not a subjectivity which then engages with the being of beings. It has no original subjectivity. *Dasein* is not what human beings are as subjectivities. Rather, *Dasein* is more fundamentally the *possibility for* every being, including being a person, in the clearing or the space between Being and beings (Heidegger, 1999). Being in this sense was dependent on the transformation of both human being and its other in the space of the clearing as *Being became* through its fundamental displacement and *not through* the single "subject" (p. 178).

The call to care (*Sorge*) is disclosed through *Dasein* as "clearing" (*Lichtung*) (Heidegger, 2001/1927, pp. 188, 232). Care simply arrives (in the clearing) apart from intersecting sociality with *others* and *things.*[2] Care, as such, is not a something, like a feeling, perhaps, but a "nothing," a possibility from which Being may gain access to itself as separate from its everyday practices (p. 263). Being's authentic singularity is rendered possible against the *in*authentic being of "the they" (*das Man*) (2001/1927). *In other words, there is a difference between being and human beings through which the individual must take responsibility in how to* *comport oneself from a mode in which human being actively opens to Being's radical alterity* (Heidegger, 1999, p. 57). One must *hold sway*, in other words, by bearing the hardship of the difference that arises between what is *both different* and *intertwined* in order to live out the fullness of one's life (p. 177). We can begin to see how Heidegger's fundamental ontology may be extended and particularized to include other alterities encountered in a differentiated humanity of beings within a widening swath of so-called identities and isms to include race, gender (queer), age, status, and so forth.

Stepping now into another important dimension of care ... *Dasein* is also in the middle between human-being and other beings (p. 211). From the in-between, *Dasein* may *reach and transform both* within their respective essences (p. 11). Here is the trans-subjective aspect of sublimation which allows the analytic patient (or any of us) to respond creatively to something beyond one's own self-interests *in a self to other engagement.*

The call of care arises with and among others but is singularly apprehended and associated with authenticity – a truth, even if transient, about oneself, about how to live, and how to conduct oneself with others when confronted with the *equiprimordiality* of Being's capacity for *untruth* (Brooks, 2011). *Dasein* is both what opens up and what closes off memory or rather a source of its knowledge *or* lack of it. Being slips back into the everyday synchrony (clock time) that reduces the past (and ways of remembering) to something "determined" through artifacts (digital archives, etc.). Thus, human being neglects the poignancy of its existential character of care that is *undetermined*, thereby *slipping into carelessness* (Stiegler, 2017, pp. 393–394). Heidegger is especially concerned with how easily whole groups may regress given our *equiprimordial* capacity for *carelessness.* "The they" (the anonymous *das Man*) is described by Stiegler as *dis*individuated. We *can* easily think or otherwise fall into this inauthenticity – it is ontologically *always* available to us – contributing to the collective's *disindividuation* (see Ross, 2018).

Stiegler is interested in what basis Being may be open to *indeterminacy.* Being is facing a new era where living toward death is no longer the crisis that awakens us to a truth of what is. My reading of Stiegler on this point is that Being's contemporary challenge is more dire because the life of the entire planet (Anthropocene) is at stake, not just our own lives. It is not only the certainty of one's own death that awakens us to an *indeterminacy* that being is, but in addition we are faced with a real possibility of not having a future *at all* beyond our death due to the accelerated status of climate change (pandemics, etc.) and subsequent threat of our species extinction *if we don't do something about it now.*

What moves a collective from its mindless disengagement requires a capacity to *hold sway* or bear the burden of Being's responsibility to care about an *indeterminate future for everybody else beyond one's own meager death*, or beyond my own *puni-verse*. Daniel Ross eloquently summarizes Stiegler on the point of indeterminacy:

> There is no access to the infinite of the indeterminate other than through the determinate. In short [realizing] both is what makes it possible to "make a difference" by caring for an indeterminate future *while also* keeping in mind our tendency to close off that possibility by reducing existence to the stereo-typical, the dogmatic or the careless "common understanding" of *das Man*.
>
> (Ross, 2018, p. 4)

Ross is amplifying in contemporary language the ontological difference between being and beings. Stiegler thus redraws the boundaries of Heidegger's notion of care beyond its own horizon of being toward death to *"being towards a life beyond my own death"* while considering the real possibility of species extinction in our present era of catastrophe (Stiegler, 2019, pp. 283–285).

From the basis of this sobering preparatory discussion, I may now lay out what I mean by the political. Politicality is the struggle to articulate the *"I"* with the *"we" toward a fruitful individuation and an indeterminate future*. Following this line of thinking, engaging the traumatizing effects of catastrophe generates the trans-subjective moment that may lead to activism. *Care consists of the cultivation and transformation of trans-individuation.*

In contrast, the *careless* insurrection, encouraged by Mr. Trump, enacted by the domestic terrorists who swarmed the US Capitol on January 6, 2021 *is not* an example of fruitful activism flowing from trans-subjective authentic (consensual) truth. The political moment, as I am using it, erupts within psyche-social sphere in-between individual and other beings mobilized by care (versus careless-ness) in response to the real of catastrophe. Catastrophe (in the material world) becomes one of the forms in which the subject encounters the traumatic real that inaugurates a call to care and political (sublimatory) possibility with and amongst others. *The trans-subjective is the link between the psyche-social subject and political possibility.*

My objective in the following section is to orient the reader to selected thought of four luminaries for whom the psyche/social was of key importance. These luminaries are Jung, Lacan, Simondon and Stiegler.

Jung and Lacan

Both Jung and Lacan viewed the collective realm as crucial for subject formation. Both conceived of a third psychical reality through which the self or subject became constituted. For Jung, the third was the extra-psychical dimension of the psychoid archetype, and for Lacan and Kristeva the third was the extra-psychical dimension of radical alterity Lacan named the Real. The Lacanian real contains *both* psychical and experiential sources of trauma characterized as radical otherness. The real as radical otherness is unintelligible, inarticulatable, may not be symbolized, has no meaning, is random, experienced as pure bodily traumatisms and intangible excesses. In other words, when we encounter the *real* of a catastrophe, say the COVID-19 pandemic, our bodies and psyches become the site for catastrophe's claims and political contestation to be worked through in psychoanalysis or elsewhere, as will be seen (Webster, 2018). By relocating the locus of subjective identity to the real (in relation to its other inter-locking imaginary and symbolic registers), Lacan and post-Lacanian theoreticians have, in my view, given us a broader theoretical basis from which to understand the effects of historical, trans-historical and catastrophic trauma on the individual and its social/political milieu across time.[3]

Jung's insight that our responsiveness to the collective was a crucial element in individuation foreshadowed later post-Lacanian thought, which understands the subject as co-constituted with the social/political dimension of reality. However, Jung's epistemological basis for the psyche does not adequately consider *how* our ontological-historical-political situation defines the very basis for how we historically enact our relationship to being. As Wolfgang Giegerich claims, and I am in agreement with him here – the great questions, deep conflicts and fundamental truths of any age come out of the effects of real, concrete historical events to which we are inured (Giegerich, 2004, p. 41). Jung's originating concern for humanity's soul and its individuation became *detached from the public sphere* of the real world.

Jung's focus was rather on the *private arena* of the individual's unconscious processes informed by the ahistorical reservoir of the trans-personal psyche. Jung's conception of a supernatural reified collective mind fails to account for how particularity *and* universality suffuses individuality within social collectives, thereby disregarding psycho/social factors that in contrast are considered to be the very locus of subjective identity in Lacan and post Lacanian thought (Goodwyn, 2012; Lu, 2020; Mills, 2018; Saban, 2020). Otherwise put, Jung did not integrate these other systems into his configuration of the self's *telos*. Nor do we find in Jung a methodological means through which a self is motivated to become collectively innovative or part of social reform. However, *we must not undermine the importance of Jung's basic insight that the collective and individual are inextricably bound* even if his "un-thought out metaphysics" falls apart under the scrutiny of contemporary psychoanalytic and psychosocial discourse (Brooks, 2011; Gullatz, 2010; Hinton, 2011; Lu, 2013).

Jung's disregard for the personal unconscious under and below his fascination with the archetypal realm is generally known and critiqued (Brooks, 2013; Saban, 2020). When a so-called archetype emerged, Jung retained a stance of epistemological authority when it came to archetypal explications regarding the patient's experience (Brooks, 2013; Jung, 1935/1989, para. 190). At the level of the personality or personal unconscious, however, Jung's method dramatically shifted. At the personal realm he conceived a differentiated humanity and addressed the patient as an individual irreducible to others including himself.

He writes: "I talk with them as one natural human being to another, and I expose myself completely and react with no restrictment" (Jung, 1935/1989, paras. 318–319, 174). Jung's phenomenological/descriptive approach was a method he developed and retained from his earlier and acclaimed word association test research conducted at Burghölzli Psychiatric Hospital in Zurich in 1901–1904 (Bair, 2003, p. 66). In this approach, Jung would enter a discursive back-and-forth process between analyst and patient following the patient's associations. We are less bound to interpretive dogma using Jung's phenomenological/descriptive approach when engaging enigmatic material and free to be shaped by an ensuing sublimatory process that emerges in between self and other and world.

I have come to think of archetypes as *provisional* universals producing cultural particularities that may be uniquely shared. When these provisionally shared realities are recognized, they may become a basis for a new consensual reality in response to a dilemma posed eventuating in a collective's fruitful individuation – or they may alternatively disindividuate into collective carelessness. These provisional universals include both psychic and/or experientially based phenomena that are inextricably bound yet distinct, and they may flash up when encountering the shared traumas of our era. *In trans-subjective moments such as these, the subject can begin to translate particularity into some kind of universality, one that levels distinctions between others by recognizing what is common amongst ourselves as peoples over time but, at the same time, does not disallow what remains irreparably separate* (Brooks, 2016).

Here is an example of what I mean by universals that colonize (totalize) versus particularize a shared truth revealed to us during the current pandemic. A maddening and ubiquitous meme we see blasted on social media and in public spaces is: *We are all in this together*. While the virus does not discriminate who it infects (a universal), some individuals live in conditions that render infection more likely (crowded structures, homelessness, living with children, frontline health/care staff with or without adequate PPE, and other essential workers). Still others are more vulnerable to its deadly outcomes (age, race, etc.), and still others have better access to healthcare, where early detection and treatment may save a life or minimize how the virus ravages the body. Memes such as this are totalizing structures that reify particularities into a universal that tacitly colonizes distinctions into propagandizing presuppositions becoming a violent Hallmark card.

For Lacan, the world takes hold of the subject through its radical encounters with catastrophe thus opening what is obscured on the socio/symbolic dimension of reality. Lacan's three registers of psychical reality provide a broader platform through which we may better theorize the effects of catastrophe on the level of the *visceral real of the subject*, the *inter-subjective imaginary*, and *socio-political dimensions of experience* in the modern world, allowing us to think into how these experiences may contribute to political agency.

Simondon and Stiegler

Gilbert Simondon was embedded in the contemporary discourses on phenomenology, general systems theory, Marxism, Lacan's linguistic interpretations of Freud's opus, and the birth of deconstruction. His thought has been taken up by Jungian scholars such as Saban and Chabot, who see in Simondon a (trickster-like) basis from which we might creatively revision aspects of Jung's thinking (Chabot, 2003; Saban, 2020). While Simondon was influenced by Jung's elaborations on psychical individuation and expanded notion of libido (in contrast to Freud), his project ventured much further into multiple co-affective modalities of individuation through which new kinds of sociality and collectivity could be imagined (Chabot, 2003; Scott, 2014). He thought of the natural, the psychical, collective, and processes as involved in *any* and *all* constructions of individuation (Simondon, 1965). Thus, his theory of individuation was also a critique of the human sciences of his time, which, in privileging the subject, disavowed the problem of the individuation of the group.

While Simondon formulated two tiers of psychical individuation, for the purposes of this presentation I will focus only on the second tier, which he referred to as "transindividuality." This is the linchpin for the possibility of collective individuation (Scott, 2014, p. 76). The transindividual is the product of a new individuation which requires a more profound engagement with itself into its affective resources. This process allows the transindividual to be able to adopt a new attitude and openness with the *other as other*.

Crucially, for Simondon, *transindividuality of one allows for other individuals to communicate at the level of their pre-individual yet authentic Being*, thus making it possible for entry into new collective individuations. From this basis we may better understand Simondon's claim that the phenomenon of collective individuation is the *true psychosocial* from which the *trans-individual* arises (Simondon, 1992).

Stiegler uses Simondon's conception of *transindividuation* as a point of departure for his vision of an alternative way of life in our present era of catastrophe. Its basis requires a return to *self-reflection as a collective practice*. Simondon's conceptualization of multiple, distinct and ontogenetically generated individuation processes allowed Stiegler to extend and amplify the uncritically held destructive effects of technological individuation on the other individuating systems.

Stiegler is concerned with what Simondon calls *thinking's disindividuation*, which is a moving away from the conditions of individuation, especially our ability to think critically into the feeling of the world's wound. This wound presents itself through the viscerality of our singular wounds. In order to invigorate thinking that can make a difference Stiegler claims we must hold on to our own minds first and, secondly, to think with others beyond the ideological frames of yesteryear, the major premises of which do not apply to our present era.

According to Stiegler, Simondon *can think* the dynamics of a relation of the "*I*" to the "*we*," but he fails to consider "the *they*" in relation to "*I*" and "*we*." Simondon, he claims, cannot fully think into the human experience of "disindividuation" at individual or collective levels, the "leveling down of all possibilities of being" in relation to advancing technology that is manipulated by the invisible hand of hyper-globalized neoliberal agendas today (Stiegler, 2019, p. 29). Recall Stiegler's observation that Heidegger *can* think the regress to collective disindividuation ("the they") but his philosophical imagination cannot grasp the possibility of a "genuinely fruitful collective individuation process" (a "we") other than the dissolution of the "I" into a "we" equated by the "*Volk*" – the tragic effects of nationalism (Ross, 2018, p. 7). Ultimately, Stiegler is concerned with conceptualizing how we may carry the weight of our existence as an inner polemic that defines our ontological struggle as it applies to whole systems. That is, our *becoming as a society* is an enactment of both "enowning" to individuate (caring) *and* disindividuate (carelessness). In this way he revises both Simondon's and Heidegger's distinct contributions to a larger vision of saving the world and ourselves from our disindividuating tendencies.

The wound of the world, according to Stiegler and echoing Heidegger, is received through the senses (affect) and evokes a kind of demand or calling to do what is necessary (Stiegler, 2018, p. 399). Put another way, thinking into the question of the Anthropocene is akin to encountering the Lacanian real (not a connection I am aware Stiegler made) through its contingent, traumatic effects whose very definition lies in its utter resistance to symbolization and is therefore unintelligible, incomprehensible and unspeakable. Such a traumatic engagement with the real opens up spaces for the ethics of singularity by paradoxically driving the subject's relation to others arousing a call to care (Brooks, 2016).

Stiegler further elaborates what he means by the mechanism through which we may save ourselves via the transindividual construction of many social systems. In this way, a catastrophic event becomes the meeting place between the individual and society where trans-subjective possibility may arise. In this sense *the trans-subjective is the link between the psyche-social and political possibility.* If one accepts the call from the wound of a dying world and the incumbent crisis of civility, eventually, society can be constituted through the *transindividual* construction of many social systems of care into a new epoch.

Stiegler does not stop here. His project is to think into the possibility of a new epoch that on the global level liberates the individual from its misery into the ability to relate to the world with others ("we") through a renewed sensible aesthetic. Such an epoch is not where he situates us now. We have since drifted past the tipping point where Anthropocenic denial advances us toward our own extinction. Stiegler places us in the precarious gap between the hyperindustrical Anthropocenic era and what he hopefully calls the *Neg-anthropocene* (2018). Such an aesthetic, he argues, is crucial so that individuation in all of its forms may occur through all dimensions of intentional experience (Stiegler, 2019, pp. 227–228). Stiegler calls on each of us to turn toward the singular wound of our existence, to think into it with others towards new subversive expressions so that, as he poignantly writes,

> the emergence of new forms of thinking is translated into religious, spiritual, artistic, scientific, and political movements, manners and styles, new institutions and new social organizations, changes in education, in law, in forms of power, and, of course, changes in the very foundation of knowledge – whether this is conceptual knowledge or work-knowledge or life-knowledge.
>
> (2019, p. 14)

I am most moved by Stiegler's optimism for the healing potential of collective life, which does not separate thought from the reals of contemporary existence and, secondly, envisions how each of us within our spheres of influence may contribute to changing the "very foundation of knowledge."

While the bones of trans-individuation are found in Simondon's and Stiegler's philosophical treatises, they do not thematize how these processes show up in clinical practice or group dynamics. Nor should they. Both have rigorously philosophized a notion of trans-individuation, breaking the trail for any of us to amend for our own purposes. Lacan does not go far enough conceptualizing the trans-subjective moment in collective life even though much of his narrative foreshadows later political theorizing by Žižek (2008), Hook (2018), McGowan (2016), and Badiou (2003) to name a few. Jung envisions the problem, but his ontology lacks a persuasive psyche/social perspective grounded in the public sphere of the real world. Kristeva is reluctant to extend her exquisite rearticulation of sublimation outside of a traditional clinical realm.

I first became aware of what I am now calling the trans-subjective dimension of group life when I was a young therapist co-leading group experiences with individuals who were living with AIDS in the terrifying early years of that pandemic long before there were any societal supports in place. Eventually an egalitarian community of care emerged manifesting in a clinic called Project Quest in 1989, which still exists today in Portland, Oregon. My process of conducting an auto-ethnographic study unearthed a visceral memory of AIDS and the transforming moments our community came together in powerful agentic surges, provoking new waves of mourning and indebtedness.

Jung gave us insight into the powerful collective forces that shape us and erupt psychically in the individual and the collective. Our task is to apply what is relevant in Jung's vision of the collective unconscious to the concrete collectivities and critical time in which we live.

Notes

1 Stiegler is my silent interlocuter throughout this book as it was through his reworking of Heidegger's analytic of care in relation to the urgency of the Anthropocene that I awakened to it (Stiegler, 1998, 2013, 2019). I attempt throughout this chapter to veer away from the many neologisms Stiegler creates to deepen his arguments for the sake of a beginning reader that may sadly dilute the richness of his text. See Daniel Ross's article "Care and Carelessness in the Anthropocene Introduction to 'Reading of Stiegler and Heidegger'" from a talk he gave at the University of Canterbury, Christchurch, 11 May 2018. Ross is a not only a translator (from the French) of Stiegler's works, but also interprets/summarizes key aspects of Stiegler's thought.
2 We might note an echo of Heidegger's notion of care in Jung's quotation referred to above if Jung had not so ardently rejected Heidegger's thought. A big difference is that Jung is making an impassioned remark while Heidegger is building a philosophical edifice premised on factical life experience (See Brooks, 2011).
3 Traditional psychoanalysis is blind to the effects of catastrophic trauma that demand historical context beyond Oedipal and infant configurations. What was central for Jung was the teleological trajectory of the self's individuation while Freud's aim was the teleological transformation of the pleasure principal by the ego (Brooks, 2016, Wallwork, 1991 p. 122).

References

Badiou, A. (2003). *Saint Paul and the foundation of universalism*. Trans. R. Brassier, Stanford, California: Stanford University Press.
Bair, D. (2003). *Jung: A biography*. New York: Little, Brown.
Brooks, R. M. (2011). Un-thought out metaphysics in analytical psychology: A critique of Jung's epistemological basis for psychic reality. *Journal of Analytical Psychology*. 56, 492–513.
Brooks, R. M. (2013). "The ethical dimensions of life and analytic work through a Levinasian lens." *International Journal of Jungian Studies*. 5, 188–199.
Brooks, R. M. (2016). The intergenerational transmission of the catastrophic effects of *Real*-world history expressed through the analytic subject. R. Naso, & J. Mills (Eds.), pp. 137–176, *Ethics of evil psychoanalytic investigations*. London: Karnac.
Butler, J. (2006). *Gender trouble: Feminism and the subversion of identity*. New York: Routledge.
Chabot, P. (2003). *The philosophy of Simondon between technology and individuation*. New York: Bloomsbury Academic.
Christakis, N. A. (2019). *Blueprint the evolutionary origins of a good society*. New York: Little, Brown Spark.
Giegerich, W. (2004). The end of meaning and the birth of man. *Journal of Jungian Theory and Practice*. 6(1), (pp. 1–66).
Goodwyn, E. (2012). *The neurobiology of the Gods*. New York: Routledge.

Gullatz, S. (2010). Constructing the collective unconscious. *The Journal of Analytical Psychology*. 55, 691–714.

Heidegger, M. (1999). *Contributions to philosophy*. Bloomington: Indiana Press.

Heidegger, M. (2001/1927). *Being and time*. New York: Harper One.

Heidegger, M. (2010). *The phenomenology of religious life*. Trans. M. Fritch & J. A. Gosetti Ferencei, Bloomington: Indiana University Press.

Hinton, L. (2011). *Unus Mundus* – transcendent truth or comforting fiction – Overwhelm and the search for meaning in a fragmented world. *Journal of Analytical Psychology*. 56, 3. 375–380.

Hook, D. (2018). *Six moments in Lacan*. London and New York: Routledge.

Jung, C. G. (1927/1970). Women in Europe. *CW*, 10.

Jung, C. G. (1935/1989). The Tavistock Lectures on the theory and practice of analytical psychology. *CW*, 18.

Kristeva, J. (1987). *Black Sun depression and melancholia*. Trans. Leon S. Roudiez, New York: Columbia University Press.

Kristeva, J. (1995). *New Maladies of the Soul*. Trans. Ross Mitchell Guberman, New York: Columbia University Press.

Lacan, J. (2006). *Écrits: The first completed edition in English* Translated with notes by Bruce Fink, in collaboration with H. Fink and R. Grigg, New York and London: W.W. Norton.

Lu, K. (2013). "Can individual psychology explain social phenomena? An appraisal of the Theory of cultural complexes." *Psychoanalysis, Culture & Society*. 18(4), 386–404.

Lu, K. (2020). Racial hybridity Jungian and post Jungian perspectives. *International Journal of Jungian Studies*. 12, 11–40.

McGowan, T. (2016). *Capitalism and desire*. New York: Columbia University Press.

Mills, J. (2018). The essence of archetypes. *International Journal of Jungian Studies*. 10(3), 199–220.

Plomin, R. (2018). *Blueprint: DNA makes us who we are*. UK: Penguin Random House UK.

Ross, D. (2018). *Care and carelessness in the anthropocene introduction to a reading of Stiegler and Heidegger*. University of Canterbury, Christchurch.

Saban, M. (2020). Simondon and Jung: Re-thinking individuation, In *Holism possibilities and problems*. C. McMillian, R. Main & D. Henderson (Eds.), 91–97, London and New York: Routledge Taylor & Francis Group.

Scott, D. (2014). *Gilbert Simondon's Psychic and collective individuation a critical introduction and guide*. Edinburgh: Edinburgh University Press.

Simondon, G. (Jan/Feb 2015, 1965). Culture and technics, *Radical Philosophy*. Found 10/19/19 http://www.radicalphilosophy.com/article/culture-and-technics-1965

Simondon, G (1992). The genesis of the individual, in *Incorporations*. by Jonathan Crary and Sanford Kwinter (Eds.). New York, NY: Zone.

Stiegler, B. (1998). *Technics and time, I: The fault of Epimetheus*, Stanford, CA: Stanford University Press.

Stiegler, B. (2013). *What makes life worth living: On pharmacology*. Cambridge: Polity.

Stiegler, B. (2017). What is called caring? Beyond the anthropocene. *Techné: Research in Philosophy and Technology*. 21(2–3), 386–404.

Stiegler, B. (2018). *The neganthropocene*. Trans. Daniel Ross, London, UK: Open Humanities Press.

Stiegler, B. (2019). *The age of disruption technology and madness in computational capitalism*. Trans. by Daniel Ross, Medford, MA: Polity Press.

Wallwork, E. (1991). *Psychoanalysis and ethics*. New Haven: Yale University Press.

Webster, J. (2018). *Conversion disorder: Listening to the body in psychoanalysis*. New York: Columbia University Press.

Žižek, S. (2008). *The sublime object of ideology*. London and New York: Verso.

Introduction to "Hillman's Ambivalence: An Inhuman Twist of Human Science"

Michael P. Sipiora outlines a genuine synthesis between Hillman's archetypal psychology and Dilthey's original conceptualization of the human sciences. He starts by addressing Hillman's polemic against any form of science in psychology, but then develops his project for archetypal psychology—personifying, pathologizing, psychologizing, and dehumanizing—using Dilthey's original terms: lived experience, expression, and understanding. In doing so, Sipiora is also offering Dilthey's terms—and hence human science psychology—psychological resonance through Hillman's archetypal project. Dilthey's appeal to lived experience (*Erlebnis*) refers to the depth of experience described by Hillman as soul; expression (*Ausdruck*) refers not to something primarily personal but to anything that marks the inner life of the human world. It follows, then, that understanding (*verstehen*) reaches beyond the personal into the cultural and imaginal background in which personal experience and expression are contained. Sipiora's chapter breathes new life into Dilthey's original project while also rooting Hillman's archetypal psychology in the origins of psychology as a human science.

Chapter 7

Hillman's Ambivalence*
An Inhuman Twist of Human Science

Michael P. Sipiora

Introduction

Over many years of teaching James Hillman's work in graduate programs in human science psychology, I have been mindful of his ambivalence regarding the idea of psychology as a human science. In *Re-Visioning Psychology*, he dismisses "human science" as an "monstrous joint title" (Hillman, 1975, p. 172) and refuses to subjugate archetypal psychology to either human or natural models of science. Elsewhere he refers to the human sciences, the "scholarly, investigative disciplines (*Geisteswissenshaften*)," with praise because they deal "with the depths of human nature" (Hillman, 2007 vol 6.1, p. 107). Provoked by this ambivalence, I consider Hillman's objections and then suggest a human science conception of archetypal psychology. The inherent tension in that conception leads to a twisting of human science's understanding of life-experience (*Erlebnis*).

Human Science and Psychology

Following Wilhelm Dilthey, the human sciences (*Geisteswissenshaften*) are to be distinguished from the natural sciences (*Naturwissenshaften*). The latter endeavors to explain (*erklärüng*) facts by way of experimental demonstration of quantifiable causes—a powerful and appropriate approach to the natural world including, to an extent, human beings. While recognizing the validity of natural science on its own terms, the human sciences argue that distinctive features of human beings elude causal explanation but nonetheless can be understood qualitatively in a scientific manner. While the natural sciences' literal explanations of facts enable control, human science interpretative understandings of meanings engage conversation. Alternative to the natural science project of "control of the surrounding world," Hans-Georg Gadamer (2001) argues that the

* Material included in this essay has drawn on my previous publication: (2023) *Psychological Citizenship and Democracy: The Political Relevance of James Hillman's Archetypal Psychology.* Spring Publications, Inc.

DOI: 10.4324/9781032694603-10

humanities and social sciences (*Geisteswissenshaften* ... bring something different into our lives through their form of participation in what has been handed down to us, something that is not knowledge for the sake of control (*Herrschaftswissen*), yet is no less important. We customarily call it "culture".

(p. 41)

He elaborates:

We participate in the essential expressions of human experience that have been developed in our artistic, religious, and historical tradition—and not only ours but in all cultures, this possible participation is the true criterion for the wealth or poverty of what we produce in our humanities and social sciences.

(2001, pp. 40–41)

Human Science psychology seeks to understand (*verstehen*) meanings by way of qualitative methods of description and interpretation of life experience. Research in such psychology embraces an array of empirical and theoretical approaches that share a qualitative orientation and concern for meaning. Meaning refers to how things matter, their significance and import which is neither solely private nor merely subjective. The meanings that inform our individual experience, while uniquely "ours," are in the first place public and shared, appearing within the context of our culture and history. It is such concrete meanings that we individually make sense of as we fashion the psychological reality of our lives. Human Science psychologies generate qualitative descriptions leading to the recognition of structures or configurations of meaning that inform human experience, the articulation of which provides insight into individual behaviors and cognitions.

Archetypal Psychology Is Not a (Natural) Science

Aligned with the impetus in Jung's later work to "solve psychological problems at a step beyond scientific models" (Hillman, 1970, p. 216), Hillman registers his resistance to a scientific approach from the very beginning of archetypal psychology. In *Re-Visioning Psychology*, he argues that the "science fantasy of psychology" arises from the historical tension between "secular" and "religious" orientations (Hillman, 1975, p. 169) that arose as monotheistic theology "tried to prevent science from turning to nature" (Hillman, 1975, p. 172). (By the same token, theology censored "the humanities from turning to the polytheistic past" [Hillman, 1975, p. 172] which, as will be discussed below, is the very heritage Hillman claims for archetypal psychology.) Attempting to break free of religious or other speculative ideologies and place itself on an empirical footing, psychology turned to the "objectivity, technology, verification, measurement, and progress" (Hillman, 1975, p. 169) offered by science. Religious and moral beliefs about human nature were surpassed by secular explanations as scientific psychology gained prominence in the late nineteenth century.

The criteria that Hillman (1975) identifies with science, the ones that "make it impossible for a psychology based on psyche to imagine itself as a science" (p. 169), are specific to a natural science model: quantitative analysis, experimentation, and causal explanation. He most objects to the reductionism and literality of the natural sciences that leads to disallowing validity to other perspectives. In a blunt evaluation of the adoption this model, Hillman (1975) laments that

> Psychology has been so trapped in the literalizations of subtlety that it now looks to stupidity as a way out. For it had hitherto mixed precision with measurement, discernment with segmentation, sophistication with technology, and differentiation with compartmentalization.
>
> (pp. 221–222)

Neglect of the soul follows natural scientific psychology's empirical equation of whatever exists with its subjugation to measurable quantities, "thereby eliminating the traditional idea of psyche altogether" (Hillman, 2021, p. 146).

Imagining Archetypal Psychology as a Human Science

Psychology, for Hillman, is first and foremost about the psyche or soul, terms he uses interchangeably, and he relentlessly critiques the discipline of psychology for its all but nominal attention to its very subject. "The human being," Hillman (2013) writes, "is set within the field of soul. Soul is the metaphor that includes the human" (p. 26). In *Suicide and the Soul*, he notes: "Experience and suffering are terms long associated with the soul" (Hillman 1964 p. 44). They point to the "inside meaning" (Hillman, 1964, p. 44) of psychological understanding and the experiential reality that cannot be empirically quantified or operationally defined. This "sense of 'in-ness' … is not a spatial idea, but an imaginal metaphor for the soul's nonvisible and nonliteral inherence, the imaginal psychic quality within all events" (Hillman, 1975, p. 173). Soul is that "unknown" (Hillman, 1975, p. x) dimension of worldly existence, a reflective perspective rather than a substance, which is the condition of possibility for the deepening of events into experiences, that is, for things to matter in the distinctive ways that give them value beyond their mere occurrence. Meaning, as the emergence of significance covered over in ordinary functioning, is the dimension of extraordinary relatedness that arises metaphorically out of this deepening. In this dimension are the matters of ultimate concern—questions of love and death, beauty and justice, religious and moral questions that are inaccessible to the instrumental calculations of the natural sciences but very much the subject of human science investigation which differentiates the qualities of lived experience instead of reducing events to measurable quantities.

Hillman (2013) positions archetypal psychology as "deliberately affiliated with the arts, culture, and the history of ideas ... rather than with medical and empirical psychologies which tend to confine psychology to the positivistic manifestations of the nineteenth-century" (p. 13), that is, the natural scientific paradigm. Following Plato in the belief that ideas are the eyes of the soul, archetypal psychology's interest is in the ideas that

> arise from the soul's relationship to death, the world, and other souls; with its body, gender and generation; with virtue and with sin, with love beauty, and knowledge; with Gods, with sickness, with creation and destruction, with power, with time, with time, history, and future: with family, ancestors, and the dead.
>
> (Hillman, 1975, pp. 117–118)

Again, these are themes of human science inquiry. The arts, humanities, and social sciences (*Geisteswissenshaften*), whose purview is culture, are the disciplines attentive to the moral, erotic, intellectual, and aesthetic dimensions of existence. For archetypal psychology, the psychological and the cultural are inextricable. As Hillman (2013) avers, "To study human nature at its most basic level, one must turn to culture" because that is where the psychological is "portrayed" (p. 14).

In *Re-Visioning Psychology*, Hillman (1975) propounds four "basic psychological ideas" (p. ix)—personifying, pathologizing, psychologizing, and dehumanizing—in service to bringing soul back into psychology. In accordance with his alliance of psychology with culture, he specifies the "traditional area" (p. xv)—mythology, psychiatry, philosophy, and the humanities—from which each is derived. These ideas are both articulations of the psychological character of experience and methods, avenues of investigation for "grasping and ordering that experience" (Hillman, 1975, pp. 37–38). Refusing the natural scientific conflation of the concrete with the literal, Hillman notes the polyvalence of our concrete experience that exceeds the singularity of literal interpretation. Psychologizing or deliteralizing, the method of seeing through the literal presentation that Hillman (1975) identifies as "the primary work of my field" (p. 127), discloses that qualitative, metaphorical multiplicity. It is "how events become experiences" (Hillman, 1975, p. 122), the process of deepening that makes soul.

Archetypal psychology's affinity with "the arts, culture, and the history of ideas," its concern with the "inside" meaning of experience, its methods of inquiry, and its pursuit of qualitative understanding recommend it as a human science. Dilthey, writes Hillman (1975), rightly saw the expanding purview of empirical scientific objectivity and thus the imperative "to refound psychology on the basis of understanding" in recognition of "the fundamental place of subjectivity in all human thought" (p. 15). He proceeds to credit Dilthey's "research into the Greeks, the Renaissance, and Giambattista Vico," the explicit lineage of archetypal psychology. In line with that heritage, "Humanistic education as conceived in Florence," Hillman (2006) asserts, "becomes a necessity again: differentiated language, the fine arts, handiworks, biography, criticism, history, cultural anthropology, manners, customs, life among the things of the world" (p. 40).

The Twist

So far, so good and relatively straightforward. Archetypal psychology is undoubtably not a natural science and stands diametrically opposed to its reductionism and literalism (but not to the natural sciences themselves, as Hillman always contended when they are also taken within a psychological context). Archetypal psychology can be imagined as a human science sharing, among other aspects, a concern for culture that disdains the project of control and eschews certainty while alternatively embracing diverse forms of knowing leading to pluralistic truths. But here's the twist: the humanism of Renaissance Florence was fundamentally different from its subsequent versions. Hillman sharply contrasts both the Humanism of the Enlightenment and its heirs in existentialism and humanistic psychology with that of the ancient Greeks as well as that of the Renaissance with which he allies "dehumanizing"—last and most profound of the four "basic psychological ideas" in *Re-Visioning*. The "inhuman" humanism of the latter understands the realities of human experience to be dependent on other than human powers and forces figured in the pagan gods. For these views, "The human was unthinkable without its inhuman background" (Hillman, 1975, p. 193). The Renaissance's "efflorescence in art, literature, music, politics, science, discovery" (Hillman, 1975, p. 193) was animated by an encounter with "the mythical persons and ideas from a pre-Christian polytheistic world" (Hillman, 1975, p. 194). Hillman (1970) inaugurated archetypal psychology in the realization that: "[t]he problems of the psyche were never solved in classical times nor by archaic peoples through personal relationships and 'humanizing' them; but through the reverse: connecting them to impersonal determinants" (1970, p. 218). The project of archetypal psychology was conceived as a restoration of these connections.

While the issue of science in Hillman's objection to the "monstrous joint title" is, for the most part, resolvable by clarifying its human science conceptualization, it is the depiction of the human operative in science that underlies Hillman's deepest concerns. Monstrousness is best referenced not to science, but to the image of the human when either science is conflated with a notion of the real as quantifiable or yet again, when it is conceived on basis of the merely human. How then to conceive of the subject matter of the human sciences? Hillman endeavored to re-humanize psychology à la ancient Greek and Renaissance humanism leading to a quite different conception of the human: our humanity rests on the claim of the inhuman. The bottom line in a dehumanized humanism is that who we understand ourselves to be and the dramas that unfolds in our individual lives have "depths that are alien, inhuman, and impersonal" (Hillman, 1975, p. 51). Instead of looking for one's true voice found deep inside one's subjectivity, Hillman (1995) contends that "the human being in these other [than modern Western] cultures reflects contested voices and is imagined always in a nexus of relation" inclusive of those with impersonal personages (p. 194). The twist: "the soul," the subject of archetypal psychology, "has inhuman reaches" (Hillman, 1975, p. 173) that condition our lived experience.

Lived experience, *Erlebnis*, is one of the three fundamental elements in Dilthey's conception of the human sciences.

> The combination of lived experience, expression, and understanding [*Erleben, Ausdruck*, and *Verstehen*] is the specific process whereby mankind exists for us as an object of the human sciences. Hence the human sciences are grounded in this connection of life, expression, and understanding.
>
> (Dilthey, 1927, as cited in Betanzos, 1988, p. 24)

Erlebnis refers to the configurations of meaning experienced in our engagement with life, as Richard Palmer (1969) notes, "a unit held together by a common meaning" (p. 107). The prethematic grasp of meaning implicit in *Erlebnis*, the subjectivity investigated by the human sciences, precedes the rift initiated by conscious reflection separating subject from object. "Experience is, in fact, not distinguished from perceiving or apprehending (*innerwerden*) itself. *Erlebnis* that direct contact with life which we may call 'immediate life experience'" (Palmer, 1969, p. 108). In Dilthey's formulation: "the reality that is lived experience is present to me in the fact that I am inwardly aware (*innerwerden*) of it, that I immediately possess it as something belonging to me in in some sense" (Dilthey, 1924, quoted in Betanzos, 1988 p. 23).

For Hillman (1975), this inside meaning of experience refers to "neither literal ownership nor to physical containment"; instead, as noted above, it manifests "the imaginal psychic quality within all events" (p. 173). The sense of "belonging to me" arises from how I belong to it. The imaginal quality, the inhuman reaches of the soul, "presents a claim—moral, erotic, intellectual, aesthetic—and demands a response" (Hillman, 2013, p. 23). The character of my experience is elicited by this inhuman reach of the soul, the depth dimension of *Erlebnis*. Our humanity, that which distinguishes us as humans and is the concern of the human sciences, arises in response to the claims of the soul. Thus, archetypal psychology's being permeated by religious thought, its attending to what obligates, binds us in the etymological sense of the Latin *religare*. However, unlike monotheistic religion, which takes its god literally, Hillman (2013) understands the inhumanity personified by gods in the metaphorical manner archetypal psychology shares with the humanities—that is, concretely but not literally—as "creating claims on each human life and giving personal acts more than personal significance" (p. 42).

"Expression" (*Ausdruck*), the second moment of the process studied by human science, concretizes the excess of personal significance inherent in lived experience thereby producing the whole of the realm of culture. As Palmer (1969) explains,

> An expression, for Dilthey, is not primarily an embodiment of one's personal feelings but rather an "expression of life"; an "expression" can refer to an idea, a law, a social norm, language—anything that reflects the imprint of the inner life on man.
>
> (p. 112)

Convergent with Dilthey is Hillman's already noted "turn to culture" as the dimension in which the psychological is "portrayed" but with a twist: the imperative to see through culture to appreciate the soul's inhuman exactments in these expressions of lived experience. Psychologizing, deliteralizing as Hillman defines it in *Re-Visioning*, is a method for understanding this deeper significance.

Dilthey's specific notion of "understanding," *Verstehen*, refers to a grasping of the significance expressed in the phenomena of culture. "We explain by means of purely intellectual processes, but we understand by means of the combined activities of all the mental activities in apprehending" (Dilthey, 1924, as cited in Palmer, 1969, p. 115). Having initially conceived of this apprehension in terms of individual psychology, Dilthey comes to recognize that understanding expressions is an interpretative, that is, hermeneutical engagement. Understanding is the interpretation of the expressions of lived experience beyond their merely personal significance. For Dilthey, expression is "not of a person at all, as in psychologizing, but of a socio-historical reality disclosed in experience, the socio-historical reality of experience itself" (Palmer, 1969, p. 114).

Hillman firmly distinguishes his idea of psychologizing from psychologism—which better describes what Dilthey references—in that the latter literally reduces all meaning to that comprehended by scientific psychology. Psychologizing, in sharp contrast, acknowledges the plurality of meanings in the diverse interpretations of the human. Hillman concurrently contends that such truths are not of themselves exhaustive and that implications for the soul abide within them. To see such implications requires seeing through the socio-historical to the deeper dimensions that link its truths to the reality of the soul. "History," contends Hillman (2014), "is not the determining factor; psyche is" (p. 313). The movements of the psyche are "an archetypal movement that is not the result of historical conditions, as much as the condition of historical results" (Hillman, 2014, p. 313). While the intrinsically historical situated significance of our prethematic lived experience provides its wider context, the soul's inhuman dimension is the deeper context of *Erlebnis*. Hillman (1975) associates this dimension with "the imaginative possibility in our natures" (p. x), the apex of "the combined activities of all the mental activities" that Dilthey identifies as understanding. "In order to be more objective" Hillman (2021) would have a human science psychology "be more subjective in examining the structures of our imagination" (p. 386), the structures that animate lived experience. Psychologizing is the imaginative interpretation of the extraordinary meaning which arises in the deepening of events into experiences. "The act of seeing through events connects them to the soul and creates experiences" (Hillman, 1975, p. 122). Just as Dilthey recognized that we know ourselves indirectly, Hillman (1975) asserts that *"Psychologizing goes on whenever reflection takes place in terms other than those presented"* (pp. 134–135). For Dilthey, we come to know ourselves through our interpretive understandings of the cultural expressions of lived experience. Hillman's psychologizing is the twist on human science interpretation that sees through the artifacts of cultural to their inhuman depths.

"Spirit understands only what it has created," asserts Dilthey. *"Everything in which spirit has objectified itself* falls within the *human sciences"* (Dilthey, 1927, as cited in Betanzos, 1988, p. 24). The human spirit responds to the soul's inhuman obligations; its creations are conditional on alien, impersonal exhortations. This twisting of Dilthey's *Erlebnis* reconciles Hillman's ambivalence toward psychology as a human science without reducing its inherent tension. "There will always be," he recognizes,

> unease when one deals—as do the scholarly, investigative disciplines (*Geisteswissenshaften*)—with the depths of human nature, because these depths remain open questions. ... these fields display the human spirit, they remain enigmatic in principle and their riddles give rise to philosophical wonder—and psychological anxiety.
>
> (Hillman, 2007, p. 107)[1]

An archetypal human science, psychology probes this "unease" without succumbing to the natural sciences' obsession with objective certainty. Instead, it cultivates the anxious wonder appropriate to our responses to the enigmatic, more-than-personal dimension expressed within the purview of Dilthey's human sciences. The encounter with the depths of life experience is invariably soul-making. It provides a perspective from which to differentiate and evaluate the meaningful character of the phenomena studied by discerning the inhuman aspect of how things matter, their significance over time, their relation to other phenomena, and their individual and communal value.

Recall Gadamer's depiction of the knowledge sought in the human sciences as a participation in an ongoing conversation for the sake of culture. "Culture" notes Hillman (2006),

> evokes an intelligentsia or initiates—and these may be everybody in a society, not only an elite priesthood of "the cultured"—who appreciate, maybe even live in terms of the occulted (like ideas, qualities, soul, virtues, forms). That is *invisible values and the value of invisibles*. The occulted is not simply given. It refers to anything artifacted.
>
> (p. 137)

The depth psychological twist of lived experience unfolds in an inhuman human science's understanding of those occulted cultural expressions, the artifacts of the human spirit that are excluded in a natural scientific, humanistic milieu. Participation in the perennial human response to the invisible inhuman dimension that lays claim to our lived experience is the "true criterion for the wealth or poverty of what we produce in our humanities and social sciences [*Geisteswissenshaften*]" (Gadamer, 2001, pp. 40–41).

Note

1 For an existential- phenomenological approach to this theme of wonder and anxiety, see my (2000) Psychology in the neighborhood of thought and poetry: The uncanny logos of the psyche. *Janus Head: Journal of Interdisciplinary Studies in Literature, Continental Philosophy, Phenomenological Psychology and the Arts*, 3(1), pp. 40–61.

References

Betanzos, R. (1988). Introductory essay. In W. Dilthey, *Introduction to the human sciences: An attempt to lay a foundation for the study of society and history* (R. Betanzos, Trans.). Wayne State University Press.

Gadamer, H. (2001). *Gadamer in conversation: Reflections and commentary* (R. Palmer, Ed. and Trans.). Yale University Press.

Hillman, J. (1970). Editorial postscript: Why archetypal psychology? *Spring: An annual of archetypal psychology and Jungian thought* (pp. 212–219).

Hillman, J. (1975). *Re-visioning psychology*. Harper and Row.

Hillman, J. (1964). *Suicide and the soul*. Spring Publications, Inc.

Hillman, J. (1995). *Kinds* of *power: A guide to its intelligent uses*. Currency Doubleday.

Hillman, J. (2006). *City & soul, Uniform edition of the writings of James Hillman*, vol. 2. Spring Publications, Inc.

Hillman, J. (2007). *Mythical figures, Uniform edition of the writings of James Hillman*, vol. 6. Spring Publications, Inc.

Hillman, J. (2013). *Archetypal psychology, Uniform edition of the writings of James Hillman*, vol. 1. Spring Publications, Inc.

Hillman, J. (2014). *Alchemical psychology, Uniform edition of the writings of James Hillman*, Vol. 5. Spring Publications, Inc.

Hillman, J. (2021). *Philosophical intimations, Uniform edition of the writings of James Hillman*, vol. 8. Spring Publications Inc.

Palmer, R. (1969). *Hermeneutics: Interpretation theory in Schleiermacher, Dilthey, Heidegger and Gadamer*. Northwestern University Press.

Introduction to "Geography of Creative Thought: Walking with Freud and Nietzsche"

If the notion of our being-in-the-world is to be taken seriously, it means our theorizing in psychology is never the result of pure abstraction, or purely logical thought based on evidence that is set out in front of us for all to see. In other words, in the human sciences there is no simplistic "correspondence theory of truth." On the contrary, even our most rigorous thinking is dependent on our being bodily situated in a specific time and place, socially recognized, and named. Huskinson's chapter illustrates the truth of this ontological and epistemological claim by tracing the daily walks and thinking of Freud and Nietzsche. What is a delightful read, as we walk with them, is also a beautiful illustration of Jung's claim that we are always in the psyche and that we can never escape the "personal equation," which is we ourselves. Readers might also notice how Huskinson's chapter is in line with the Dutch phenomenological tradition, describing our psychological lives as mirrored in the material reality of architecture and the times.

Chapter 8

Geography of Creative Thought

Walking with Freud and Nietzsche

Lucy Huskinson

Introduction: Relationships between Geography and Philosophy

It is commonly said that our best ideas come to us when we are not trying to think about them, when we occupy ourselves with other activities and when we change our location. Archimedes' legendary "eureka moment," when he was relaxing in the bath, is a case in point. Although a fundamental connection between place and creative thinking is regularly reported, serious investigation into this connection and the cognitive opportunities and benefits it could provide is relatively scant.

Investigations into the nature of creative thought tend to approach creative thinking as resulting from combinations of previously unconnected mental representations and the evidence they draw on is mostly anecdotal (Boden, 2004; Koestler, 1957; Stewart, 1792). This chapter explains how walking through places enhances creative thinking by encouraging the interplay of mental representations, and it employs anecdotal evidence from two iconic thinkers who were also prolific walkers: Friedrich Nietzsche (1844–1900) and Sigmund Freud (1856–1939).

While creative thought is the fundamental currency of Philosophy and arguably also depth psychologies, the interpretation of physical environments and place is often reserved for Geography. The absence of serious study into the relationship between walking through physical places and creative thinking thereby suggests a disconnect between academic approaches of Philosophy and Geography with their tendencies to prioritise either creative thought or the physical/human environment to the detriment of the other. But to treat place and thought separately leads to artificial conclusions about human experience.[1]

While Geography has relied extensively on philosophical ideas in the development of its discipline, the use of Geography by philosophers is less obvious and trickier to pin down. Philosophy has provided the foundation for core arguments and ideas in Geography since antiquity, with investigations by the pre-Socratics into the nature of the world, and analyses of place in Plato's *Timaeus* and Aristotle's *Physics*.[2] Throughout the Medieval era, Arab philosophers such

DOI: 10.4324/9781032694603-11

as Al-Bakri (c.10-40-1094) and Muhammad al-Idrisi (1100–1165) strongly influenced the study of cartography. And early modern philosophy saw debates emerge between rationalists and empiricists on the value of the phenomenal world, drawing together key ideas from René Descartes (1596–1650), Baruch Spinoza (1632–1677), and Gottfried Leibniz (1646–1716) on the one hand, and John Locke (1632–1704), George Berkeley (1685–1753), and David Hume (1711–1776) on the other. Immanuel Kant (1724–1804) sought to reconcile the two positions of experience and reason, leading to his understanding of Geography as a counterpart to History as a means of organising knowledge and perceptions of space alongside time. In the modern era, philosophical arguments have contributed broadly and deeply across a spectrum of approaches and themes in Geography, from positivist theories to humanistic concerns and ethical issues.

A veritable "philosophical geography" can be readily conceived. But what of examining Philosophy from the position of Geography? Philosophers tend to associate specific epistemological approaches to geographical regions. They refer for instance to "continental philosophy," "Western philosophy," "German idealism," the "European Enlightenment," "Scottish Enlightenment," "American pragmatism," "French existentialism," and so on. But these ideas are not confined by the boundaries of these places—to assume they are is to encourage artificial bonds between creative thought and place. As Elden writes, a "geography of philosophy" could lead us into a dangerous "geographical determinism" (2009, p. 149). We must tread carefully if we are to locate kinds of thoughts within specific places. Elden rightly acknowledges that more productive studies in this area are achievable.

There are more helpful ways to postulate a "geography of philosophy." Notable attempts include the following. Gaston Bachelard's *Poetics of Space* (*La poétique de l'espace*), which calls us to conduct a "topoanalysis," which is to say, a "systematic psychological study of the sites of our intimate lives" (1957/1958, p. xxxvi). According to Bachelard, an analysis of place—irrespective of whether the place is real, remembered, dreamt, or imaginary—is inextricably linked to our sense of being and to the continuity of our everyday experiences. Later, in *What Is Philosophy?* (*Qu'est-ce que la philosophie?* (1991), Gilles Deleuze and Félix Guattari propose the term "geophilosophy" in their attempt to re-orientate philosophy away from unhelpful transcendental ideas and metaphysical posturing to engage instead with ideas of immanence, intuitions, and experimental thoughts that are grounded in lived experience. Their geophilosophy was influenced by the work of Nietzsche—with his simultaneous rejection of metaphysical constructs of thought (which were, he claimed, unhelpful inventions designed to make us feel more comfortable in an uncertain world) and his rousing call for us to "remain true to the earth" (Nietzsche, 1883–1885/1969, Prologue 3). And, also, Nietzsche's brief attempts to "determine the national characteristics of French, English, and German philosophy" (Deleuze & Guattari, 1991/1994, p. 102).

Neither Bachelard's topoanalysis nor the geophilosophy of Deleuze and Guattari developed into an established approach of "geographical philosophy" per se, but their ideas continue to inspire geographers and philosophers alike. For instance, topoanalysis was intended by Bachelard to uncover the places to which a person feels most attached, to expose, he says, their "topophilia": their relationship to a physical environment infused with personal and cultural history. The humanist geographer Yi-Fu Tuan continues this idea, notably in *Topophilia: A study of environmental perception, attitudes, and values* (1974). Further investigation into Deleuze and Guattari's term "geophilosophy" may shed light on its relationship to another, similar term—"geosophy"—coined decades earlier by American geographer John K. Wright. Wright popularised the term in the late 1940s to denote the variety of ideas, true and false, that people have in relation to places. Wright was concerned with the geographer's "aesthetic imagination" and its impact in determining the "distinctive or characteristic" aspects of a place, and the acquisition of geographical knowledge more generally (Wright, 1947). "Geosophy" was the name given to the processes by which geographical concepts are shaped by perception and imagination. According to Keighren, it is surprising that, although Wright's contributions to the academic and professional study of Geography have been "seminal," few geographers are aware of his work, and his concept of geosophy "remains obscure at best" (2005, p. 548).

More recently, geographers have variously sought to explain the significance of place in the creation and interpretation of knowledge. David N. Livingstone, for instance, argues that "scientific objectivity" within the "Geography of Science" is not a "view from nowhere," but "turns out to have always been a 'view from somewhere.'" The recognition that rationality is not disembodied but *situated*, he argues, has significant implications for understanding science and scientists (2003, p. 184). Charles W. J. Withers (2007) similarly argues that the philosophical period of Enlightenment or "age of reason" was not a uniform experience, but a collection of assorted epistemological activities and experiences dispersed across countries and cities. Key to understanding it, Withers argues, is the "travelling nature of knowledge" between places.

This chapter investigates the potentials of a "geography of philosophy" by exposing fundamental connections between creative thoughts and physical environments not only in the experiences of iconic thinkers who are known for their scientific discoveries or philosophical formulations, but in creative ideas of people on an everyday basis. It questions interrelationships between the physical features of the places we walk in and the ideas we subsequently have. It investigates the curious link between walking and wondering.

Walking Philosophy

Many philosophers have professed the need to walk to think and to think well. "Never trust a thought that occurs to you indoors," warns Nietzsche, for "all truly great thoughts are conceived by walking" (1889/1990, aphorism 34).

Søren Kierkegaard cedes that "I have walked myself into my best thoughts" on the streets of Copenhagen (1847/1978, p. 214). Immanuel Kant is famously alleged to have walked the same route in Kōnigsberg (now Kaliningrad) at the same time every day to order his ideas and tame his more compulsive thoughts (Caird, 1889/2000, pp. 63–64). Jean-Jacques Rousseau, who walked up to twenty miles a day on the outskirts of Paris, went as far as to claim, "My mind only works with my legs … When I stop walking, I cease to think" (1782/1953, p. 382). Freud and Jung appear to be aware of the cognitive merits of walking. The earliest therapy sessions given by Freud involved him taking his patients out for a walk—taking advantage, perhaps, of the merits of the *"walking cure"* as much as the "talking cure." "To go for a walk," Jung writes, "is both a search and a succession of changes" for a good walk incites transformation for the individual and groups alike (1944/1954/1968, para. 101). Although many thinkers have earnt their reputation as hardened walkers they rarely reflect on or philosophise about the walks themselves and do not question the relationship between the places they walk within and the ideas they have.

The caricature of the walking philosopher is traceable to ancient Greece, where legend speaks of toga-clad philosophers discussing higher truths along the colonnades of the polis. Aristotle's School was known as the "Peripatetic" School of Philosophy due to the alleged habit of its scholars who would walk while philosophising and lecturing. Despite the long-established connection between philosophising and walking, it is usually either from the personal letters or diaries of philosophers rather than their published works that we glean information about where they walked and their perceptions and feelings along the way, or from contemporaneous accounts of those who observed them at a distance.

Indeed, the works of scholarly thinkers who were renowned walkers tend to focus on their ideas and the places of their philosophising fade into the background as an irrelevance. Their ideas are subsequently presented as if conceived in a vacuum, within a mind isolated from its immediate environment and detached from its moving body.[3] The notion that ideas take place within a mind set apart from the external world is one often attributed to the legacy of Descartes' (1641/1996) ontological distinction between an interior place of subjective reflection and the physical world. This dualistic interpretation of human experience has shaped other disciplines, including early modern psychology and psychiatry, which inadvertently conflated its understanding of the "psyche" with the notion of a mind abstracted from its nonhuman environments (See Brooke, 2009). Harold Searles, a psychiatrist writing in the 1960s, claimed, for instance, that Sigmund Freud and his followers were too preoccupied with the intrapsychic workings of the mind and interpersonal human relations that they simply did not have the time to consider the impact of the nonhuman environment on a person's well-being (Searles, 1960, p. 25). To this day, mainstream psychotherapeutic thought falls short in its considerations of the physical and material environment and the extent to which the places we inhabit—such as cheap housing blocks, overly stylised urban parks, traffic jams, the glare of artificial lighting, and so on—may be contributing to our psychological problems (See Huskinson, 2019).

The philosopher Martin Heidegger is perhaps an exception.[4] In his later writings, Heidegger posited human "being" or *Dasein* as "being in the world." To be human, he argued, is to dwell, and through dwelling we find ourselves inextricably linked to our physical environments (1954/1975, p. 147). Human being is actualised, he says, in what he conceived as the "fourfold": the earth, sky, mortality and immortality or "gods." The landscapes and places we find ourselves in "preserve" and "gather" our being (Heidegger, 1954/1975, pp. 151, 158). In this scenario, the environment is integral to our self-reflection. Heidegger is concerned, however, with a metaphysical explanation of our being, and not with the relationship between specific environments and the thoughts or ideas they give rise to.[5]

I wish to bring our physical places back into our philosophical speculations and to foreground the places where prominent thinkers walked. In doing so, I am keen to begin to understand how places are more integral to the development of ideas than we perhaps realise, and I suggest that the legacies of philosophers and scholars are shaped by the landscapes they walked in. The remainder of this chapter will outline the relationship between walking and thinking and question whether one's "walking style" influences the kinds of ideas had when walking. I go on to examine the regular walks of Nietzsche and Freud to spotlight some of the prominent physical features they encountered along the way to suggest how these may have shaped the ideas they have become known for.

Walking and Thinking

Research across various disciplines has tried to understand the correlation between walking and thinking, and why walking, for instance, is conducive to problem solving and for disclosing ideas that we struggle to formulate while immobile, sat at a desk or in front of a computer screen.

For example, in the 1920s the social psychologist Graham Wallas concluded that walking encourages the incubation of ideas that a person had started to establish through more direct cognitive efforts. Walking, he says, acts as a catalyst to complete the idea, bringing it to conscious awareness (1926/2014). A clear illustration of this theory is described by the nineteenth-century mathematician Henri Poincaré in *The Foundations of Science* (1908/2012). There he explains the circumstances of his discovery of several mathematical formulas, and from these, his deduction of a method for problem solving and creative thinking. "Every day," he says, "I seated myself at my desk, stayed an hour or two, tried a great number of combinations and reached no results." That's when I decided to take leave of my studies and "forget my mathematical work," by "walking along the streets" or "on the bluff." When walking, "the solution to the difficulties which had stopped me, suddenly appeared to me, with a feeling of perfect certainty." He deduces from his experiences that rational deliberation alone is unproductive: but "when conscious deliberation has failed to achieve its desired results such efforts have not been as sterile as one thinks, for they have set going the unconscious machine" (1908/2012, pp. 387–9).

The cognitive sciences have explored relationships between walking and thinking more widely. The incubation period of Wallas' model, for instance, has been developed by the cognitive psychologist Guy Claxton, who concludes that intelligence and problem solving increase when we stop chasing after data and engage instead in "loafing" activities. Walking as a *loafing* activity may seem to remove us from our attempts to formulate theories or solve problems, but it grants "access to mental places which are otherwise inaccessible to earnest, purposeful cognition" (1997, pp. 14, 49). A series of experiments by researchers at Stanford University concluded that walking enhances creative thinking in adults by an average of 60 per cent (Oppezzo & Schwartz, 2014). Participants in these studies were asked to think of alternate uses for common objects and original analogies for complex ideas. The investigation found that the group who had walked while pondering possible solutions were able to provide several novel solutions, demonstrating a consistently higher capacity for divergent thinking compared to their counterparts, who undertook the task while seated and sedentary.

When it comes to explaining the mechanisms or processes that underpin the cognitive powers of walking for the incubation of ideas, there is no clear explanation or interdisciplinary consensus, but a complex variety of speculations which are customarily categorized according to their biological or psychological aspects. For instance, some conclude that walking enhances creativity due to the increased perceptual stimulation that occurs when moving through an environment; others focus on mood enhancement as key, suggesting walking increases positive mood states which in turn heighten creative thinking (Rethorst et al., 2009; Akinola & Mendes, 2008). Others pinpoint biological mediators, such as changes to chemical composition in the body, to blood pressure (Hartig et al., 2003) or increased blood circulation in the neural circuits involved in cognitive functioning (Erickson et al., 2012), which leads to changes in neuroplasticity (Mandolesi et al., 2018, p. 509; Fernandes et al., 2017). Some suggest that walking restores powers of concentration after it has been depleted or exhausted (Berman et al., 2008; Norman & Shallice, 2000; Pearson & Craig, 2014). Others suggest walking reduces the suppression of memories, thereby increasing divergent thinking (Chrysikou & Thompson-Schill, 2011). A psychodynamic model would favour several aspects here, focusing on the potential freedoms granted to unconscious reveries and non-directed ways of thinking as and when the preoccupations of the ego are distracted by changing perceptions and sensations from the moving landscape (Jung, 1911–12/1952/1990).

Does the Way We Walk Influence the Kinds of Ideas We Have?

Few have speculated on this question, but it is a curious issue to ponder. Take, for example, the experience of walking on a treadmill. Although the treadmill represents perhaps the most mundane of walks—forcing a person to move with regimental strides in a straight line while going nowhere—these walks can be surprisingly insightful. Rebecca Solnit in *Wunderlust: A History of Walking* is particularly scathing of the treadmill, regarding it as the "most perverse of all the devices in the gym" because it "simulates the surfaces on which walking takes place" and the "disappearance" of "space." As a result, the "multifaceted experience of moving through the world" is rendered "dull" (2001, p. 264). Solnit correlates this dull experience with the muted and uncreative mindset of the treadmill's users and their "suburbanized minds" which are "more comfortable with quantifiable and clearly defined activity than with the seamless engagement of mind, body, and terrain to be found walking out-of-doors" (Solnit, 2001, p. 265). The treadmill is the rationalised walk par excellence through its numerical assessments of speed and virtual distance covered. As such, Solnit concludes that it reduces the chances of creative thoughts emerging: "it eliminates the unpredictable and unforeseeable from the routine," which means there are "no sudden revelatory sights around a bend" and "far fewer experiential connections" available (Solnit, 2001). Those who agree with Solnit's criticisms may be surprised to learn that experiments undertaken in the 2014 Stanford study (above) found little difference in creative outputs from walks on a treadmill compared to walks outside. A walk on a treadmill in a room facing a blank wall still enhanced creative thought by 50 per cent compared to a sedentary person seated at a desk.

Walking leads to creative ideas—even it would seem, a walk conducted under strict conditions in a straight line and with regulated pace. But does the way one walks—one's walking "style"—influence the content of ideas? The 2014 Stanford study sought to test only the variety, appropriateness, and novelty of ideas and did not hypothesise about the relationship between environmental conditions and specific content of ideas. Can we suppose that the rationalised rhythms of a walk on a treadmill led participants, not so much to "dull" and "muted" ideas as Solnit suggests, but to novel ideas that were more precisely defined and structured compared to ideas formulated with freer strides and wanderings outside? In the context of our investigation into the walks of philosophers, we could rephrase this question to ask whether Kant's purposeful daily strides up and down the same street led him to compose his efficient and systematic philosophical prose, and, by the same token, whether Heidegger's meandering and convoluted prose was shaped by his rambles and jaunts along the twisting paths of the Black Forest.[6] In other words, is there a correlation between how we walk and the kinds of ideas we have? Some theories go so far as to posit a correlation between the physical gait of a person when walking and their personality type—a curious take on personality tests, perhaps? (Satchell et al., 2017). There appears to be just one empirical study of note that touches on an answer. C-Y Kuo and Y-Y. Yeh (2016) from National Taiwan University tested the efficacy of creative thinking of a group of students who wandered freely about campus against a group who walked a straight path. They conclude that "free-walkers" achieve greater cognitive flexibility, with a diversity of novel solutions to problem-solving, compared to the other group, whose solutions were less sophisticated and more uniform.

Does the Environment We Walk in Shape the Content of Our Ideas?

What of the places we walk, and the material features we perceive when walking? Do they shape our ideas? Jung's famous dream of walking the streets of a place called Liverpool suggests they do (1961, pp. 198–199). There, in dark, wet, and sooty streets, which radiate from a central plaza dimly illuminated by streetlights, he discovers the soul of the city: a blossoming magnolia tree. Jung interprets the features of the environment as a spatial topography for the psyche and his walk through it as a psychodynamic movement towards the Self.

If we were to conflate Solnit's comments about treadmills with the findings of Oppezzo and Schwartz's Stanford study, we might be led to assume that walking on a machine that "negates place" is as conducive to creative thinking as walking outdoors. However, I wish to propose an alternative approach by suggesting that a walk on a treadmill placed before a blank wall will shape the content of ideas in the same way as a more varied walk taken outdoors, but the thoughts or ideas that result in these different situations will contrast in their form or content. Broadly speaking, Oppezzo and Schwartz support this view insofar as they concede that "walking appears to prompt high structure and novelty" in one's thoughts, but "the outdoors seems to influence novelty" in their content (2014, p. 1147).

While philosophers and their commentators are keen to discuss the need to walk to think well, they do not consider the specific walks taken and how they may have influenced the ideas conceived at the time. Of course, such considerations will inevitably be speculative, but they can lead to curious insights. For the remainder of this chapter, I will briefly analyse the walks of Nietzsche and Freud to speculate on how some of the distinctive material features of the places they regularly walked in are potentially traceable in their key theories. We shall accompany Nietzsche along his walks in northern Italy to trace the contribution of his steps to his ideas of the "noble" and "upright" person, who is compelled to *go beyond* conventional ideals and into *the heights* of their own creations. Thence to Freud, whom we shall accompany on his various walks including his daily walk along the Ringstrasse—a three-mile horseshoe-shaped boulevard that encompasses the old city centre of Vienna—to imagine how it influenced his celebrated metaphor of the unconscious as an eternal city.

Nietzsche's Thinking Places

Nietzsche treated with suspicion the kinds of metaphysical systems and ideals that are rationally deduced without recourse to feelings and instincts. He asserts that "our most sacred convictions" and "highest values are judgements emanating from our muscles" (1883–1888/1977, p. 169). This notion underpinned his philosophical outlook, which valorised bodily instincts and a physiological engagement with the world and the places we visit and inhabit. In this context his walks are a veritable medium through which to examine his key ideas—and Nietzsche certainly liked to walk! He walked several hours each morning, accompanied with a notebook for jotting down ideas that sprung to mind. Later, in the afternoon, he would sit at his desk to write his thoughts intensively. In a letter to a friend, he says he needed to walk six-to-eight hours every day (1880–1884/1967, p. 60), and to his sister, Elisabeth Förster-Nietzsche, he says he requires "a *great variety* of walks to choose from" (Nietzsche, 1880–1884/1967, p. 845). It is widely thought that Nietzsche sought variety in the cool Swiss mountains during the summer months and the warmer climes of Italy in the winter to temper the illnesses that plagued him throughout his life. It is also assumed he favoured his aphoristic writing style because it was kinder to his poor eyesight, enabling him to commit his ideas to paper quickly. However, I wish to explore another perspective and stake a claim for the places he walked in as key to the shaping of his ideas and writing style.

The figure of Nietzsche and his fictional spokesperson, Zarathustra, are depicted as lonely wanderers on mountainous paths. Soon after Nietzsche's death, his mountain walks achieved cult-like status, developing into a lucrative tourist industry with his ardent followers seeking inspiration by walking in his footsteps, retracing his pathways (Aschheim, 1994, p. 35). But it is the material features of his walks that interest me. For these treacherous pathways provide topographical spatial arrangements for his principal ideas, including his vision of noble creativity, often described by him as a "struggle to the summit," and the moral frameworks to which he aspired, described as "the edge of the horizon," and the "depths the abyss." Collectively, these emphasise the challenges we face in our self-development and self-overcoming. Nietzsche's philosophy for life is described by him as dangerous and risky, where comfortable and deep-seated values are tested, with the distinct and ever-present possibility that one may slip and fall. We can also point to his nomadic wanderings in contrasting Swiss mountain paths and North Italian city streets as indicative of Nietzsche's insistence on competing perspectives—a theme that runs throughout his writings, and is expressed through his aphoristic writing style, with its predilection for ambiguity and contradiction (Huskinson, 2014).

Nietzsche gives insights into how his walks influenced his ideas. One specific mountain walk attracts scholarly attention due to his claim that it was there, by a specific rock on the shores of Lake Silvaplana in the Upper-Engadine valley of Grisons, that he arrived at one of his most important ideas, as if out of the blue. This was his idea of the "eternal recurrence," which Nietzsche referred to as an idea "6000 feet beyond humanity and time" to honour the location that inspired the idea (1908/1967:295). There are several other mountain walks that shaped his ideas, including walks in Sorrento with a view to the island of Ischia, which became the model for the "Blissful Islands" in *Thus Spoke Zarathustra* (D'Iorio, 2016, pp. 4–5).

Nietzsche's walks in natural landscapes appear to mold his ideas. Mark E. Bolland (1996) argues that it was the topography of the mountain-form that influenced Nietzsche's interpretation of culture as having a pyramid hierarchical structure, with exemplary individuals at the heights of the summit, and the inferior herd, residing like sheep in the valleys below. But what of Nietzsche's walks in the towns and cities he frequented? Their potential influence on his ideas is rarely discussed. A closer look at Nietzsche's comments about his urban walks is revealing, especially in relation to his later ideas about the noble and higher self, who exudes "the grand style," which is to say, the one who lives a potent, creative life encouraged by intense self-reflection and mastery of instinct. In the brief accounts he gives of various buildings he saw on his walks through Genoa and Turin, he alludes to the grand style in relation to the architecture of buildings and personality alike (Huskinson, 2024). But there is one building in Turin that sparks greatest excitement for Nietzsche, for he sees in it, reflected back, his own noble self.

Before Nietzsche visited Turin, he wrote of the need for each of us to find a place that is "still, wide, [and] expansive," a place "for reflection," "with high, spacious, long colonnades … buildings that express as a whole the sublimity of stepping aside to take thought for oneself" (1882/1974, aphorism 280). Such an environment is conducive, he thought, for our noble development, and in Turin he seems to have found it.

Just a ten-minute walk along the arcades and cobbled pathways from his lodgings at the corner of Palazzo Alberti, Nietzsche came face-to-face with the material embodiment of his "grand style."

This was the Mole Antonelliana (built 1863–1889). This was a building with which Nietzsche felt greatest affinity, and with which he identified both himself and his creative achievements. I think it's fitting that the building was still under construction when Nietzsche saw it, for its unfinished state expresses the dynamic self that Nietzsche wrote about, with its aspirations to develop ever-onwards or, in the case of the Mole, ever-upwards. By the same token, it is perhaps fitting too—though sadly so—that Nietzsche's famous fateful collapse in a street or square (depending on which report you consult) a few blocks away from the Mole occurred just before his cherished building was finally completed.

Four days before his collapse, Nietzsche writes to a friend: "Earlier I passed the Mole Antonelliana, the greatest structure that may ever have been built out of an absolute instinct for height—suggestive of nothing so much as my Zarathustra. I have christened it 'Ecce Homo' and mentally surrounded it with immense open space" (1880–1884/1967, p. 565). *Ecce Homo*, "behold the man," was the title of his final work—regarded by some as a quasi-autobiography. It was symbolically significant to Nietzsche that he completed this work soon after the death of the building's architect, Alessandro Antonelli. He writes, "I was present at the funeral of Antonelli this November—He lived until Ecce Homo, the book was finished—The book *and* the human being" (Nietzsche, 1880–1884/1967, p. 566). Nietzsche writes this in one of his final letters—the last of several known as "the delusional letters" written after his collapse. He wrote it to his former colleague and cultural historian Jacob Burckhardt. In the last sentence of his final letter, he writes again to Burckhardt, giving the impression that he thinks he, Nietzsche, *is* Alessandro Antonelli, before telling Burckhardt that he really ought to come to Turin to see his building (Nietzsche, 1880–1884/1967, p. 577).

Standing at nearly 170 metres high, the Mole was in Nietzsche's day the tallest unreinforced brick building in Europe, and analogous to Nietzsche's "instinct for height"—one of the core principles of the "grand style," and comparable to the mountain peaks with which Nietzsche and his Zarathustra are more commonly associated. Indeed, the building's design, with its observational deck is a suitable illustration of Zarathustra's description of a building that enables the elevation of life:

> Aloft will [life] build itself with columns and stairs—life itself into remote distances would it gaze, and out towards blissful beauties—therefore does it require elevation! And because it requires elevation, therefore does it require steps, and variance of steps and climbers! To rise strives life, and in rising to overcome itself. … He who here towered aloft his thoughts in stone, knew as well as the wisest ones about the secret of life! … How divinely do vault and arch here contrast in the struggle: how with light and shade they strive against each other, the divinely striving ones.
>
> (1883–1885/1969, p. 125)

Let us leave Nietzsche now as he wanders and wonders along the streets of Turin and catch up with Freud on his walks about town.

Freud's Thinking Places

It is perhaps unsurprising, given Freud's early interest in hysteria and psychosomatic complaints, that most of his allusions to walking appear in his case studies of patients who find themselves unable to walk due to mysterious paralysis or pains in their feet or legs. And it is no secret that Freud himself suffered from ailments often brought about by walking—namely, his self-professed agoraphobia, which was widely believed at the time to be linked to anxieties of walking in open urban spaces and in close proximity to large buildings that dwarf the individual, as if threatening to swallow them up into the fabric of the city. But what I am interested in is Freud's daily walks in Vienna to ascertain how his walking style and the features he perceived as he walked may have influenced his key idea: the characterisation of the unconscious.

Freud's eldest son, Martin, compared his father's walking style to a marching soldier. Martin recounts how his father preferred to walk in a straight line, and would walk with purpose, taking long strides at terrific speed (M. Freud, 1983, p. 27). Each summer, Freud would take a break from his work to holiday with his family in the countryside, often going for long woodland walks with his children, where they would enjoy foraging for mushrooms. On such occasions, we might expect the meandering paths and the juiciest mushrooms far from the well-worn track to encourage Freud to wander, dawdle, and saunter. But instead, as his son recounts, he approached these occasions like an army exercise, rallying his troops to compete to find the best mushroom—a competition his father would usually win! According to Martin, his father would insist that they all stick to the path (Freud, 1983, p. 59).

Freud's regimental strides along pathways purposely taken are reminiscent of Kant's. They suggest a mindset that is meticulous and restrained—one, perhaps more firmly led by rational deduction than disjointed intuitions. In terms of Jungian typology, we might interpret the purposeful stride as indicative of a dominant thinking function, in contrast to the free intuitive wanderer. Like Kant, Freud was known to take his walk at the same time each day and to stick, whenever possible to the same pathway—the celebrated Ringstrasse, to which I return shortly (Freud, 1983, p. 27). Unlike Kant, however, Freud's mind was intent on uncovering and exploring the realm of the unconscious mind. We could interpret Freud's regimental walking style, therefore, as an attempt to contain, ground, and perhaps to control the ideas that came to his mind—which is perhaps especially important when trying to make sense of something so unruly as the unconscious.

One of the most recognisable of Freud's characterisations of the unconscious, which he happens to describe in the context of walking, is his theory of the uncanny (1919). The uncanny, from the German *Ünheimlich*—commonly mistranslated into English as "unhomely," but more accurately defined as "unconcealed," "unhidden," or "unsecret"—is an experience of the "return of the repressed." It is both familiar and unfamiliar because it expresses the return of a forgotten experience that has been recalled to mind but without the memory of its original context. To illustrate the idea, Freud employs anecdotal examples of walking in environments that appear strangely familiar. For instance, an occasion when he found himself lost in the deserted streets of an Italian town. Although he encountered familiar landmarks as he walked, he kept returning to them, as if walking in circles, unable to get his proper bearings on the place. Another example is the occasion he wandered about a dark and unfamiliar room, searching for the light switch, colliding time after time with the same piece of furniture. Each case describes a walking style that contrasts strikingly with Freud's own—a meandering which thwarts his intentions and leads to an experience out of his control.

While Freud is keen to interrogate uncanny experiences to uncover the origins of repressed experiences and to make sense of the person's inability to manage them, I am interested in the evocative qualities of uncanny environments that trigger, for Freud at least, the return of the repressed. For instance, in the examples just cited, I question the extent to which the features of the Italian town helped to facilitate Freud's uncanny encounters. Could the winding cobbled streets and its haphazard alignment of mediaeval buildings that jut out from the twists and turns of Freud's pathway to thwart his determined strides have played a significant role in his experience? And by extension, a role too, in the formulation of his theories about the uncanny unconscious that resulted?

Freud provides another useful example of a walk he took, which highlights the different emphases that he and I place on the significance of his walks. This is the occasion he walked around the ruins of the Acropolis in 1904, which he recounts several years later in 1936 in the paper "A Disturbance of Memory on the Acropolis." As the title suggests, Freud seeks to explain an uncanny experience he had on this walk, which he describes as a surprise upon realising that the Acropolis exists even though he had known of its existence all along. He diagnoses his experience as the return of repressed feelings he harboured towards his father and the dawning realisation that he has finally surpassed his father's authority. The details of his diagnosis are not relevant here. What is under investigation is the role of the material landscape of the Acropolis that Freud perceived just before and during his uncanny experience (see Huskinson, 2019). Freud barely mentions the physical features of the place, only passing comment on its historical significance. The evocative sights of the crumbling ruin, with large chunks of rock strewn across his path, having fallen from the once pristine and coherent building seems wholly irrelevant to his explanation. So tied up is he in the intra-psychic and interpersonal origins of his experience that he is unaware of the possible impact of the immediate nonhuman environment on his experience.

When I imagine Freud walking around the ruins of the Acropolis, I imagine him walking around his own spatial archaeological metaphors of the psyche. There, the remnants of past ages are unearthed by the archaeologist, a figure whose work corresponds to the psychoanalyst, for both expose formerly repressed meanings by interpreting them in the current day. The Acropolis is akin to Freud's own "memory Palace," if you like, which is to say it presents to Freud the possibility of recalling past experiences as he walks about a place that is charged with evocative ideas and meanings. I would like to think that the material features of the Acropolis somehow encouraged the return of Freud's repressed feelings—an experience that contributed to the formulation of his theories.

Freud's regular walk in Vienna provides fuel for thought for another of Freud's well-known metaphors of the unconscious: the eternal dream city of Rome (1930–2001). Freud's walk along the wide, tree-lined Ringstrasse was part of his daily routine. He dedicated precisely one hour to walking the three kilometres pathway after lunch, and I suggest this specific walk had greater impact on Freud's thoughts than he perhaps realised. Indeed, I think it pertinent to replace Rome with Vienna as Freud's veritable city of the unconscious. And I would like to think of Freud's well-known allusion to "the royal road to the unconscious"—the proverbial road of dreams or dream-like thinking—as the Ringstrasse (a road established by royalty: by Franz Joseph, emperor of Austria).

Freud walks along this road every day, with specific purpose and focus. Because the boulevard is so familiar to him, we may assume he is inclined to "switch off" from his surroundings and focus on his thoughts, in a manner that, as Wallas suggests, is crucial for the incubation of thoughts. Nevertheless, this boulevard is far from dormant. It is undergoing radical material transformation—in step perhaps with the development of Freud's ideas—slowly changing from a messy building site to the pristine, coherent row of elegant buildings we can visit today. Freud first moved to Vienna soon after construction work on the Ringstrasse began, and this work would continue for another fifty years. He began walking this street shortly after moving into his apartment at Bergasse IXX in 1891, when several buildings were complete and several were undergoing construction. His walk took him through an environment rich in latent meaning and tantalising in its promise of revealing its final manifest form.

Freud remarks that, as he walked around the ruins of the Acropolis, he felt compelled to imagine what the place looked like in its original pristine condition, and we can imagine him attempting to picture how the Ringstrasse will appear upon completion. And I imagine that the finalised form of the Ringstrasse may have impacted on the nature and content of some of Freud's ideas. Its massive size, with vast elegant buildings lining its wide and expansive street, may have been of sufficient magnitude to encourage Freud's agoraphobia. Certainly, we know there were occasions when Freud would start to shake when crossing large streets. In this context, his regular regimental walks along the Ringstrasse could be interpreted symptomatically as a repetition compulsion, indicative of an unresolved conflict.

The architecture of the buildings that line the Ringstrasse exemplify the historicist style—an eclectic array of different historical architectural styles placed together, side by side and occasionally within one and the same building. The result is an ornate collection of buildings that somewhat bewilders in their architectural presentation. Freud's daily walk in this context is analogous to a walk through architectural history—an encounter with neo-Classical, neo-Gothic, Renaissance, and Baroque architecture all present in the same walk, and all under construction and coming to completion in a relatively short span of time. The beguiling and eclectic array of designs, although probably not sufficient to trigger an uncanny experience akin to Freud's experience within labyrinthine Italian streets, may well have stirred his imagination, especially given his broad, more conscious interests in architecture.

When discussing his celebrated characterisation of the unconscious as the "eternal city," Freud asks his readers to imagine the architecture of Rome, and to visualise every building and monument that has ever been constructed there—both ancient and modern—appearing immediately at one and the same time in its original location and original form. Freud invites us to look upon this eternal city and to perceive every one of its historical layers at once. This image, Freud says, characterises the timeless unconscious where all experiences are conserved and where "nothing which has once been constructed can perish" (1930–2001:69). The unconscious occupies an eternal space, where past materials or forms have not been erased or replaced. The Ringstrasse provides Freud with a particularly apt urban landscape of the kind he encourages us to imagine.

Conclusion

Walking is conducive to creative thinking, and the physical features of the environments we walk in may shape the kinds of ideas we have when walking. Anecdotal evidence provided by Nietzsche and Freud about the natural and urban landscapes they regularly walked in suggests a correlation with the ideas and theories they developed. This implies that the legacies of their thought are inextricably linked to the places they walked in. The examples of the walks of Nietzsche and Freud can be treated as case studies of the wider investigation into relationships between walking and thinking. As such they furnish relatively undeveloped empirical investigations into the cognitive advantages of walking outdoors in urban or natural environments. The approach of this chapter is a foray into, and a step towards, reconciling the disciplinary interests of Geography and Philosophy from the overlooked perspective of a "geographical philosophy." The potentials of examining philosophical theories from the perspective of geography are relatively untapped, and it is hoped that more work will be done in this area to the benefit of both subjects. Finally, it would seem Jung was right to insist that we are always in the psyche. The "personal equation" which always founds our theorizing is thoroughly embodied and is evident in the architecture and landscapes of our material environments. We do not need to study dreams to find archetypal images; we can simply open our eyes and look outside.

Notes

1 Although there are some overlaps between the two disciplines, they tend to be offshoots of mainstream academic discourse, such as for instance the investigatory areas of environmental aesthetics, eco-philosophy, and psychogeography.
2 For a succinct summary see Elden (2009).
3 Rousseau is perhaps a notable exception. His *Reveries of a Solitary Walker* (*Les rêveries du Promeneur Solitaire*, 1782/2004) comprises ten chapters, numbered as a sequence of walks, each of which comprise autobiographical anecdotes and

descriptions of physical features (especially plant life) he experiences along the way, on the outskirts of Paris. Peter France, the English translator of the work, describes the work as an exploration of the state of "mental wandering." He notes a "telling phrase jotted down" by Rousseau on a "playing-card at the time when he was writing this book" that says: "My whole life has been little else than a long reverie divided into chapters by my daily walks" (France, 2004, p. 12). However, France notes, "Not many of the Walks are directly concerned with the walks around Paris, though they may record some of the thoughts that filled Rousseau's head as he walked" (France, 2004, p. 13). Nietzsche is another exception to the rule, as I go on to show.

4 And some of those who were immediately influenced by his ideas such as Maurice Meleau-Ponty.
5 Heidegger's work *Country Path Conversations* (1944/1945/2010) (*Feldweg-Gespräche*) may imply from its title that it is a study about walking, but its focus is a series of philosophical dialogues and not a reflection on the physical "country path." However, I wish to suggest that the forest path is implicit in Heidegger's meandering philosophical approach and thereby relevant in the shaping of his ideas (see also note 6).
6 Speaking of the entwined nature of Heidegger's Black Forest walks and Heidegger's ideas, Bret W. Davis (the English translator of Heidegger's work *Country Path Conversations*) notes: his ideas "veer off the pavement of our accustomed ways of speaking and at times venture into a thicket; their ponderous yet radical manner … frequently transgresses the limits of our familiar horizons and goes several strides beyond our established 'clearings' of intelligibility" (Heidegger, 1944/1945/2010:xx).

References

Akinola, M. & Mendes, W. B. (2008). The Dark side of creativity: Biological vulnerability and negative emotions lead to greater artistic creativity. *Personality and Social Psychology Bulletin*, 34: 1677–1686.
Aschheim, S. E. (1994). *The Nietzsche legacy in Germany 1890–1990*. University of California Press.
Bachelard, G. (1957/1958). *The poetics of space*. (M. Jolas, Trans.). Beacon Press.
Berman, M. G., Jonides, J., Kaplan, S. (2008). 'The cognitive benefits of interacting with nature'. *Psychological Science, 19*: 1207–12.
Boden, M. (2004). *The creative mind: Myths and mechanisms*. Routledge.
Bolland, M. E. (1996). *Nietzsche and mountains*, Durham University Doctoral Thesis. Durham: Unpublished.
Brooke, R. (2009). The Self, the psyche and the world: A Phenomenological interpretation. *The Journal of Analytical Psychology, 54*(5): 601–18.
Caird, E. (1889/2000). *The critical philosophy of Immanuel Kant*, Vol. 2. MacMillan.
Chrysikou, E. G. & Thompson-Schill, S. L. (2011). Dissociable brain states linked to common and creative object use. *Human Brain Mapping, 32*: 665–75.
D'Iorio, P. (2016). *Nietzsche's journey to sorrento*. Chicago University Press.
Deleuze, G. & Guattari, F. (1991/1994). *What is philosophy?* Verso.
Descartes, R. (1641/1996). *Meditations on first philosophy*. (J. Cottingham, Ed. & Trans.) Cambridge University Press.
Elden, S. (2009). Philosophy and human geography. In (R. Kitchin & N. Thrift, Eds.) *International encyclopaedia of human geography*. (pp. 145–50). Elsevier
Erickson, K. I., Miller, D. L., Weinstein, A. M., Akl, S, & Banducci, S. (2012). Physical activity and brain plasticity in late adulthood. *Ageing Research, 3*: 34–47.

Fernandes, J., Arida, R. M., & Gomez-Pinilla, F. (2017). Physical exercise as an epigenetic modulator of brain plasticity and cognition. *Neuroscience & Biobehavioral Reviews, 80*: 443–456.

France, P. (2004) Introduction'. In J. Rousseau, *Reveries of a solitary walker*. Penguin.

Freud, M. (1983). *Sigmund Freud: Man and father*. Jason Aronson.

Freud, S. (1930–2001). Civilisation and its discontents. In (J. Strachey & A. Freud, Eds.). *The standard edition of the complete psychological works of Sigmund Freud*. vol. 21. Vintage.

Hartig, T., Evans, G. W., Jamner, L. D., Davis, D. S., & Gärling, T. (2003). Tracking restoration in natural and urban field settings. *Journal of Environmental Psychology, 23*(2): 109–123.

Heidegger, M. (1944/1945/2010). *Country path conversations*. (B. W. Davis., Trans.) Indiana University Press.

Heidegger, M. (1954/1975). Building, dwelling, thinking. In (A. Holstadter, Trans.). *Poetry, language, thought*. Harper.

Huskinson, L. (2014). *Nietzsche and Jung: The whole self in the union of opposites*. Brunner-Routledge.

Huskinson, L. (2019). *Architecture and the mimetic self: A Psychoanalytic study of how buildings make and break our lives*. Routledge.

Huskinson, L. (2024). *Nietzsche and architecture: The Grand style for modern living*. (in press). Bloomsbury.

Jung, C. G. (1911–12/1990). 'Two kinds of thinking'. CW5. Trans. R. F. C. Hull, Princeton University Press.

Jung, C. G. (1961). *Memories, dreams, reflections*. (A. Jaffé, Ed., & R. Winston and C. Winston, Trans.). Fontana.

Keighren, I. M. (2005). Geosophy, imagination, and *Terrae Incognitae*: Exploring the intellectual history of John Kirtland Wright. *Journal of Historical Geography, 31*(3): 546–62.

Kierkegaard, S. (1847/1978). Letter to Henrietta Kierkegaard. In (H. Rosenmeier, Ed. & Trans.). *Kierkegaard letters and documents*. Princeton University Press.

Koestler, A. (1957). *The act of creation*. Dell.

Kuo, C-Y. & Yeh, Y-Y. (2016). Sensorimotor-conceptual integration in free walking enhances divergent thinking for young and older adults' *Frontiers in Psychology, 7*. https://doi.org/10.3389/fpsyg.2016.01580

Livingstone, D. N. (2003). *Putting science in its place: Geographies of scientific knowledge*. University of Chicago Press.

Mandolesi, L., Polverino, A., Montuori, S., Foti, F., Ferraioli, G., Sorrentino, P., & Sorrentino, G. (2018). Effects of physical exercise on cognitive functioning and well-being: Biological and psychological benefits. *Frontiers in Psychology, 9*. https://doi.org/10.3389/fpsyg.2018.00509

Nietzsche, F. (1880–1884/1967). *Nietzsche Kritische Gesamtausgabe*. (G. Coli & M. Montinari, Eds.). de Gruyter.

Nietzsche, F. (1882). *The gay science*. (W. Kaufman, Trans.). Vintage.

Nietzsche, F. (1883–1885/1969). *Thus spoke Zarathustra*. (R. J. Hollingdale, Trans.). Penguin.

Nietzsche, F. (1883–1888/1977). *Sämtliche Werke: Kritische Studienausgabe*. (G. Colli & D. M. Montinari, Eds.). vol. 13. de Gruyter.

Nietzsche, F. (1889/1990). *Twilight of the idols.* (R. J. Hollingdale, Trans.). Penguin.

Nietzsche, F. (1908/1967). *On the genealogy of morals and Ecce homo.* (W. Kaufmann, Ed.). Penguin.

Norman, D. A. and Shallice, T. (2000) Attention to Action: Willed and Automatic Control of Behaviour. In M.S. Gazzaniga (ed.) *Cognitive Neuroscience: A Reader*, Blackwell: Malden, pp. 376–90.

Oppezzo, M. & Schwartz, D. L. (2014). Give your ideas some legs: The positive effect of walking on creative thinking. *Journal of Experimental Psychology: Learning, Memory, and Cognition, 40*(4): 1142–1152.

Pearson, D. G. & Craig, T. (2014). The great outdoors? Exploring the mental health benefits of natural environments. *Frontiers in Psychology, 5.*

Poincaré, H. (1908/2012). *The foundations of science, science and hypothesis: The value of science and method.* (G. B. Halsted, Trans.). The Science Press.

Rethorst, C. D., Wipfli, B. M., & Landers, D. M. (2009). The antidepressive effects of exercise. *Sports Medicine, 39*: 491–511.

Rousseau, J. (1782/1953). *Confessions.* (J. M. Cohen, Trans). Penguin.

Rousseau, J. (1782/2004). *Reveries of a solitary walker.* (P. France, Trans.). Penguin.

Satchell, L., Morris, P., Mills, C., O'Reilly, L., Marshman, P., & Akehurst, L. (2017). Evidence of Big Five and aggressive personalities in gait biomechanics. *Journal of Nonverbal Behavior, 41*: 35–44.

Searles, H. (1960). *The nonhuman environment in normal development and in schizophrenia.* International Universities Press.

Solnit, R. (2001). *Wanderlust: A history of walking.* Granta Books.

Stewart, D. (1792). *Elements of the philosophy of the human mind.* Strahan, Cadell & Creech.

Tuan, Y. (1974). *Topophilia: A study of environmental perception, attitudes, and values.* Prentice-Hall.

Wallas, G. (1926/2014). *The art of thought.* Solis.

Withers, C. W. J. (2007). *Placing the enlightenment: Thinking geographically about the age of reason.* University of Chicago Press.

Wright, J. K. (1947). Terrae incognitae: The place of the imagination in geography. *Annuals of the Association of American Geographers, 37*(1): 1–15.

Introduction to "An Archetypal Perspective on Anti-Homeless Architecture"

Adam J. Schneider's research on anti-homeless architecture explores the interface between the archetypal psychology developed by James Hillman and the metabletic phenomenology of the Dutch psychiatrist J. H. Van den Berg and those who were inspired by him. This psychological method describes the material realities of the human world, its architecture, as revealing and mirroring how we emerge and understand ourselves as human. This environmental world is not merely factual, nor is it external to our psychological lives. It is, rather, the aesthetics, ethics, and politics of our psychological lives made visible. By using phenomenology in this way, Schneider's chapter pushes research in analytical psychology into the public sphere. He also provocatively suggests that psychotherapy in its various contemporary forms participates in the splitting, ugliness, and politics of anti-homeless architecture. This chapter reads especially well as a response to the appeals by Brooks and Sipiora in this book.

Chapter 9

An Archetypal Perspective on Anti-Homeless Architecture

Adam J. Schneider

Introduction

Archetypal psychologist James Hillman (1926–2011) detailed throughout his text *City & Soul* (2006) the inherent political nature of psychology. He argued this inherent political nature has been forgotten by contemporary practitioners. Hillman's conceptualization of archetypal psychology sought to restore this vocation, to understand patients as citizens, and for therapists to engage their work and world as psychological activists. Archetypal psychology is the practice of "soul making." Hillman (1992) defined soul as "a perspective rather than a substance, a viewpoint towards things rather than a thing itself" (p. x). The soul is reflective in nature, it mediates interactions and engagements in life, and, most importantly, is independent (cannot be identified with any *thing*) (Hillman, 1992, p. x). Psychologists cannot control the soul but can facilitate or hinder its presentation.

Hillman outlined three primary areas of activism in the work of soul making: justice, destiny, and beauty. Each of these areas experiences repression by contemporary society. Where the soul is a "deepening of events into experience," society seeks a surface-level engagement with the world. Where the soul has a "special relation with death," society seeks to avoid engagement with death. Where the soul engages in fantasy, or conversation with images, society seeks only rational reality (Hillman, 1992, p. x).

Anti-homeless, or hostile, architecture is a concrete example of the repression of beauty through the pursuit of surface-level order. This architecture includes sidewalk spikes placed on the border of buildings, public benches that are sloped so that a body, if sleeping, would slide onto the ground, artificially rocky pavements, sprinklers that randomly start despite there being nothing to water, and more.

An analysis of this architecture must attend to the social constructions that contributed to their development. As Cushman (1995) argued, "One task of human science is to develop understandings about the contextual meanings and functions of these artifacts" (p. 19). These contextual meanings are dynamic; they are not merely theoretical. As Crawford (2006) noted, "meanings have consequences. They are not only derivative of social reality; meanings are also real in

DOI: 10.4324/9781032694603-12

that they shape and transform experience, behaviors, and institutions" (p. 402). Architecture constructed to prevent homeless people from sleeping in public spaces holds meaning that is derived from a social reality that sees the homeless person as less than human. These structures shape and transform the experiences of the homeless but also people with more normative homes, as well as the relationships between the two groups (to be hostile or afraid of one another).

This inquiry is influenced by the metabletic approach pioneered by J. H. Van den Berg (1971). The metabletic approach articulates a fundamental principle: every artifact provides a partial answer to the question of what it means to be a human being in relationship to reality. Conceptualizing anti-homeless architecture as an artifact in this sense allows for a nonliteral consideration of its impact on the phenomenological existence of being human. Indeed, Van den Berg and Romanyshyn (2008) traced the beginning of his metabletic approach to the connection he observed between discoveries in human physiology and the development of specific styles of architecture.

Metabletics also facilitates observations and descriptions of the change in meaning of being and reality across time. "The claim of metabletic phenomenology about the changing nature of reality is, therefore, a claim about the relation between humanity and reality" (Romanyshyn, 2008, p. 506). What it means to be human is contingent on the reality in which humans live, including their cities and dwellings.

Metabletics aims to enliven what has become concretized in the natural science model. As Romanyshyn (2008) described, "What we would take for granted; what we would culturally live out as a necessity of fate; what we would live out forgetfully and literally as a fact in itself is thereby re-membered and de-literalized" (pp. 522–523). Anti-homeless architecture aims to blend into the existing natural and designed landscape and have normatively homed people relate to it, and its consequences, as a given fact. This chapter follows the metabletic aim to address the collective amnesia regarding the anti-homeless architecture often taken for granted in daily life.

The first step of this study is a critical analysis of the language used in this phenomenon. Anti-homeless architecture is considered within the category Crime Prevention through Environmental Design (CPTED) (Chellew, 2016). Hillman's notion of depersonification is used to demonstrate how this term uses exaggerated language but the words are essentially meaningless. This term contains no soul. Enacting this language through concrete architecture then depersonifies the people who inhabit these spaces.

Second, Hillman's interrogation of contemporary notions of pathology is applied to stereotypes of the homeless person. Whereas psychiatry distinguishes between health and sickness, Hillman understood these notions as two essential sides of how the soul expresses itself. Both are necessary to recognize and express the soul. The attempt to eliminate sickness, through a projection onto homeless communities, is to attempt splitting the soul.

Finally, the stories of two homeless men who found viral fame and assistance are used to identify and criticize the societal value of action. Because the stereotyped homeless person is seen as lazy, they are not likely to receive attention or help unless they show themselves willing to act (Pellegrini et al., 1997; Wusinich et al., 2019). This value of action is also represented in popular modalities of psychotherapy, such as cognitive behavioral therapy (e.g., exposure, modification, imagery, reframing, etc., see Beck, 2020) and dialectical behavioral therapy (e.g., opposite action, half-smiling and willing hands, observe/describe/participate, protocols for sleep/nightmares, see Linehan, 2014). In other words, psychotherapy can hinder, force, or facilitate the expression of beauty in its participants' lives. Therefore, clinical interventions are ethical decisions brought to bear on the expression or hindrance of beauty in their world.

The Ethics of Beauty

Hillman's historical engagement with architecture is complex and, at times, contradictory. Hillman continued from Freud and Jung in using architecture as a metaphor for psyche (Huskinson, 2015). Hillman often used pathological language to describe environmental concerns. Hillman saw buildings as representations of "pathological egos" (Huskinson, 2015). This perspective risks seeing all human construction as soulless. But as Giucastro Fabio (2017), an architectural professor inspired by Hillman, made clear,

> The architecture we propose has the ethical duty of connecting individual and collective feelings, man and the world, autobiography and sociality, soul and city, declaring and adapting the specificity of places and their corporeal connection (Material) and sentimental (Soul) with man.
>
> (p. 2)

Hillman's approach to architecture was first and foremost a division between the natural and made worlds, but only insofar as one illuminated the other. The criticism is intended to evoke the sense that there is a proper, meaningful way for beings, their constructions, and the natural environment to engage with one another. This chapter builds on Huskinson's (2015) reading of Hillman, that human constructions often (but not always) represent an egoic attempt to control what defines beauty. Criticizing anti-homeless architecture, then, is not a broadside against all human construction. Anti-homeless architecture is a particular way in which human buildings not only repress meaningful aspects of the soul but fight against them.

Hostile architecture represents literal attempts to displace and deny the messages the phenomenon of homelessness conveys to society. To pathologize the homeless person, which evokes a normative view of home, is a projection.

These designs are ugly. Hillman understood beauty not through subjective perception or objective measurement, but somewhere between the two as an instinctual, epistemological display. Beauty is the way things present themselves, without distortion. In other words, beauty is "the manifest visible image, the displayed presentation" (Hillman, 2014, p. 56). The result architects hope to achieve through anti-homeless designs – people avoiding these spaces because of bodily discomfort – is how such designs are recognized as distortions of beauty. This result is the consequence Hillman outlined when he wrote, "the ugly makes us withdraw, shrink into ourselves, turn away" (2006, p. 144). Hillman referred to this response as the "soul's reaction" (Hillman, 2006, p. 144).

Not only is such design a consequence of the depersonification of the environment but consequently depersonifies the people who inhabit these spaces. Many of the people impacted by the hostility are not afforded the clean spaces of elite private therapy practices but instead wherever their state-subsidized insurance allows. Their distraught sensory, bodily experiences are either metaphorized away as being representative or symbolic of something intrapsychic and infantile or worked too concretely, too individually, in the person's body.

Both detours miss how these lived experiences are indicative of societal, systemic issues. Should they be recognized as such, Hillman suggested, psychotherapy would be much more intentionally invested, compelled to enter, the polis. Such motivation is not only an objective, ethical imperative. As Hillman argued, ethics requires the passion of beauty, the impulse of the id, to be motivated into such action. Ego alone does not express the soul. So long as physical contexts remain ugly and oppressive, so long will souls be suppressed under this weight. What is needed is an architecturally/archetypally minded focus on the beauty and ugliness in society and how people might better participate in, or un-hinder, their unfolding presentation.

Depersonification through Language

Hillman's first chapter of *Re-Visioning Psychology* (1992) outlined the consequences of decades, if not centuries, of both *de-personification* of being and a *narrow personification*, regarding human beings as the only kind of being that has soul (pp. 1–2). One component and area of consequence of de-personification is language. Hillman (1992) argued a twofold move occurs in society's discourse in which certain words take on exaggerated value while being empty of substance. Words lose any inherent meaning and are separate and reducible things distinct from any notion of truth. Words become variables in a mathematical equation.

Within public policy such hostile design is incorporated into Crime Prevention through Environmental Design (Chellew, 2016). This term identifies the purpose of environmental design is crime prevention. This purported purpose suggests the hostility and defensiveness of the architecture is targeted at crime. Yet as Hillman (2006) argued,

> It is not enough well known that you are more likely to be raped, beaten, or killed in the home than out in the street. The private home – that essential image of the American Dream – is in general the most dangerous place to be.
>
> (p. 362)

The crime to be prevented by anti-homeless architecture, then, is loitering, Orwellian Newspeak for homelessness.

Locating the cause of crime in the homeless population is a projection indicative of one of Van den Berg's (1969) neuroticizing factors in Western society: the mobility of people. As Mook (2008) wrote, "This factor led to an increase in superficial contacts between people, in comparison to a limited number of familiar relationships in the past, resulting in possible social misunderstanding, conflict and social isolation" (p. 469). Rather than take responsibility for population growth, fewer resources, and architecture which distances people, the homeless population is used as a scapegoat for the crime in major cities. The use of situational crime prevention, a form of CPTED, confuses the victims of crime for the perpetrators (Bryar, 2006; Rayman, 2016).

The second word, prevention, again betrays the directionality of the action. The act of prevention is the crime itself. As Ocean Howell, professor of architectural history and former skateboarder stated, "The message is clear: you are not a member of the public, at least not of the public that is welcome here" (Omidi, 2014). Even if the design was initially intended to promote social interaction, to bring people out into the streets and thus reduce crime as a natural consequence of greater socialization, there was always a shadow to this idea. "Ideas we do not know we have," like complexes, "have us" (Hillman, 2006, p. 360). More to the point, as Huskinson (2018) wrote, "Buildings design us as much as we design them" (p. 1). Without design that neither allows our public spaces to manifest their beauty nor allows people to exist in these spaces without penalty, the world is soulless, the social pathology of the present moment. But as Fabio (2017) wrote, "We need places for the body. Places where bodies can be seen, meet, come in contact with each other," for cities, and their beauty, are dependent on places for bodies to gather (in a Heideggerian sense) and contact one another (p. 4).

Therefore, it is not crime that is being prevented, but the symptoms which indicate the repression of beauty. Like effective manualized psychotherapy interventions, the goal of anti-homeless architecture is to eliminate the symptom. If the people displaced, the people the architects and pedestrians consider ugly, are not present in public, then people do not have to confront the ugliness of their lives and the dangers "homed" people pose to public safety. Public spaces are then privatized, criminalizing those who apparently trespass. Pfeffer

(2006) uses the example of young people being confronted in a shopping mall to illustrate the growing illusion of public spaces. There is, then, a link between crime prevention strategies and corporate profit.

Crime Prevention through Environmental Design also includes the environment. The usage of the term *environment* in this way is egocentric and exclusionary. It is egocentric in the way it conceives the environment as defined by developmental design. It implies a separation between the designer and the designed. Environmental design is in direct opposition to Hillman's (2006) "responsive environmentalism" (p. 320). Not only is the designer apparently endowed with creative energy, but the designed environment is robbed of it.

This process violates the first core component Hillman articulated: engagement with the environment must come from a personal response. Hillman (2006) wrote, "The organic health of human beings, their sensory systems and psychic awareness, are in constant reciprocal relationship with a world that *acts upon us as much as we act upon it*" (p. 321, emphasis added). To repress the responsive soul of the environment is to repress the soul of the Other, and this is evident in the hatred of the homeless communicated through environmental design. The environment, Hillman (2006) argued, must be seen as a gathering "place," a change in discourse that encourages greater participation and care for everything in society: nature, concrete, and people (p. 321).

The last term in the phrase is design. The aesthetic perspective promoted by Crime Prevention through Environmental Design is of the shallow quality Hillman (2006) defined as "quite free of moral and ethical value" (p. 144). Hillman argued that beauty (and therefore ethics) is not solely found in the surface level appearance of objects but is grounded in their functional impact on people who use them. Designers of anti-homeless architecture create pretty flowers and pretty people, but in the end, petty happiness. The archetypal perspective sees the comfort and cleanliness pursued by these means as an illusion. No matter how well trimmed the sidewalk dividers, regardless of the creativity in the mold of the sliding bench, they remain fundamentally ugly. The homeless – and the ugliness of the society to which they direct our attention – do not actually disappear when they are cleared from the streets. Should the designing process include "artists and critics of the arts," as Hillman (2006) suggested, their aesthetic response would likely offer an explicit rebuke of the current pattern (p. 322). Crime Prevention through Environmental Design is therefore a soulless term that, when enacted, promotes soulless places and people.

Whose Pathology?

Another consequence of the CPTED perspective is that it locates the ugliness, the pathology, within the homeless, and wrongly believes that in getting rid of the homeless on the streets, the pathology is gone. Hillman (1992) criticized the lower-class category to which psychopathology has been relegated (pp. 64–66). Such a perspective is representative of an illusory split between "health" and "sickness" when these are both part and parcel of soul. One cannot speak about soul, or hear the soul speak, without hearing both health and sickness. In this way, the supposed depression or psychosis of the homeless person is on a lower rung of mental health hierarchy than, say, the discomfort of those with homes and wealth. The homeless are seen as the (caricatured) primitive, in need of insight and perhaps a job.

This "transcendence" from primitive to modern is one form of a denial of depression, of death, that Hillman detailed. These individuals might be considered by behaviorist Albert Ellis (1968) as those people who "have probably remained disturbed for most of their lives largely because they will not get off their asses and take risk after risk" (p. 318). Contemporary self-help movements elaborate such a perspective, prioritizing and valorizing health, hope, courage, love, maturity, warmth, wholeness, but doing so dismisses the intelligibility and necessity of sickness, despair, fear, hatred, childishness, cold, and fragmentation. Such a position privileges one aspect of soul over another and sets an impossible teleology of happiness.

The same is true with anti-homeless architecture, those who design it, and those who are intended to enjoy it. They split off and displace their ugliness for the sake of superficial comfort and illusory safety. Hillman argued such a perspective is simplistic, naïve, delusional, and moralistic. Hillman (2006) wrote, "We need to recognize here how much contempt for all human nature, and not only the nature of the poor, is insinuated by this idea of laziness" that accompanies the stereotype of the homeless (p. 365). This contempt ignores the "degrading conditions to which the other submits ... hunger, poverty, ugliness, dirt, and bureaucracy" (Hillman, 2006, p. 366).

The use of the term "homeless" to describe a person, which even this chapter employs, is indicative of displacement and splitting defenses. By defining where most people live as home, and anything outside of it as not-home, people are not responsible for what happens "out there," and likewise the people who choose (or are forced) to live "out there" are not others' responsibility, and at worst, are not fully human. After all, people with modern dwellings are not referred to as "homed people." Home is equated with civilization, and anything not-home is uncivilized, including the people existing in those spaces. Yet people in society are not content with their homes. Hostile architecture functions as an effort to colonize and enlighten these wild spaces. Shadows, in a Jungian sense, are projected onto these people to concretely attempt to rid society of these qualities. The presence of the differently homed person forces society to question the psychological cost of its homes and the subjectivity these homes shape.

Society needs differently homed people to hear that message, not because they are "sick" but because they teach something about the soul. This may be what Jesus was alluding to when he taught that the poor will always be present (Matt. 26:11). Their presence is meaningful. One comes to recognize the soul's autonomy in its creation of (what the public perceives as) disorder and abnormality. Hillman argued for a foundational perspective that needs to be enacted prior to any consideration of diagnosis or treatment, because such a perspective can and should change the way mental health workers diagnose and treat. He favored some diagnostic categories but only in their utility to help the soul express itself and for it to be understood, only so long as they assist in expanding the room in which soul can and should be present, not cover over or "contain" its message. Otherwise, the width and breadth of the soul's language is suppressed and constricted.

How, then, can environments be designed in such a way that welcomes differently homed people? Pro-homeless architecture? Vulnerable design? But beyond the literal homeless person; how can environments recognize and welcome the general ugliness that leads cities, neighborhoods, and benches, to be designed with such hostility? Recognition of complicity is the precondition for the aesthetic response to become appropriate action. Acting on the delusion that neighborhoods become safe by removing people from the streets makes communities more at risk for succumbing to the consequences of repressing symptoms. The primary consequence is the numbing of the aesthetic response. Van den Berg (1969) termed this neuroticizing factor "the ambivalence of society" (Mook, 2008, p. 469). The more people are encouraged and feel capable of ignoring and displacing the homeless, the number they become to those parts of themselves.

This numbing starts small. Hillman (2006) wrote, "By repressing our reactions to the basic ugliness of simple details, like ceilings, by denying our annoyance and outrage, we actually encourage an unconsciousness that estranges and disorients the interior soul" (p. 189). The estrangement grows as people learn not to mind the slant of their seat or begin to see the sidewalk spikes as simply modern design. It estranges people from their souls and from those who are more directly impacted by these designs. Seeking small comforts costs meaningful pain (Hillman, 2006, p. 195). "But this pain to our senses," Hillman (2006) wrote, "may be the entrance fee, the cost required for attaching ourselves to the world, re-finding our love for its beauty" (p. 195). Symptoms, like the thousands of homeless people and the efforts made to displace them, point society in the direction of what most needs attention. Putting their light out leaves neighborhoods ironically in the dark.

The Dangers of Action

Two recent stories are relevant. First, a man named Ted Williams was living homeless after succumbing to the consequences of drug addiction. He stood on the street with a sign that read: "I have a God-given gift of voice. I'm an ex-radio announcer who has fallen on hard times." He was videoed by an off-duty reporter and dubbed "The Golden Voice." He received viral fame and was offered high-paying employment and residence by the Cleveland Cavaliers (Memmott, 2011). Second, a homeless man in Silicon Valley stood on the street, notably in a suit and tie, with a sign that read, "Homeless hungry for success take a resume." He received more than 200 employment offers (Zdanowicz & Vera, 2018).

What do these stories demonstrate, given these men received help when thousands of others do not? What do their signs have in common? They were communicating a message of action; these men once worked and were ready to work again. Their signs and words were effective precisely because they played to the idea which Hillman (2006) described, that "stupidity and inertia are more fundamental than enterprise and ambition" (p. 365). Hillman astutely recognized the danger of idolizing action.

The problem is not that these men were willing to act to improve their lives. The issue is they were seen by others as *deserving* of resources and opportunities because of their insistence on action when thousands of others struggling without homes are not given similar support. The implicit assumption from those with the resources is that not everyone is willing to act (which explains their homelessness) and therefore not deserving of support. In other words, if you act, you will become homed. But this superficial logic exacerbates homelessness through ignoring the complex psychological, economic, and sociological factors which contribute to homelessness. Two men were helped while nothing about the wider social circumstances affecting thousands of people changed.

Current expressions in psychology which risk such a danger are behavior-focused therapies. Whether cognitive, dialectical, or applied behavioral, these are therapies that drive patients into action through education and practice of skills. These treatments correspond to the action-based terms of diagnosis: oppositional-defiant, attention-deficit, antisocial, dependent, and so forth. There is a fundamental belief undergirding these approaches that people are in control of their behavior and their lives. The client is expected to act to change and the psychotherapist facilitates change through their active teaching and interventions. Contrary to Freud, they insist ego *is* master in its own house. But these so-called developments are for Hillman (1992) simply an expression of "semantic anxiety" and hamper the capacity to tell stories, and for stories to say something about people and society (p. 217).

Hillman (2006) recognized "beauty arrests motion," that is, action-oriented therapies work against the grain of beauty (p. 175). Beauty encourages one to pause, reflect, and change. Psychotherapists should be cautious of acting too quickly or aggressively to change, rather than first hear, client stories. In the situations described above, the observers of the homeless men did not pause and reflect on the reasons which led to their homelessness and were, therefore, ignorant of their fundamental needs. Instead, they immediately acted through the provision of employment and providing luxurious housing. Unfortunately, Ted Williams's sudden fame and wealth triggered an alcohol relapse, prompting him to seek rehabilitation (Duke, 2011). Fortunately, Mr. Williams became sober and now leads a healthy life. But his story is a cautionary tale about idealizing action, which can become ugly interventions. Beautiful interventions, on the other hand, prioritize context, in clinical and social work. Such context implicates *everyone* in the action which needs to be taken at each level of the issue (individual, societal, etc.).

Psychologist as Activist

Those practicing in the field of psychology have a responsibility and role to play in this work. Hillman argued psychotherapy is the "talking cure," and yet it has sought to become an authority on using large, technical words that mean almost nothing. In this sense, psychology communicates its own CPTED. This is the practice of diagnostics seen in the DSM, what Hillman considered symptomatic of the profession's disorder. On the other hand, contemporary preoccupation with nonverbal communication and affect is an example of how literal clinical practice has become because of losing Hillman's (1992) metaphorical recognition that "words, too, burn and become flesh as we speak" (p. 9). Words have their own subjectivity apart from their utility in communication. Acknowledging such inherent and independent status is to acknowledge indebtedness to "archetypal significances," for without them no message could be sent or received between people. The irony of the attention to affect and gestures is that the meaning to be found in such communication is grounded in the soul-full-ness of words-as-persons. Otherwise, speech is about as stirring as an Ikea manual. The lived experience of the homeless person becomes a lifeless stereotype.

Hillman returned to this topic when he discussed the overcorrection of psychology to its loss of soul in words. He identified two extremes: attention to language at the expense of affect or ignoring speech altogether in favor of "inchoate feeling" (Hillman, 1992, p. 214). Separately, these poles miss the importance of how the soul expresses itself in the interplay between the two. Hillman (1992) referred to this interplay as "rhetoric" and its primary expression as "eloquence" (p. 214). Rhetoric returns language to its place in psychotherapy not as an organizing system of diagnosis or empty philosophy and theory but as its "method," a method which facilitates the experience of soulfulness, whereas diagnosis and empty philosophy foreclose on such meaningful experience. One of the most important productions of such speech is narrative. Hillman referred to this work as the "rectification of language," in speaking and listening to one another, people move closer to an ever more accurate expression of soul.

How do agency-employed therapists and social workers have time for narrative when they have a caseload of thirty to forty clients who need to be cycled every three to eight weeks? How many therapists continue such plot-less work without using their narratives to speak against such "symptom prevention through treatment design"? Such a schedule risks another of Van den Berg's (1969) neuroticizing factors: "the pressure of time." As Mook (2008) summarized it, "Experiencing the pressure of time in the present while obscuring the influence of the past and the expectations of the future could lead to stress and to direct bodily manifestations of neurotic disturbances" (p. 469). Effective psychological work takes time. Hillman (2006) wrote, "The road to beauty means for the ego to enter conditions like those of beauty" (p. 175). Those working in the field of mental health must have the time and their own experience of beauty to know how to facilitate those experiences for their clients.

If ugliness makes bodies withdraw and recede, Hillman (2006) wrote, "does this not as well suggest that what we turn toward may become beautiful?" (p. 177). In other words, the individual response to architecture can itself become a posture that *in turn* changes the architecture. Environments remain ugly because people are not conscious of them. The clients and diagnoses which clinicians judge to be outside their scope of practice may find their evaluation changing were they to turn toward and engage those people. The modality of psychotherapy matters, but the directionality of psychotherapy matters more.

Conclusion

Anti-homeless architecture is a strategy to repress aesthetic ugliness but instead represses ontological beauty. The terms in Crime Prevention through Environmental Design act like slips of the tongue, and the designs are bungled actions that, like any effective symptom, return what has been repressed. The anti-human construction of public spaces consists of the neuroticizing factors outlined by Van den Berg (1969). Therefore, anti-homeless architecture makes people sick. Public spaces have become more broadly anti-communal over time, in the interest of individual, illusory comfort. "The devastating availability of images and information of our present made us blind, unable to see and ignorant, incapable of understanding and knowing. Being no longer able to see and know, we are no longer able to design" with beauty (Fabio, 2017, p. 2). No longer the product of beautiful design, formerly communal, public spaces become controlled, private, and ugly defenses.

Psychologists are ethically obligated to respond to this reality, but observing egos are often directed inward. Hillman (2006) directed the discipline of psychology to dismantle its narcissism (another consequence of the repression of beauty) if it is to recover its aesthetic response (pp. 169–170). Psychologists are uniquely situated to educate city planners, architects, lawmakers, and the public at large about the psychological and sociological dangers of ugly design. In other words, to better facilitate the expression of archetypal beauty, psychologists must move beyond the consulting room and enter the polis. Doing so will enable practitioners to aid people most impacted by the ugliness of anti-homeless architecture to make sense of their experience within the context of larger manipulations at work around them.

References

Beck, J. (2020). *Cognitive behavioral therapy: Basics and beyond*. New York: Guilford Press.
Bryar, T. (2006). Public space and violence in young people experiencing homelessness. *Parity*, *19*(1), 90–91.
Chellew, C. (2016). Design paranoia. *Ontario Planning Journal*, *31*(5), 18–21.
Crawford, R. (2006). Health as a meaningful social practice. *Health*, *10*, 401–420.
Cushman, P. (1995). Selves, illnesses, healers, technologies, and the self in America. In *Constructing the self, constructing America: A cultural history of psychotherapy* (pp. 15–90). New York: Addison-Wesley Publishing Co.
Duke, A. (2011). 'Golden voice' Ted Williams departs drug rehab. *CNN*. Retrieved from http://www.cnn.com/2011/SHOWBIZ/celebrity.news.gossip/01/24/ted.williams.rehab/index.html
Ellis, A. (1968). Is psychoanalysis harmful? *Psychiatric Opinion*, *5*(1): 16–25.
Fabio, G. (2017). *Soul making in the places: The awareness of the archetypes in the creative process of architecture*. Paper presented at the *UIA 2017 Seoul World Architects Congress, Seoul, Republic of Korea*.
Hillman, J. (1992). *Re-visioning psychology*. New York: Harper Perennial.
Hillman, J. (2006). *City & soul* (Vol. 2, Uniform ed.) (R. J. Leaver, Ed.). Putnam, CT: Spring Publications.
Hillman, J. (2014). *The thought of the heart and the soul of the world*. Putnam, CT: Spring Publications.
Huskinson, L. (2015). James Hillman's approach to architecture and the built environment: Some conceptual complications and an attempt to resolve them. *International Journal of Jungian Studies*, *7*(2), 154–164.
Huskinson, L. (2018). *Architecture and the mimetic self: A psychoanalytic study of how buildings make and break our lives*. New York: Routledge.
Linehan, M. (2014). *DBT skills training manual* (2nd ed.). Guilford Press.
Memmott, M. (2011, January 5). Must-see video: Homeless man with a golden voice. *NPR*. Retrieved from https://www.npr.org/sections/thetwo-way/2011/01/05/132677065/must-see-video-homeless-man-with-a-golden-voice
Mook, B. (2008). J. H. Van den Berg revisited: Reflections on the changing nature of neurosis. *Janus Head*, *10*(2), 461–475.
Omidi, M. (2014, June 12). Anti-homeless spikes are just the latest in 'defensive urban architecture.' *The Guardian*. https://www.theguardian.com/cities/2014/jun/12/anti-homeless-spikes-latest-defensive-urban-architecture
Pellegrini, R. J., Queirolo, S. S., Monarrez, V. E., & Valenzuela, D. M. (1997). Political identification and perception of homelessness: Attributed causality and attitudes and public policy. *Psychological Reports*, *80*, 1139–148.
Pfeffer, R. (2006). Losing control: Regulating situational crime prevention in mass private property. *Oklahoma Law Review*, *59*(4), 759–808.
Rayman, T. (2016). Designing-in crime by designing-out the social? Situational crime prevention and the intensification of harmful subjectivities. *The British Journal of Criminology*, *56*(3), 497–514.
Romanyshyn, R. (2008). The despotic eye: An illustration of metabletic phenomenology and its implications. *Janus Head 10*(2), 505–527.
Van den Berg, J. H. (1969). *De zuilen van het Pantheon*. Nijkerk: Callenbach.

Van den Berg, J. H. (1971). Phenomenology and metabletics. *Humanitas*, *7*(3), 279–290.

Van den Berg, J. H., & Romanyshyn, R. (2008). Jan Hendrik van den Berg answers some questions. *Janus Head*, *10*(2), 377–383.

Wusinich, C., Bond, L., Nathanson, A., & Padgett, D. (2019). "If you're gonna help me, help me": Barriers to housing among unsheltered homeless adults. *Evaluation and Program Planning*, *76*.

Zdanowicz, C., & Vera, A. (2018, July 30). A homeless man handing out resumes in Silicon Valley gets more than 200 offers. *CNN*. Retrieved from https://www.cnn. com/2018/07/30/us/homeless-man-hands-out-resumes-trnd/index.html

Introduction to "Encounters with African Elephants: Transformative Gatherings"

One of the gifts of Jung's archetypal and phenomenological approach is to provide mental space for resonating with the symbolic realities of cultures very different from his own. Euvrard's chapter invites us with warm hospitality into her world, the South African landscape with its elephants and Xhosa tales. What she offers, though, is much more than an aesthetic experience. If we think of aesthetics as the physiognomic ground of our ethical imaginations, then Euvrard's chapter draws us into the Jungian imagination as an ecopsychological and multicultural reality with a strong ethical as well as aesthetic appeal.

Chapter 10

Encounters with African Elephants

Transformative Gatherings

Gwenda Euvrard

Introduction

I want to invite you to explore how a sense of our interconnected humanness might come into deepened and expanded being in our encounters with African elephants. In protected wilderness areas such as those which surround my home in the Eastern Cape of South Africa – a multitude of biomes alive with grassy plains, thorny thickets, coastal dunes, mountains and valleys – we humans can, respectfully and for a moment, open ourselves to encounters with the wild animals which inhabit the elemental indigenous landscape, never knowing what will be activated. This is not dissimilar to a psychotherapist entering each therapy session; we open ourselves to the edge of possibility and the potential that it carries. As African elephants and water are inseparable, a good place for a potential encounter may be a waterhole. Waiting at the waterhole for the enormous mammals to come and drink, douse their bodies and wallow in mud gives us time to attune ourselves to the environment: listening, feeling, seeing, being stirred, opening ourselves to the world we are in and to being surprised. Suddenly we sense a presence: for their size, elephants move amazingly quietly. A matriarchal family group emerges from the bush. Some elephants run gleefully towards the water. The herd drinks, splashes, swims, rolls, plays, all the while interacting, touching, stroking each other with their trunks. Nearby a small adolescent bachelor group recently separated from their matriarchal herd spar playfully, and an adult bull who has taken them under his wing to guide them to adulthood grazes.

I have been encountering African elephants my whole life. Every year I gift myself a solo day in the Addo Elephant National Park, a vast wilderness area in the Eastern Cape, set aside for the preservation of African elephants. It was during one such day, in a space of withdrawal and meditation, of contemplation, connection and joy that I first became aware that this chapter was being called into being. Sitting in my sturdy offroad vehicle, alone in the open veld, surrounded by grazing families of African elephants, I entered a state of reverie. To my surprise, I was transported to the imaginal International Association for Jungian Studies conference at far off Duquesne University then planned for 2020. A few months earlier, when I had been invited to think of presenting a paper, I had thought, "That would be absolutely terrifying", and simply

DOI: 10.4324/9781032694603-13

bracketed the idea. However, in my state of reverie, I found myself answering an unknown question at this conference, in response to an as yet unknown paper on the African elephant. In my transported state, my answer was borne on a deeply lived conviction of interconnectedness across time, space, worlds, people, environments, our histories-and-our-future, the ancestors and those yet to be born. So, this chapter is an attempt to explore that numinous experience of connectedness which was activated in my encounter with the African elephants in the indigenous Addo wilderness on that day, and to begin to explore the ontological questions evoked in my reverie.

I am African. Africa plants and grounds me. The crackling droughts prick my skin, while deep underground waters whisper in my veins. Thorn trees flicker light and shadows as I squint through the hot glare at distant mountains. And when the rains come, my heart lifts with the massed choir of the charging river. Yet African elephants seem to carry something which speaks to everyone, across continents, cultures and time. When diverse people hear of my interest in exploring our connection with African elephants, almost everyone, no matter where they call home, has a story or image they want to share. What psychic mysteries do our encounters with African elephants presence which activate a connection in so many people?

Elephants seem to attune us beyond time and space to a world where the seemingly unconnected *is* connected. Through many evolutionary and migratory phases, their earliest ancestors, traced back to North Africa 58 million years ago, eventually populated almost every landmass. Although most became extinct, zoologist Lyle Watson (2002) writes of modern-day people's intuitive experiences of connections with elephant ancestors in both the United States and the United Kingdom, millions of years later. In unexpected connections, using fossil, anatomical and molecular data, evolutionary palaeontologists hypothesise that the giant modern-day African elephants' closest living evolutionary descendants are marine dugongs (sea-cows) found in the Indian and Pacific Oceans and the small rabbit-like South African *dassie* (hyrax) (Shoshani, 1992a). The mystery of elephants surprises us with connections in unexpected relationships across time, as well as across now disconnected continents which, throughout Earth's history, have themselves been in the slow, continuous and ongoing process of connection, disconnection and coming back together again in different configurations (McCarthy & Rubidge, 2005).

As Jungians we understand the self as that process of being human which both calls us into connection and is simultaneously the felt connection. I have always resonated with Brooke's description of the self as a gathering of potentiality and relationships in the lived world of our psychological experiencing (whether actualised or not) as well as the resonancing of that experience of gathering (Brooke, 1991, 2009). While taking liberties in the expression of Jungian theory, as a watercolour artist I like to imagine the process of self's gathering and expression as being similar to the process of painting: broad sweeps of colour and water meet the paper so that, in an alchemical process, the painting begins to appear and come alive. This requires an intuitive, feeling and sensate attitude of openness to what is emerging. Then there is a subtle shift as, still holding the aliveness of these attitudes, as artist I invite an attitude of more rational consciousness and begin to work on the detail which completes the artwork, making it both uniquely mine and also more accessible to others. In a similar way, the realization of the gathering of deepened and broadened potentialities of self in more conscious daily living requires the active participation of the ego. Colman makes the distinction between being a self, the overall psychosomatic process of the self beyond consciousness in the elemental world with other creatures, and knowing the self, the self-reflexive process of awareness of being and having a self (2008). We could understand this as being in the presencing of connections, and the process of coming into conscious reflective resonancing of these connections.

Our patients enter therapy because they are disconnected. A young woman started therapy with me at a time when she felt cut off from every aspect of her daily lived world. Undifferentiated from her mother, she was restricted in venturing out by an ever-growing dance of obsessive-compulsive rituals. She began to weave through our psychotherapy sessions stories of her delight in her encounters with African elephants in various ways. The elephants came into presence in multiple modes of being: a bull in the threatening thrall of hormonal musth, allomothers (aunts and sisters in the matriarchal herd) assisting a vulnerable youngster struggling to get out of a waterhole, elephants grieving a loss, the constant interacting of the herd. Slowly she began to encounter her own traumas and grieve her losses, differentiate from her mother and experience a widening and deepening of her world and her connections in it. Then one day, as she was talking about the many different experiences and expressions of African elephants in the wild, she paused. With simple clarity she said: "Elephants move about interacting in world, but they also stand firm in who they are, and can look upon it." After a moment she took a deep breath, then said: "I feel alive, awake … I've tried so hard to be good, now I'm being human". On reflection, I wondered if her encounters in the gathering presence of African elephants in their many various aspects had invited a gathering of potentials outside the narrow confines of her undifferentiated state, allowing her slowly to became conscious of a widened, deepened and more centred self. As these potentials were slowly differentiated in her interactions in her daily world, it seemed she was increasingly able to maintain a sense of balance in her various relationships, with a more reflective sense of herself which was at the same time both more centred and spacious.

As a keystone species, African elephants in the wilderness co-exist and are interconnected with other creatures and with the elemental landscape in such a way that their presence opens up, expands and activates that gathering of relationships which is the ecosystem. The African elephants' daily activities of feeding, drinking, dousing themselves and moving in the wilderness open up paths and waterholes and ensure an ongoing availability of food and water for all creatures, while pruning and replenishing the environment, and maintaining the delicate balance between destruction and construction which is pivotal to a balanced ecosystem (Figures 10.1–10.3).

Figure 10.1 Matriarchal family group

Figure 10.2 Mourning elephants turning the bones of a departed family member

Figure 10.3 Baby and mother

Due to their intelligence and longevity, African elephants pass on from generation to generation the knowledge of where to find essentials and how to access them throughout the seasons: food, water and mineral salts (Redmond, 1992). As they move between these vital resources they compact the soil, linking feeding areas to waterholes and rivers, and creating corridors or highways which other wild creatures also use (Thompson, 2019). Water is a scarce resource in many parts of Africa. Not only do elephant trails lead to available water, they also create runoff which enlarges the water supply. And when water is unavailable, these "water diviners of the African savanna" (Fynn & O'Connor, 2019, p. 103) provide water for themselves and other species by digging wells to over a metre deep down to underground streams in dry riverbeds. In addition, "most waterholes in a wild ecosystem were engineered by elephant action over millennia" (Thompson, 2019, p. 111). As African elephants excavate mineral-rich soil to eat salt, they create depressions which fill with rainwater, providing wallowing holes for many creatures, which ultimately become larger waterholes. And as elephants plaster their bodies with mud (essential to cooling, as they have no sweat glands), dams continue to increase in size.

Being megaherbivores, the African elephant's long survival is attributed in part to its adaptability in browsing and grazing on a wide variety of plants. In the process they break off various parts of the vegetation: leaves, fruit, seed pods, roots, bulbs, twigs, branches, sometimes uprooting whole trees in the process. Elephant "pruning" modifies and shapes the environment: keeping vegetation at browse level for all leaf eaters, ensuring the regenerative growth of plants, and clearing areas of thicket, thereby converting them into grassland habitats for other species (Shoshani, 1992b; Thompson, 2019).

Elephant dung is a wonderful example of how this keystone species brings into being the interconnected cosmos: the moist, mineral-rich dung provides water for insects, while largely undigested particles in the dung provide food for birds and other creatures. Many varieties of seed are germinated and distributed in the dung, which provides a womb for the eggs of dung beetles and migrant butterflies, while the nourishment of the dung maintains the biodiversity of the soil (Shoshani, 1992b; Thompson, 2019).

"Co-existence has always been at the core of ecological webs" (Henley, 2019, p. 95). African elephants play such a pivotal role in structuring, modifying and maintaining the delicate balancing and diversity of the dynamic wild ecosystem that Shoshani (1992b) suggests they can be considered a "*super-keystone* species" (p. 229). In contrast, we humans are not a keystone species. Instead, our greed and our detachment from other creatures and the from the elemental landscape is not only contributing to environmental destruction and the extinction of various species but also impacting on our isolation from our interconnected humanness. Abram (2010) and McCallum (2005) both call attention to how our disconnection from our wild origins affects not only other creatures and the elemental environment, but our human being too. "When we speak of the human animal's spontaneous interchange with the animate landscape, we acknowledge a felt relation to the mysterious that was active long before any formal or priestly religion" (Abram, 2010, p. 277). In opening ourselves to encountering a deepened and expanded connection with the elemental earth and other creatures, we open ourselves to the attunement and animation of our interconnected wild being. "[T]o enter into the wild places of the Earth is to enter into the wild places of the human psyche at the same time – it is both a reaching out and a homecoming" (McCallum, 2005, p. 125).

McCallum (2019) suggests that, in addition to their pivotal role as a keystone species in their ecosystem, African elephants are an indicator species to our human being, "large grey mirrors of the fate of all other wild creatures … and [the] crisis of human character" (2019, p. 17). An aspect of the mystery of African elephants is that, for many of us, our encounters with these sentient giants open up and presence the psychic space of interconnectedness which reaches across space and time, from far-off ancestors to the depths of human intimacy, an interconnectedness of all creatures, plants and the elemental world. This experience of self is exactly the understanding that Africans, growing up in the world of elephants through the ages, have developed. The Nguni AmaXhosa people who live in the Eastern Cape of South Africa call this *ubuntu* – the experience of self and what it means to be human, our engagement in a spiritual and moral kinship and interconnection of relationships across time.

The Nguni understanding of personhood was brought to a more universal consciousness by Archbishop Desmond Tutu in the 1990s, at the time of the liberation of South Africa from the apartheid regime, which enforced disconnection between people, and during the subsequent Truth and Reconciliation Commission's attempts to find a connecting way forward through restorative justice (Tutu, 1999). This new consciousness of *ubuntu* opened up vigorous explorations and debates in public, political, theological and academic spheres. While disconnection, exclusion and dehumanization by the dominant Western colonial ideology had previously typified the experiences of black South Africans, *ubuntu* offered an opportunity for an indigenous reconsideration, within an African moral understanding, of the complex lived experiences of what it means to be human (Peterson, 2019).

An *ubuntu* attitude understands the presencing of humanness through participation in the cosmology of interconnected relationships with ancestors, other humans, the elemental earth and other creatures. Humanity is achieved through active involvement in these relationships. *Ubuntu*

> speaks of the very essence of being human. When we want to give high praise to someone we say " *Yu, unobuntu*"; hey, so-and-so has *ubuntu*. Then you are generous, you are hospitable, you are friendly and caring and compassionate. ... It is to say, "My humanity is caught up, is inextricably bound up, in yours". We belong in a bundle of life.
>
> (Tutu, 1999, p. 31)

Ubuntu presences a gathering of interconnection including but also beyond the interpersonal, "a range of related relations between humans and nature that are fundamental in Nguni cosmology" (Peterson, 2019, p. 74). In this gathering, the potentialities for "personhood, identity and morality ... are achieved in relation to and through social interaction based on ethical conduct with others especially in conditions that are marked by imbalances in social and personal power" (Peterson, 2019, p. 75). Thus, we might understand that our humanness is constantly given the opportunity to come into being and actively express itself through the process of reciprocity, as if the ideal interconnected cosmos was already in existence. Our encounters with African elephants bring us into an experience of a relational and keystone cosmology, which might similarly call us to participate actively in bringing our humanness into being in a more interconnected ethical *ubuntu* consciousness with the elemental earth, other creatures, and in our human relationships. We can understand this process of coming into consciousness of these interconnections, differentiated and resonant, as describing the experience and integration of the self. Hence its numinosity. At its heart traditional *ubuntu* consciousness provides a spiritual and ethical calling to live the depth and breadth of one's humanity within the moral order of the interconnected environment and pastoral economic Nguni homestead (collections of family homes with animals, crops, the elemental environment and ever-present ancestors).

However, Peterson notes that in current South African black intellectual thinking and artistic expression, *ubuntu* is facing "a crisis of legitimacy – between its intention and realization" (2019, p. 91). The challenge is finding alternate ways for understanding and expressing individuality (rather than Western individualism) while identifying with and actively living *ubuntu* kinship, community and culture. Ultimately however, for Peterson, *ubuntu* ontologically gathers "the needs and responsibilities of personal and communal imperatives" and the "contingent achievement of reciprocity, compassion and humanness [which] are at the centre of the possible conferment of personhood" (2019, p. 92). Ogude notes that *ubuntu's* modern understanding of community is "a network of mutuality" (2019, p. 5) which transcends the specificity of the everyday cultural context and points to the potentiality of its global relevance, enabling engagement by underscoring our interdependence in creating a world in which we can all potentially experience agency and live a deepened and expanded humanity.

Brooke proposes that *ubuntu* consciousness awakens us to a reimagining of individuation within a network of facilitating social relationships and calls up an animating ethical dimension to this process (2008, 2019). *Ubuntu*

> reaches outwards, towards the stranger and the Other, to the living and even the dead, to our animal cousins, and to the wider earth and sky. From infantile dependency to mature spirituality our expanding community is the psychological home in which we become fully persons.
>
> (Brooke, 2019, p. 150)

Ubuntu constantly activates this gathering and calls us to action. Since coming into international consciousness, the most often cited Nguni proverb is: *umntu, ngumuntu, ngabantu* ("a person is a person through other persons" or "I am because you are, we are because you are"). The fullness of Nguni cosmology (expressed here as "people") both presences the ambit of relationships in which our humanness can come into expression and provides the ongoing ethical challenge for our conduct (Peterson, 2019). "What persons are and what persons should become – the ontological and the ethical – are mutually implied" (Brooke, 2019, p. 149). In this context, Brooke reframes an understanding of the central process of individuation, the withdrawal of projections, as a process that listens to what presences and, with awakened, expanded and deepened connection, reflectively responds. In this way "psychological life becomes more deeply embodied, spacious, and differentiated" (Brooke, 2019, p. 153).

Many African folktales carry the collective mystery of our encounters with elephants. African orature (oral literature, including folktales) has traditionally formed part of "the individual's, homestead's, and clan's sensual and reflective interactions and deliberations" (Peterson, 2019, p. 77), conveying the moral wisdom of *ubuntu* cosmology. Thus, the carrier of *iintsomi* (isiXhosa folk tales) is a *makhulu*, a grandmother in the homestead, because she has lived a long life, so carries and passes on the connection between the ancestors and the living. The *iintsomi* she tells bring into presence and activate the depth and breadth of what it means to be human in the interconnected Nguni world. As my interest in IsiXhosa *iintsimi* deepened, I was privileged to meet isiXhosa writer and literary scholar Ncedile Saule. We grew up on different sides of the Eastern Cape Winterberg mountains during the apartheid era, a political and social structure designed to prevent connection. Maybe it was the great mountains that held and connected us: our first meeting was a meeting of souls. The experiences and stories we shared brought us to laughter and left us so deeply touched that we were both in tears. I am honoured by his sharing with me the richness of the isiXhosa *iintsomi* told to him as a child by the carrier of this aspect of isiXhosa cosmology in his family, *Makhulu Tyebileyo*, "the fat grandmother", his great aunt.

Here is one Nguni isiXhosa folktale or *intsomi* (*intsomi* singular/*iintsomi* plural).

Umfazi Othile (a certain woman) sets off to collect firewood, leaving her two beautiful younger children in the care of *Umkhuluwa* (an older brother). Various animals approach and, seeing the children, remark on their beauty and wonder whose children they are. The children become afraid and call for their mother, "Mama, Mama, *uphi, uphi?* Where are you? Where are you?" An enormous African elephant emerges from the bush, scoops the children up in its trunk, and swallows them. *Umfazi Othile* arrives home carrying a large bundle of firewood on her head. On hearing her children's fate, she immediately makes preparations to look for Elephant. She cooks a big pot of *ipapa* (porridge), adds *amasi* (sour milk), puts the pot on her head, picks up her knife and sets off. The animals tell her to follow the tracks to the beautiful place with white stones under the tall trees in the forest, where she encounters the biggest elephant she had ever seen. She demands that her children be returned to her, but she too is swallowed. *Umfazi Othile* descends into the darkness deep in Elephant's belly, where she finds a land of mountains, forests, rivers, cattle, goats, sheep and dogs, as well as her children, and many, many people who had disappeared a long time ago. *Umfazi Othile* gives her children food. But everyone is hungry. *Umfazi Othile* is scornful that they have not eaten the meat that surrounds them in Elephant's belly. She hacks off a piece of Elephant meat, makes a fire and begins to roast it. Everyone joins in gathering meat and feasting. Elephant's groans can be heard from far away until finally Elephant dies. *Umfazi Othile* carves a door between the giant ribs, light streams in, and everyone walks out, gifting *Umfazi Othile* cattle, sheep and goats.

Our *intsomi* carries a deep layering of *ubuntu* redemption. It is a story about the gathering of potential and bringing that gathering into a more reflexive resonance in daily life. Central to the story is the African elephant which, when it withdraws to the numinous place with the tall trees and the white stones, provides a liminal place in which transformation can happen. In her storytelling, *Makhulu Tyebileyo* never used the isiXhosa word for elephant, *indlovu*, but spoke instead of *Bade-uBade*, the Very Huge One, the presence. And in the gathering of ancestors, animals, land, mountains, rivers and people, Elephant, *Bade-uBade* brings into presence the fullness of the Nguni world itself.[1] This liminal world is pregnant with possibility. However, just as the realisation of a deepened and expanded expression of the self requires the active participation of the ego, the realisation of our humanness in *ubuntu* cosmology is achieved through coming into resonant awareness of our interconnected being, and the calling for our active participation in realizing this ideal.

A certain woman goes about the rhythm of her daily work in an unreflective way, making practical provision for her home and family. She is unaware that the beauty of her two younger children will activate the entrancement of the animals, which will become so overwhelming that they will be abducted into darkness. Here they, and those who have gone before, live in an unconscious and undifferentiated state in the numinosity of the interconnected *ubuntu* world. As noted earlier, being a self can be overwhelming, thus metabolizing the experience of self, knowing the self, is also important (Colman, 2008). The resilient woman makes preparation and sets out to find her children.[2] But she too must encounter the darkness where the interconnected Nguni world can be revealed and where she can activate the work which will bring about the reflexivity and reciprocity of *ubuntu* redemption. So the people's hunger calls her enterprise and generosity into being, even though she chides them for their passivity. Awakened, the people feed on the meat in Elephant's belly. In Nguni consciousness, it is not the heart, but the *umbilini*, the gut, where emotion is stirred and experienced. Enlivened and enlightened, the people are freed to take into daily life the new, enriched *ubuntu* community which was brought to consciousness by the actions of an ordinary woman. She will earn the high praise, "*Yu, unobuntu*": you live the essence of being human! And she in turn is more reflective and enriched with gifts, in a world where cattle are the measure of wealth. Her ordinariness calls us too to take up the task as our own.

For one of my long-term patients who had increasingly experienced an opening of the world and her authentic engagement in it, the African elephant provided the container for her expression of this connection and simultaneously ushered in the termination phase of her therapy. She brought the following dream to a session:

> I dreamt I made a gift for you, a ceramic pot in the shape of an elephant. I wanted to write a letter to put in the pot, but in the end I didn't need to write a long letter. I simply wrote

thank you "on a card and placed it in the elephant pot". The patient paused, then exclaimed: "*Elephants are everything, as opposed to one thing!*" She mused: *"they are almost prehistoric, huge, strong and unwavering, but can be flexible, play and be vulnerable, and they know what's needed to take care of themselves"*.

And full circle. As I steeped myself in working on this chapter, knowing that the threads which were gathering intuitively seemed to make sense, but grappling with how to express the connections which were emerging, I realised that I was engaging with the very process that I was writing about. In my numinous experience with the keystone African elephants in the Addo wilderness, a gathering of worlds, relationships, connections and potentials was brought into presence and called this chapter into being. In that moment I knew my interconnectedness. But there was more. Writing the chapter asked of me that I reflect on and actively engage with the meaning of the experience. I too needed to be awakened from the darkness of my undifferentiated state of numinosity, feed on the rich meat in the belly of the elephant, engage in the enterprise of grappling with words and ideas, metabolize the experience and find a renewed light and enterprise. The telos of that numinous encounter invited me into a deepened and broadened community, knowing myself in a new way while finding my voice as a passionate writer among respected academic peers, opening an enriched interconnectedness and my active participation in it.

Acknowledgements

Thanks to Professor Ncedile Saule, Department of African Language Studies, Rhodes University, isiXhosa novelist and writer.

Notes

1 This world is described by many mystics and echoed in the words of Origen of Alexander in *Leviticum Homiliae* V2, quoted by Jung:

> Seek these sacrifices within thyself, and thou wilt find them within thine own soul. Understand that thou hast within thyself flocks of cattle ... flocks of sheep and flocks of goats ... Marvel not if we say that these are within thee, but understand that thou thyself art even another world, thou hast within thee the sun and the moon, and also the stars.
>
> (Jung, CW 9i par. 624)

2 Oral literature offers as many variations of a story as there are grandmothers to tell them. In another version of this *intsomi*, *Umkhuluwa* (the older brother) temporarily leaves the children who have been placed in his care, to go and look for *iimpuku* (rats) and gets back to find the children missing. When *Umfazi Othile* returns, she and *Umkhuluwa* set off together to look for the children. On encountering the very large elephant, *Umfazi Othile* demands her children be returned to her, but she too is swallowed and finds herself in the world with those who have disappeared long ago, including her parents and the chief. He assures her that, if they wait, her son will rescue them all. *Umkhuluwa* runs away from Elephant. When he grows up, he is told by the animals where he will find Elephant, and sets off with his knife.

References

Abram, D. (2010). *Becoming animal*. New York: Vintage Books.

Brooke, R. (1991). *Jung and phenomenology*. London: Routledge.

Brooke, R. (2009). The self, the psyche and the world: A phenomenological interpretation. *Journal of Analytical Psychology, 54*, 601–618.

Brooke, R. (2008). Ubuntu and the individuation process: Towards a multicultural analytical psychology. *Psychological Perspectives, 51*, 36–53.

Brooke, R. (2019). Jung's fantasies of Africa and Africa's healing of analytical psychology. *International Journal of Jungian Studies, 11*, 140–159.

Colman, W. (2008). On being, knowing and having a self. *Journal of Analytical Psychology, 53*, 351–366.

Fynn, R., & O'Connor, T. (2019). Conserving elephants and biodiversity in Africa's savannas. In D. Pinnock & C. Bell (Eds.), *The last elephants*. Cape Town: Struik Nature.

Henley, M. (2019) Big trees, big elephants and big thinking. In D. Pinnock & C. Bell (Eds.), *The last elephants*. Struik Nature: Cape Town.

Jung, C. G. (1959). The archetypes of the collective unconscious. *Collected Works, 9i*. H. Read, M. Fordham, G. Adler (Eds.). Trans. R. F. C. Hull. Routledge and Kegan Paul: London.

McCallum, I. (2005). *Ecological intelligence: Rediscovering ourselves in nature*. Colorado: Fulcrum.

McCallum, I. (2019). Elephants: A human-animal crisis. In D. Pinnock & C. Bell (Eds.), *The last elephants*. Struik Nature: Cape Town.

McCarthy, T., & Rubidge, B. (2005). *The story of earth & life*. Struik Nature: Cape Town.

Ogude, J. (2019). Introduction. In J. Ogude (Ed.), *Ubuntu and the reconstitution of community*. Bloomington: Indiana University Press.

Peterson, B. (2019). The art of personhood: Kinship and its social challenges. In J. Ogude (Ed.), *Ubuntu and the reconstitution of community*. Bloomington: Indiana University Press.

Redmond, I. (1992). Erosion by elephants. In J. Shoshani (Ed.), *Elephants*. Checkmark Books: New York.

Shoshani, J. (1992a). The elephant's relatives. In J. Shoshani (Ed.), *Elephants*. Checkmark Books: New York.

Shoshani, J. (1992b). Why save elephants? In J. Shoshani (Ed.), *Elephants*. Checkmark Books: New York.

Thompson, G. (2019). Constant gardeners of the wild. In D. Pinnock & C. Bell (Eds.), *The last elephants*. Struik Nature: Cape Town.

Tutu, D. (1999). *No future without forgiveness*. Random House: New York.

Watson, L. (2002). *Elephantoms: Tracking the elephant*. Penguin: London.

Introduction to "Anatomy of a Vision: A Psychological Approach to the Papua New Guinea UFO Sightings, June 26–27, 1959"

David J. Halperin applies hermeneutic guidelines from Jung's essay on flying saucers to analyze in detail the famous Boianai UFO sighting in 1959, exploring the imaginal space between what was looked at astronomically and what was seen experientially. Readers will enjoy his chapter for its historical, narrative detail as well as for his integration of Jungian archetypal theory with sociological and religious analysis. Perhaps more than any other chapter in this volume, Halperin's essay illustrates the power and epistemological subtlety of Jung's thinking with regard to phenomena that are at the same time experientially real, religious, psychological, and embedded in contexts reaching across disciplines.

Chapter 11

Anatomy of a Vision
A Psychological Approach to the Papua New Guinea UFO Sightings, June 26–27, 1959

David J. Halperin

Introduction

On Friday and Saturday nights, June 26 and 27, 1959, at Boianai on the coast of Papua New Guinea, a young Anglican priest named William Booth Gill and twenty-five of his Papuan parishioners experienced a series of what would later come to be called "close encounters of the third kind." Mysterious disks came from the sky, hovered low above the Boianai mission, seemed on the verge of landing. At one point they exchanged signals with the witnesses. The pilots of one disk emerged and walked about its surface, like sailors on the deck of their ship. They were not, however, the spindly-limbed aliens with the light-bulb shaped heads and enormous oval eyes that we've come to expect of UFO beings. Instead they seemed in all respects like male humans, except for one detail: their bodies were self-luminous. For two nights they visited Boianai. Then they disappeared, never to be seen again (Clark, 2018; Hynek, 1972, pp. 145–150, 241–242; Klass, 1974, pp. 234–244; Kottmeyer, 1995; Menzel, 1972, pp. 146–153).

The mystery of the Boianai UFOs has in one sense been solved. In another sense, it remains profoundly baffling. We know pretty clearly what Father Gill and his followers were looking at those two nights: bright stars and planets—specifically, the planets Jupiter and Saturn, the stars Spica and Rigel Kentaurus—which gave the illusion of approaching the witnesses and departing from them as clouds dispersed or thickened (Kottmeyer, 2007, 2017). But if that was what they were looking at, it wasn't what they saw. The heavenly bodies triggered in them a collective vision that has to be understood as coming from within the witnesses, bearers of meaning—as I will argue, religious meaning—for them. This is the true UFO mystery, located not in the sky but in the soul; and it's at least thinkable that Jungian psychology gives us the tools with which to explore it.

Nineteen-fifty-nine, the year of the Boianai sightings, was also the year that saw the appearance in English translation of the last book Carl Jung would publish before his death. It had come out in Switzerland the year before under

DOI: 10.4324/9781032694603-14

the title *Ein Moderner Mythus von Dingen, die am Himmel gesehen werden*. The American edition made more explicit what these "things" were: *Flying Saucers: A Modern Myth of Things Seen in the Skies* (Jung, 1958/59).

By calling "flying saucers" a myth, of course, the last thing Jung intended was to disparage them. "Myth," for Jung, was not falsehood but the profoundest truth of all, a sort of collective dream of the entire species. As myth, UFOs had irrupted into the anxiety-ridden malaise of the post-war world, conveying hope and healing with their very shape. Aerodynamically, flying disks might not make much sense. But psychologically, these sky-borne visions could be understood as *mandalas*, modern-dress specimens of the age-old

> *symbol of order*, which organizes and encloses the psychic totality … impressive manifestations of totality whose simple, round form portrays the archetype of the self, which we know from experience plays the chief role in uniting apparently irreconcilable opposites and is therefore best suited to compensate the split-mindedness of our age.

As images, they're profoundly religious; for is not God Himself "a circle whose centre is everywhere and the circumference nowhere" (Jung, 1958/59, paras. 619–622)?

Was it conceivable that UFOs were also physical objects, whether extraterrestrial visitors or something else beyond our ability to grasp? In his various pronouncements, Jung seemed uncertain. The aviator Charles Lindbergh visited him in July of that same year, 1959, and was astonished to find Jung insisting the UFOs were physically, materially real; Lindbergh's objections were dismissed with a variant of Hamlet's more-things-in-heaven-and-earth-Horatio-than-dreamt-of-in-your-philosophy (Bair, 2003, pp. 572–573; Berg, 1998, pp. 511–512; Miller, 2009, pp. 244–246). But in the final chapter of his *Flying Saucers* book, entitled "Ufos Considered in a Non-Psychological Light," Jung admitted his own confusion. Surely UFOs were manifestations of the human psyche; their appearance in dreams and art, their parallels in religious and mythological tradition, guaranteed that. How was it, then, that they'd been photographed? That they appeared on radar screens? "It boils down to nothing less than this: that either psychic projections throw back a radar echo, or else the appearance of real objects affords an opportunity for mythological projections" (Jung, 1958/59, para. 782).

I am not aware that Jung ever commented on the Boianai sightings. If he had, he would surely have noted the presence in the Papuan sky not only of the mandala but of another key archetype: the quaternity, like the mandala a symbol of wholeness, the Four of which one is somehow different from the other three. Jung (1958/59, para. 738) invokes in this connection the vision described in the first chapter of the Book of Ezekiel, of the four "living creatures" with three animal faces and one human face. (Or, in ancient rabbinic expositions of

Ezekiel's vision of which Jung had no knowledge, three faces that are divine and one, the ox, that is demonic; Halperin, 1988, pp. 189–193.) "The heavens were opened," Ezekiel says at the beginning of his account of the vision, "and I saw visions of God." That is precisely what happened at Papua New Guinea, only in a technological guise suited for the mid-twentieth century.

I

The primary source for Gill's experience is a report he prepared for the Victorian Flying Saucer Research Society (VFSRS) on July 14, 1959, about two and a half weeks after the event. This was incorporated in a longer document submitted on November 25 by the VFSRS to Australian prime minister Robert Menzies, with the recommendation that the Australian government take UFO incidents seriously and investigate them (*Victorian Flying Saucer Research Society Report 1959*).[1]

Gill is described in this document as

> Aged 31 years. Married with two children. Educated Trinity Grammar School, Melbourne, and St. Francis College, Brisbane. Ordained priest of the Anglican Church. Licentiate in Theology. A qualified teacher, he completed over eight years of service as a missionary in New Guinea.

Gill's report opens with a first-person account of a UFO sighting by Stephen Gill Moi, a Papuan teacher at the Boianai mission school, in the small hours of the morning of Sunday, June 21. It seems in retrospect like a prelude to the more dramatic events of the following weekend. Moi told of having seen "a bright light (white) silently coming out of the sky from a point about a quarter of a mile out to sea," then descending to a height of about 300 feet. Its light dimming, it took on the shape of an inverted saucer. It tilted backwards so Moi could see its base, where he observed four black spots—the first of the foursomes (quaternities) that are a recurrent feature of the Boianai UFOs. Then it rose into the clouds and disappeared. This also is a recurrent feature, a clue to the identification of the physical stimulus for the sightings as heavenly bodies.

That was Sunday. On Tuesday, Moi related his experience to Gill, who prepared to forward it that Friday to his colleague David Durie. In his letter to Durie, which he signed "Doubting William," Gill pronounced himself "inclined to believe that probably many UFO's are … electric phenomena," or possibly effects of nuclear explosions. "That Stephen should actually make out a saucer could be the work of the unconscious mind as it is very likely that at some time he has seen illustrations of some kind in a magazine." Before he had his own experience, Gill could intuit the presence of unconscious factors, which would afterward seem to him inadequate to account for what he saw or thought he saw in the sky. He was "Doubting William"; which, to anyone familiar with the

Gospel story to which this was an allusion (John 20: 24–29), was a clear sign that he expected soon to be relieved of his doubts.

Which, not many hours later, was precisely what happened.

The report here incorporates a series of notes from the evening of Friday the 26th, which give every sign of being jottings made on the spot.

> 6.45 Sighted bright white light from front direction N.W. 6.50 Call Stephen and Eric—Langford. 6.52 Stephen arrives. Confirms. Not star like other night. Coming closer, not so bright. Coming down 500 ft?, orange?, deep yellow? 6.55 Send Eric to call people. One object on top, move—man? Now three men—moving, glowing, doing something on deck. Gone.

Two of the "men" reappear at 7:00, are "gone again" four minutes later. At 7:10 they're back—this time four of them. Then: "Thin elct. Blue spot light. Men gone, spot light still there." The first two men reappear. But at 7:20, "Spot light off, men go. UFO goes through cloud."

By this time thirty-eight people had gathered and were brought by Gill into a "well-lighted room." In separate corners of the room, Gill, Stephen Gill Moi, and a third man named Ananias Rarata set about sketching what they thought they'd seen. The sketches, done independently, showed a disk with a broad dome, four human-like figures emerging from the top, and four legs—equivalent to the "spots" seen by Moi?—jutting out from the bottom.

> All observers were briefly addressed by the reporter [Gill] and given the opportunity of signing a paper stating that a UFO as described in the sketches was seen by them. ... 27 observers of a total of 38 voluntarily signed.

The names of the signatories, beginning with Gill and including six teachers and two medical assistants, are given later in the report. They number only twenty-five, and I can't explain the discrepancy. The number is impressive, but leaves me wondering: why weren't the other eleven (or thirteen) out of the thirty-eight willing to sign? May we assume that, despite their best efforts, they weren't able to see what the majority saw?

By 8:30 the skies had cleared and the UFOs were back. (As might be expected, if the physical stimuli for the vision were stars and planets.) First the original one—"Not so big, but seemed nearer than before"—then a second, then a third, then a fourth. "8.50 Big one stationary and larger—the original (?) Others coming and going through clouds. ... All UFO's very clear—satellites? 'Mother' ship still large, clear, stationary."

The three "satellites" are gone by 9:05, but the "Mother" intermittently disappears and reappears for the next hour and a half. By 10:50, it's "Very overcast, no sign of UFO," and "Heavy rain" soon begins to fall. The sighting is over.

II

Only to be followed by a still more dramatic event the following evening (Saturday, June 27).

> Large U.F.O. first sighted by Annie Laurie at 6 p.m. in apparently same position as last night (26/6/59) only seemed a little smaller when W.B.G. saw it at 6.02 p.m. I called Ananias and several others and we stood in the open to watch.
>
> Although the sun had set it was quite light for the following 15 minutes. We watched figures appear on top—four of them—no doubt that they are human. Possibly the same object that I took to be the "Mother" ship last night. Two smaller U.F.O.'s were seen at the same time, stationary. One above the hills west another overhead. On the large one two of the figures seemed to be doing something near the centre of the deck—were occasionally bending over and raising their arms as though adjusting or "setting up" something (not visible). One figure seemed to be standing looking down at us (a group of about a dozen). I stretched my arm above my head and waved to our surprise the figure did the same. Ananias waved both arms over his head and then the two outside figures did the same. Ananias and self began waving our arms and all four now seemed to wave back. There seemed to be no doubt that our movements were answered. All mission boys made audible gasps (of either joy or surprise perhaps both).
>
> As dark was beginning to close in, I sent Eric Kodawara for a torch [flashlight] and directed a series of long dashes toward the U.F.O. After a minute or two of this, the U.F.O. apparently acknowledged by making several wavering motions back and forth. Waving by us was repeated and this followed by more flashes of torch, then the U.F.O. began slowly to become bigger, apparently coming in our direction. It ceased after perhaps half a minute and came in no further. After a further two or three minutes the figures apparently lost interest in us for they disappeared "below" deck. At 6.25 p.m. two figures reappeared to carry on with whatever they were doing before the interruption (?). The blue spot light came on for a few seconds twice in succession.
>
> The two other U.F.O's remained stationary and high up—higher than last night (?)—smaller than last night.
>
> 6.30 p.m. I went to dinner.

To UFO skeptic Philip Klass, these last four words gave the lie to Gill's whole story. How was it possible, Klass demanded (1974, pp. 240–244), that someone on the verge of an earth-shattering event—the first ever communication with extraterrestrial visitors—could interrupt the historic occasion to go eat dinner? What were those "mysterious hunger pangs" that could take precedence over the thrilling events outdoors? Wasn't it evident from this that Gill was making the whole thing up, presumably to please an ecclesiastical superior with a known interest in UFOs?

It does seem odd. Odder still, that at 7:00, dinner presumably finished, Gill found the "No. 1 U.F.O. still present but appeared somewhat smaller," whereupon "observers go to church for Evensong." Forty-five minutes later, "Evensong over," they found the sky overcast and the UFOs gone. Again, how bizarre a set of priorities! On this evening of all evenings, wouldn't it have been worthwhile and forgivable for Gill and his parishioners to skip church and stay outdoors, where the action was happening?

Unless their UFO encounter was in its essence a religious vision, and the impulse, first to eat and then to worship, was not a distraction but an inextricable part of it.

And [Abraham] lifted up his eyes and looked, and lo, three men stood by him: and when he saw them, he ran to meet them from the tent door, and bowed himself toward the ground, and said, My Lord, if now I have found favour in thy sight, pass not away, I pray thee, from thy servant ... and I will fetch a morsel of bread, and comfort ye your hearts ... And Abraham ran unto the herd ... and he took butter, and milk, and the calf which he had dressed, and set it before them; and he stood by them under the tree, and they did eat.

(Genesis 18: 1–8)

No doubt that they are human, Gill said in his report. Years afterward, recalling the event, he repeated this judgment: "The figures inside looked perfectly human. In fact, I thought they *were* human, that if we got them to land we would find the pilots to be ordinary earthmen in military uniforms and we would have dinner with them" (Clark, 2018, p. 535). Yet "ordinary earthmen" don't "glow," as the beings aboard the UFO did; and on another occasion Gill recalled that "I thought they were angels" (Bates, 2004, p. 221).[2] Similarly, Abraham's encounter with the three "men" (as they're called throughout Genesis chapter 18) is introduced: "And the LORD appeared to him ... [as] he sat in the tent door in the heat of the day." The paradox, that the visitors were human but also more than human, must be allowed to stand.

Gill's flashlight signals were an invitation, like Abraham's, for those superhuman humans to join him and his followers for a meal that would have been a communion. For a time, it looked as though they would accept. "The U.F.O. began slowly to become bigger, apparently coming in our direction." But then "it ceased ... and came on no further"—being in reality, after all, the planet Jupiter, millions of miles distant. Gill (and the Papuans with him? the point is unclear) must dine alone.

III

The real UFO mystery: not the physical identity of the objects in the sky over Boianai—that seems clear enough—but the psychic alchemy by which these heavenly bodies, which all the witnesses must have seen hundreds or thousands of times before, became transformed on those few June nights into something extraordinary and itself potentially transformative.

That such things happen, we well know. I give multiple examples in Halperin (2020), of which the best known is perhaps the "Miracle of the Sun" at Fátima, Portugal, on October 13, 1917. On that day, many thousands of men and women—not a mere twenty-five as at Boianai—watched the sun do things it couldn't possibly have done. It danced in the sky; it changed colors; it appeared to some as "a metallic disk as if of silver"—a UFO-mandala if there ever was one—and then it fell to earth.

Why at Boianai? Why in June 1959? The circumstances of the sighting offer a few clues. "I was sent to Boianai to sort things out," Gill would explain years later, "because there were certain problems caused by a growing anti-European feeling." (Papua New Guinea was then a "territory" governed by Australia; it wouldn't get its independence for another sixteen years.) "They didn't want a European there at all, really, and they wanted me least of all because I was a stranger to the district. ... We had some real difficulties" (Clark, 2018, p. 535).

In these circumstances, the mandala—that "impressive manifestation of totality," unifier of "apparently irreconcilable opposites"—was precisely what was needed. And it came. It came in the form of a quaternity of mandalas: three "satellites" plus one "Mother" (gathering to Her all Her children, European and Papuan alike?), each with four "spots" on the bottom that metamorphosed into four legs. It came bearing four "men" who were vastly more than men. It came—but it wasn't quite enough. Whatever those "difficulties" were that Gill spoke of, they must have proven intractable. In September 1959, three months after his UFO experience, he left Boianai (Clark, 2018, p. 534).

Yet on the nights of June 26 and 27, Gill and the Papuans were bound together by a shared experience of the numinous, which they must have constructed together through overt and subtle communication even while it was happening. *In that act of construction was their most profound communion, which all must on some level have longed for.* Gill brought to the joint project his awareness of the Western UFO myth as it was known in 1959, twelve years after "flying saucers" first irrupted into the Western consciousness. But the Papuans also had their contributions to make, and if I'm not mistaken theirs outweighed his.

A belief widespread in the Papuan Highlands held the sky to be inhabited by humanlike ghosts or spirits who sometimes take full human form and descend to earth (Gammage, 1998, p. 1). This was the land of the cargo cults, religious movements aimed at manipulating the ancestral sky beings into disgorging plentiful "cargo" for their children on earth, as the Japanese and Americans did for their soldiers during World War II (Lawrence, 1964; Trompf, 1990, 2003; Worsley, 1968). In 1981, twenty-two years after the shared experience at Boianai, a Papuan university student who "was trying to be very respectful of the traditions of his people" told his Australian professor how he had once seen "the heavens open and a group of angels in white clothing high in the sky. I saw it with my own eyes" (Trompf, 1991, pp. 123–126).

Yes. So did William Booth Gill, Stephen Gill Moi, and some two dozen others. But they saw it not with the eyes but with the mind, using universal unconscious patterns to shape what they'd acquired from their varied cultural heritages and to turn that into divine vision. What Ezekiel said might be said by them: "The heavens were opened, and I saw visions of God." In their experience, as filtered through Gill's narrative and interpreted in the light of Jung's psychology, we get some inkling of how such things might come to be.

Notes

1 I am indebted to Martin S. Kottmeyer for providing me with a copy of this vital document.
2 Statement attributed to Gill, not by name, but by clear allusion.

References

Bair, D. (2003). *Jung: A biography*. Little, Brown.
Bates, G. (2004). *Alien intrusion: UFOs and the evolution connection*. Master Books.
Berg, A. S. (1998). *Lindbergh*. Putnam.
Clark, J. (2018). Gill CE3. *The UFO Encyclopedia: The phenomenon from the beginning* (3rd ed.), Vol. 1, pp. 533–536. Omnigraphics.
Gammage, B. (1998). *The sky travellers: Journeys in New Guinea 1938-39*. Miegunyah Press of Melbourne University Press.
Halperin, D. J. (1988). *The faces of the chariot: Early Jewish responses to Ezekiel's vision*. J. C. B. Mohr (Paul Siebeck).
Halperin, D. J. (2020). *Intimate alien: The hidden story of the UFO*. Stanford University Press.
Hynek, J. A. (1972). *The UFO experience: A scientific inquiry*. Henry Regnery Company.
Jung, C. (1958/59). Flying saucers: A modern myth of things seen in the skies. C.W. 10, 307–433.
Klass, P. J. (1974). *UFOs explained*. Random House.
Kottmeyer, M. (1995, November). Gill again: The Father Gill case reconsidered. *Magonia*, 54. http://magoniamagazine.blogspot.com/2013/12/gill-again-father-gill-case-reconsidered.html
Kottmeyer, M. (2017, May 16). *Gill's sketch of 8 UFOs——A solution*. Facebook. https://www.facebook.com/la.wan.3538/posts/1895276350714620
Kottmeyer, M. S. (2007, May). The astronomical solution to Father William Gill's position sketches of 5 UFOs seen over Papua, New Guinea on the evening of June 26, 1959. *The REALL News*, *15*(5), 1, 4–9. https://www.facebook.com/la.wan.353/posts/pfbid0vX1ptX LBrE7wbKRYvdY2f5oiHFRvnbBT3 e6UuA7DRjSwuzN2pH5Yw5HCYbaeHuCUl
Lawrence, P. (1964). *Road belong cargo: A study of the cargo movement in the southern Madang District, New Guinea*. Manchester University Press.
Menzel, D. H. (1972). UFO's—The modern myth. In C. Sagan & T. Page (Eds.), *UFO's—A scientific debate* (pp. 123–182). Cornell University Press.
Miller, A. I. (2009). *Deciphering the cosmic number: The strange friendship of Wolfgang Pauli and Carl Jung*. W. W. Norton.

Trompf, G. W. (Ed.). (1990). *Cargo cults and millenarian movements: Transoceanic comparisons of new religious movements.* De Gruyter Mouton.

Trompf, G. W. (1991). *Melanesian religion.* Cambridge University Press.

Trompf, G. W. (2003). UFO religions and cargo cults. In C. Partridge (Ed.), *UFO religions* (pp. 221–238). Routledge. *Victorian Flying Saucer Research Society Report 1959.* (n. p.)

Worsley, P. (1968). *The trumpet shall sound: A study of "cargo" cults in Melanesia* (2nd ed.). Schocken Books.

Part 3

Psychotherapy and Analysis

Introduction to "Jung's Personal Confession"

Common to both the Jungian tradition and the broader human science field is the assumption that what is perceived or understood always reflects a certain perspective, one that is typically present in our engagements or efforts but is not reflectively thought about. This assumption underlies the general recognition that one's own analysis is the most important aspect of training as an analyst. We need to work through our complexes sufficiently to be able to allow the meanings of a patient's experience and behavior to emerge to our (Jungian) psychoanalytic ears relatively free of our personal distortions (complexes). While this truism is almost a platitude, it is not so for Betsy Cohen, who takes up the question of Jung's "personal equation" with regard to his famous essay "The Psychology of the Transference." What she finds in Jung's fascination with the erotic woodcuts of the 16th century alchemical text, the *Rosarium Philosophorum*, is not only a symbolic presentation of certain dimensions of the transference we all recognize at times. She argues that Jung's imagination found a home in these pictures because they were overdetermined by his own erotic struggles with three women patients, Sabrina Spielrein, Maria Moltzer, and Toni Wolff. While angels might fear to tread into these contentious areas, Cohen does so with nuance and compassion, encouraging us all once again to become conscious of the way our struggles might both reveal and conceal the erotic dimensions of our relationships with others, especially our patients. We also think that, by showing Jung's essay on the transference to be so personal to Jung, she effectively lifts the relevance of the essay out of the Jungian tradition and shows its value to the broader human science field.

Chapter 12

Jung's Personal Confession

Betsy Cohen

Rosarium Drawings

Jung's primary way of describing the delicate transference phenomena of the analytic relationship is depicted in the symbolism of an alchemical opus, the *Rosarium Philosophorum*, which he discovered at age seventy-one. But why did he choose arcane, sometimes distant drawings to describe the most personal aspect of his theories for how we, as analysts, are to help our patients heal? What is the subjective confession behind Jung's choice of the *Rosarium* drawings as a template for our deep work with patients, an illustration of the analytic relationship?

These drawings have taught decades of future therapists an ideal to deepen the work with their patients. I contend, however, that Jung's own erotic experiences led him to choose the drawings of the *Rosarium Philosophorum*. I assume his subjective confession is related to his personal experiences in relationship with three former patients: Sabina Spielrein; perhaps Maria Moltzer, though less is known about her; and Toni Wolff. Through the language of psychology and analysis, Jung (1946/1954) interpreted a series of woodcut illustrations, boldly reasoning that the stages of transformation in the series of pictures symbolically illustrated the *opus alchymicum*, the features of archetypal transference phenomena in psychoanalysis. The ten pictures in Jung's *Psychology of the Transference* are from a famous series of twenty woodcuts that were first printed in the second volume of *De Alchimia Opuscula Complura Veterum Philosophorum* in Frankfurt in 1550 (Fabricius, 1994).[1]

Jung sought an analogy between the healing power of the transference and these alchemical drawings, reasoning that if the analyst was not an obstacle to the process, and if the patient was allowed a full range of dreams and fantasies, then the patient was more likely to develop an integrated personality. Jung believed that the structure of the *opus alchymicum* reflected the process of individuation, the transference in psychoanalysis, and the intimacy of the doctor and patient. He made the striking statement: "Everything the doctor discovers and experiences while analyzing the unconscious of his patient coincides in the

DOI: 10.4324/9781032694603-16

most remarkable way with the content of these pictures" (Jung, 1946/1954, CW 16, ¶401).

This chapter explores the power of Eros in Jung's life with his patients and how it might have shaped his theory about how we heal in psychoanalysis. I guide the reader through current thinking about Jung's shadow and vulnerabilities and his life with these patients, all which remain a personal confession.

The *Rosarium* Today

If a person considering Jungian analysis were to look at these erotic drawings, this person would see Jung's image of a symbolic individuation process. Six are clearly erotic woodblocks. The male and female, the king and queen, disrobe, become nude together, sink into the depth of a bath. Jung knew that "sexual fantasies color the transference" (1946/1954, CW 16, ¶456). Andrew Samuels reminds us that to understand the alchemical symbolism, "sexuality has to be present for its symbolic meaning to be interpreted. In order for psychological transformation to result from analytical interaction, that interaction must acquire and radiate something of an erotic nature" (2016, p. 187). Intertwined in an embrace in the fifth drawing, called *The Conjunction*, the king and queen play in the bath, become one, create, and produce something new together from their union. Call it what you will—a child, the analytic third, a homunculus, new insights, new behavior. "Hmmm," a prospective patient might muse, "what in the world will happen to me when I enter that therapy office?"

The drawings remain an avenue for erotic aliveness in the psyche. The symbols capture for some the actual experience of being with another human being. We know that we connect, combine, change roles, distance, and unify with our patients. In modern relational analysis, patient and therapist penetrate one other, share mutuality and vulnerability, are deeply influenced by the other. Both are changed by the process (transform) and something new emerges. In a good analysis, do we not have merger, spiritual sex, the deepest of intimacies? In the last drawing, *The New Birth*, the king and queen become one figure, one body with the wholeness of two heads, male and female, a unity. Jung deepened the concept of an analytic relationship by his attention to the king and queen as analogous to analyst and patient, here, as equals in an erotic embrace and connection.

The pictures, sexual and erotic, are an expression of the intensity of such feelings in the analytic relationship. Jung reminded us that the desire for union in the *coniunctio* was not a real union—but "was always incestuous" (1946/1954, CW 16, ¶415). It is confusing because by incest he meant not just a sexual wish, with Freud's emphasis on our early incestuous wishes and the primacy of the Oedipal complex, but "union with one's own being, it means individuation or becoming a self" (¶419).[2]

For Jung, the union, the wholeness in the drawings or in the therapy relationship was not to be acted out but understood as analogous to the union of opposites—instinct transformed into symbol, not the actual coitus (1946/1954, CW 16, ¶460). The union is about transcendence, whose ultimate outcome is an integration of the patient with the Divine, within and without. We know that seeking oneness with one another, as in the patient and analyst seeking oneness, is a desired state. Finding it is fleeting or unrealizable.

Jung reminded us these drawings from the Middle Ages were archetypal, not personal (1946/1954, CW 16, ¶354), nor pornographic (¶460). One has to dig under the theory to find Jung's personal equation. He stated that the analyst was infected, affected, and had "as much trouble distinguishing himself from what has taken possession of him as the patient himself has ... [that] leads both of them to a direct confrontation with the daemonic forces lurking in the darkness" (¶376). What daemonic forces lurked in the darkness for Jung? He did enter the "bath" with loved ones. Did Jung contain these "opposites" with his patients, Sabina Spielrein, Maria Moltzer, and Toni Wolff?

Jung rarely spoke from the personal. His need was to be respected, accepted, scientific, and to remain at the objective level. He was an avowed scientist, professor, and psychologist who did not include the "he said, she said" of clinical descriptions, writing at a more general, universal level. My conjecture is that he felt vulnerability. Although Jung avoided owning his direct experiences in his clinical theories, he had experienced the heat expressed in the drawings with three female patients with whom he had affairs, sexual (Toni and perhaps Maria) and emotional (Sabina).

He suggested a divide of the personal and impersonal (archetypal, objective) psyche, but we know they cannot be divided (Brooks, 2012, p. 8).[3] Today we understand that the archetypal and personal realms of the psyche are both/ and, not either/or. They inform, respond, and interact with each other. We experience the archetypal realm through our personal lens and from our unique history. Analysis is both archetypal and personal, but it is the personal that makes each analysis unique.

Jung's Shadow: Love Affairs with Ex-patients and His Fear of Vulnerability

Jung's Eros flamed into desire with Sabina, Maria, and Toni. In alchemy, he found a metaphor to stir, contain, and bring his emotional being to these drawings. It has been said that all writing is essentially autobiographical. Jung claimed all psychological writing, his included, to have "the character of a subjective confession" (1929/1961, CW 4, ¶774). In his alchemical model, the symbol came out of his gut. Jung discussed the inherent possibility of "falling victim" to our shadow, the necessity of our shadow side being integrated into the work, how the shadow teaches us how difficult we truly are (1946/1954, CW

16, ¶452), and that we have to consciously "decide not to become its victim" (¶420). Were his erotic preoccupations destructive to Jung or these women? Was he able to know?

Many of Jung's vulnerabilities are described in his familiar autobiography, *Memories, Dreams, Reflections*. After the death of three babies in a row before Carl's birth, his mother, "Emilie withdrew, takes refuge in the private interior visions of the spirits" (Bair, 2004, p. 18). When Jung was only three years old, his mother was hospitalized for severe depression. Her tendency to dissociate created deep, lasting anxiety in him and a lasting mistrust of love. He relied on his maid, and, subsequently, perhaps he learned not to put all his faith and trust into one woman (Feldman, 1992, pp. 262–264). "The feeling I associated with 'woman' was that of 'innate unreliability,'" which he called his "handicap" (Jung, 1961, p. 8). His ensuing vulnerability and tenderness were activated by his first analytic patient, Sabina Spielrein. We find another deep hurt when Jung wrote Freud that he had been "sexually assaulted" at age 18.[4] A further trauma for Jung was to have this confession dismissed by Freud, on whom he had a "religious" crush. Today we know that childhood trauma like Jung personally suffered and endured is predictive of having to consolidate an identity around certainty, being intact by being in control, being one up on others, as well as a fear of vulnerability. These qualities were mirrored by Jung's being a white heterosexual male, inflated by his privilege.

Importantly, at the time when Jung was with Sabina, Maria, and Toni as patients and then intimates, there were no analytic rules or boundaries established. Analysts were friends, teachers, social friends, and lovers with their patients (Bair, 2004, p. 260).

Sabina Spielrein, MD (1885–1942)

One place to find Jung's analytic vulnerability with love and his patients is in the intimate analytic relationship with Sabina Spielrein, more than in his theoretical writings about the *coniunctio* or the *Rosarium* drawings. Jung's relationship with Sabina, as we read in Jung and Freud's correspondence, scared Freud more than Jung. In 1911, Freud wrote Jung, "We must never let our poor neurotics drive us crazy" (McGuire, 1974, p. 476). Freud's advice, impossible to follow, was far too late for Jung! We begin to learn the erotic arena of Jung's history from his and Sabina's mutual correspondence, which has been publicly available since 1980. Jung was Sabina's analyst, and he discussed with her his skinless vulnerability and feelings toward her. Many psychoanalytic researchers have explored Sabina's diaries, her letters to her mother, and those to and from Jung. Jung and Sabina "were both in the soup, and both analyzing the madness of what was happening to them" (Owens, 2005, p. 28). The complexity of their feelings weaves through their letters. As noted by Mark Saban, "What is clear from the letters between Carl Jung and Sabina Spielrein …: Jung became the patient and Sabina the analyst" (2019, p. 106).

We sense Jung knows the erotic quite well. A young man at the time, twenty-nine years old, an inexperienced psychiatrist, he was four years into his first psychiatric position. Four years earlier he had read and lectured on Freud's *Interpretation of Dreams*. Sabina became his first psychoanalytic patient. He fell in love with and was deeply attached to this patient, a beautiful and brilliant Russian Jewess, a true other, part of his fantasy anima. Sabina was nineteen, three years younger than Emma, when Sabina and Jung met. She was highly intelligent, intense, outgoing, dark-haired, with a predisposition for hysteria; both of her parents suffered from it as well. She was well traveled, fluent in Russian, Polish, French, and German, and also knew English, Latin, and Greek.

By June 1905, after a successful psychoanalytic treatment with Jung, Sabina progressed, became a medical student at the University of Zürich and a medical doctor (1911), a theorist, and wrote many important influential theoretical papers. In 1911, Freud accepted her into the Vienna Psychoanalytic Society, its second female member.

In 1906, Sabina came to Jung's office at the Burghölzli for six or eight months. Not a paying patient, they were having confidential talks, which could be construed as therapy (Bair, 2004, p. 108). Sabina's and Jung's boundaries were blurred. They were unable to analyze the erotic transference so early in the history of psychoanalysis because they had no theoretical understanding of it. Freud warned against such therapeutic intimacy and believed the feelings of the analyst should never enter the therapy. Leaving out one's feelings, of course, creates more anxiety and conflict for the analyst, who naturally has such emotions. Apart from their therapy relationship/friendship, Sabina helped Jung and Franz Riklin with their word association experiments. Jung even asked Sabina to analyze Emma's results when she was a subject in the word association experiment (Jung, 1904–7, 1910/1973, CW 2). And Jung later became Sabina's dissertation adviser.

Sabina's erotic transference to Jung (as well as his countertransference and real feelings toward her) de-centered him, and in October 1906, he wrote Freud for help (McGuire, 1974, p. 7). The first appeal for psychoanalytic supervision (Kerr, 1993, p. 122)! Jung took responsibility for his feelings toward Sabina when he told Freud in March and in June 1909: "I have acted the gentleman toward her ... nevertheless don't feel clean ... and that is what hurts the most ... until now I had a totally inadequate idea of my polygamous components despite all self-analysis" (McGuire, 1974, p. 207). Perhaps Jung was again alluding to his sexual attraction for Sabina when he analyzed his dream in a letter to Freud in December 1906, early in their relationship He also admitted "an illegitimate sexual wish had better not see the light of day" (p. 15). "Actually, Jung was very emotionally embroiled with Sabina. Jung's Eros was engaged in all the excruciating ways we well know and hear about even forty years later in *The Psychology of the Transference*" (Tresan, 1992, p. 87).

Sabina confessed to her mother in August 1910 that Jung told her in an intense conversation that he knew it would be dangerous were they to fall in love again. In a further example of Jung's honesty and vulnerability with Sabina, he again took responsibility for his feelings:

> I have removed all the bitterness that still existed in my heart toward you. In truth this bitterness did not emanate from your dissertation—but from the inner anguish I suffered because of you—and you because of me. I truly wish you happiness from the bottom of my heart and will always think of you with such a feeling.
>
> (Kerr, 1993, p. 349)

Jung, a victim of himself, was internally embattled and confused by their relationship. He acknowledged his painful alchemical journey when he wrote in a letter to Sabina on September 1, 1919:

> The love of S. for J. made the latter aware of something he had previously only vaguely suspected, namely of a power in the unconscious which shapes one's destiny, a power which later led him to things of the greatest importance. The relationship had to be "sublimated" because otherwise it would have led to delusion and madness (a concretization of the unconscious). Sometimes we must be unworthy to live at all.
>
> (cited in Covington & Wharton, 2015, p. 124)

The tone suggests sadness, humility, gratitude, the sense of a theory that incorporates personal failure. Sabina's having met Jung as a patient in a mental hospital provided a frame to their relationship that could not be overlooked or overcome. Without the wisdom of what it is to be in the grip of Eros, both benefited and felt damaged by their lack of theory, yet neither was ultimately destroyed by it.

For Jung, with Sabina, it would have been a madness, unintegrated with reason, not to have sublimated his passion. Analyst and historian Zvi Lothane, borrowing from all extant sources, presents a strong case that Carl and Sabina's love was tender, loving, intimate, anguished at times, intellectual, but not sexually consummated (Lothane, 1999; in Covington & Wharton 2015, pp. 139–155). No one, but the two of them, will ever know.

Katherine Olivetti understands the connection between Sabina and Jung's choice of the *Rosarium* drawings:

> Jung's experience, his countertransference with Sabina was early in his career as a psychiatrist, and he was in love with her, too. When he came upon the Rosarium drawings, he thought, "Oh, my God." He saw that the archetypal pattern manifests in a personal way … he articulated an archetypal process from his personal experience—he gave Sabina her life back in a transformative process, and was deeply affected by it … Their two unconsciouses were creating an experience which has to be brought into consciousness.[5]

Maria Moltzer, RN (1874–1944)

Maria was tall, thin, ascetic, contemplative, determined, forceful. An heiress of Bols liquor, Maria became a nurse to protest alcohol abuse and met Jung working as a nurse with him at the Burghölzli (Bair, 2004, pp. 192, 713). With Jung as her analyst and control analyst, she, too, became an analyst and opened her own practice in 1913. She became his (and Franz Riklin's) trusted assistant, seeing patients that Jung referred to her. Jung, as with Sabina and Toni Wolff, discussed his theoretical concepts with Maria. Before Maria's help, in Jung's initial schema of psychological types, there was only the introverted/extraversion function duality. Jung, to his credit, acknowledged her importance in a footnote in his book on *Psychological Types*: "The credit for having discovered the existence of the intuitive type belongs to Miss M. Moltzer" (1921/1971, CW 6, ¶773, note 68).

Some scholars assume that Jung developed his concept of anima from his intense relationship with Sabina. But Jungian historian Sonu Shamdasani believes the more forceful argument for the woman behind the concept was Maria Moltzer, rather than Sabina (1998, p. 16). Probably it was an amalgam. Jung talked with Aniela Jaffé, his enduring assistant and biographer, about Moltzer:

> I had a Dutch patient, a woman, a terrific creature who had an enormous transference to me. Through her, the anima dawned on me. In the beginning, when I wrote these things there was this voice whispering to me "this is art," and that was her.
>
> (Owens, 2005, p. 70; from Roelli typescript, 31, Protocols)[6]

Moltzer looked after his correspondence when he was traveling. She also offered Jung her case material, which he presented in 1912 at Fordham University in New York, "A Case of Neurosis in a Child" (Jung, 1913/1961, CW 4, ¶¶458–522). She and Jung jointly translated his 1912 Fordham lectures, later published as *The Theory of Psychoanalysis* (Saban, 2019, p. 111).

Two sources indicate that Jung had a sexual affair with Maria. Jung wrote Freud that, unlike Freud, Jung had been analyzed. Freud assumed Jung's analyst was Maria Moltzer. Furthermore, Jolande Jacobi, Jung's pupil, remembers that "I heard from others, about the time before he (Jung) met Toni Wolff, he had a love affair there in the Burghölzli with a girl—what was her name?—Moltzer" (Shamdasani, 1998, p. 57, note 3).

Perhaps Jung and Moltzer had a mutual and reciprocal analytic space, as he had developed with Sabina and later with Toni Wolff. There were no rules. The creativity and theory making that transpired with Jung and these women was also erotic. Lance Owens, Mark Saban, and I describe these relationships as "quasi-analytic ... a mutual psychological understanding of some depth enabled a fruitful though challenging engagement of ideas and emotions, leading to new insights, on both sides" (Saban, 2019, p. 113).

By 1914, Moltzer had a good private practice in her apartment, showing no signs of her inherited wealth, and had a purely professional and somewhat thorny relationship with Jung. She held her own in discussions at the Zürich Psychological Club, where Toni and Emma were finding their way into the inner circle and Maria was resentfully not (Bair, 2004, p. 260). Maria felt rebuffed. Before quitting the club, Maria and Jung had a long correspondence where she asked him to take her thinking seriously and not be sarcastic or ridicule her in the meetings. Jung believed that his friendships and socializing with his patients at the Zürich Club were "harmless intercourse" (1917, lecture by Maria Moltzer to Zürich Psychology Club). Maria, unlike Jung, believed these interactions were harmful to the patient who was emotionally intimate with Jung. She labeled it an "incestuous collectivity." She correctly understood that the patient, or ex-patient, couldn't feel equal to Jung in "simple sociability" (Moltzer, quoted in Shamdasani, 1998, p. 104). Her pleas failed.

Enter Toni Wolff

On September 20, 1910, Toni Wolff's mother brought her oldest daughter, Toni, to C. G. Jung for analysis. Toni Wolff's mother was concerned about Toni's depression following the death of her beloved father. Jung was 35; Toni was 22. He was no longer seeing Sabina as she had just left Zürich to study in Munich and then headed to Vienna. At first, Jung had difficulty engaging Toni's feelings that were causing her melancholy. However, after interpreting her emotional state with the help of a Greek myth, he discovered she had spent several years studying Greek myths and knew more about Greek mythology than he did. She would correct his "sloppy informality." Jung's and Toni's minds meshed and blended, and this intellectual excitement and companionship lifted her dark spirits (Bair, 2004, p. 199). Toni's mind became alive with a partner and her depression lifted. In 1912, she wrote in her diary that she would answer Jung's psychological questions and could envision "an entirely new theory of the psyche" (Healy, 2017, p. 38).

Toni, like other women to follow, began doing research for Jung and would bring piles of books to him several times a week. Jung did acknowledge her (though not by name) during a German seminar when he admitted he had been quite captivated with a beautiful, aristocratic, female analysand who introduced him to "Oriental thinking" (Baynes Jensen, 2003, p. 245). Jung's mind was more alive when in dialogue, and in his 1925 seminar Jung lectured that he could share his thinking and feelings more freely with a woman because she wasn't an intellectual threat (Jung, 1989, p. 33). He did imply he felt helpless when speaking about feelings and that men didn't like to be "helpless … and inferior" (p. 33). And, like a man of his time, he wrote the essays and took credit for the content.

About a year after terminating her therapy, as Jung explained to Aniela Jaffé, his dreams revealed he was having difficulty emotionally separating from

Toni. Jung had a nightmare in which he feared losing her in the Swiss Alps. In the dream, a band of singing elves lured her into a grotto. Toni sank into the rocks. Jung, fearing losing her forever, forcefully saved her. Another night Jung dreamt he had a leg cramp and feared drowning while swimming in Lake Zürich. He interpreted the drowning to be blocked life energy and creativity. He understood the dreams as omens to rekindle his connection with Toni, because he worried that, if he didn't try to reconnect, his life was in danger (Shamdasani, 1995, p. 40).

Jung contacted her via letter, and the rest is a history of thirty-three years of closeness, romance, creativity, love, and then deep hurt. But, at this point in Jung's life, Joseph Henderson, the co-founder of the San Francisco Jung Institute, believed Jung "found two wives in these women and so provides no model for the rest of us" (Henderson, 1982, p. 32). While wanting his family and home life to remain intact, he chose Toni as his spiritual wife. He told Barbara Hannah (an intimate friend of Jung, Toni, and Emma) and Marie-Louise von Franz that if the father does not live "the whole of (his) erotic life, which is seldomly contained in the marriage ... the outside attraction which had come to him entirely from the unconscious against his will, he would inevitably ruin his daughters' eros" (Hannah, 1997, p. 119).

In 1916 Jung determined that truly loving another who stood for his soul, since it was true love, was a guide to the Self and a gift from God (1916/1989, CW 18, ¶¶1103–1105). I assert he was struggling with his feelings toward Toni:

> Sexuality as an expression of love is hallowed ... If (a man) acts from love or in the spirit of love, then he serves a god; and *whatever he may do is not ours to judge*, for it is ennobled.
>
> (1928/1964, CW 10, ¶234, italics mine)

With Toni, Jung chose what was considered a mystical marriage, a spiritual wife seeking an "inner integration," despite his "unfaithfulness" (1925/1954, CW 17, ¶334). For a long while, allowing separate but powerful relationships with two women worked for him. Emma had begged Jung to be his confidant in reading and discussing the *Black Books*, but he believed he could find this help only from a woman outside his marriage (Bair, 2004, p. 250). How could he not feel vulnerable with his new attachment!

He shared with Toni his descent into the unconscious. Toni was not afraid of the black chaos of his unconscious *prima materia* and disorientation. She explored it alongside him, coming to his home most days during these years. The housekeeper would let her into the family home, and she would go upstairs to his library, where the two of them discussed and analyzed his visions and dreams of the night before. She was his helper, mutual explorer, his guide, anchor, for what became six volumes of the *Black Books*. She had faith in his images and simultaneously encouraged his letting go of their hold on him (Healy, 2017, p. 124).

From about 1911 until he immersed himself in alchemy, Toni was Jung's muse, intimate friend, and primary intellectual partner. She was elegant, mysterious, sophisticated, cultured (p. 3). Joseph Henderson wrote that Toni was Jung's other half, feminine counterpart, "complementary opposite" (Henderson, 1975, p. 117) in the "creation of one of the grand mythic patterns of the twentieth century: the Jungian model of the human psyche" (Healy, 2017, p. 1). Joseph Wheelwright concurred: "Toni Wolff was Jung's *femme inspiratrice*; she helped him get going and contributed much of the creative ferment in his work, especially its mystical side" (Douglas, 1990, p. 49). Wheelwright also felt that Toni was the best analyst he ever had, and they shared a profound intimacy (Healy, 2017, p. 23). Tina Keller (2011), who saw both Jung and then Toni for analysis, agreed.

Throughout her life, Toni's passion remained her personal and professional dedication to Jung and their relationship, a dedication that was intertwined with her commitment to the psyche. Most who knew her found her to be a genius, and Jung often described her as a beautiful mind, an exceptional poet, and yes, brilliant (Healy, 2017, p. 23) Without her having any formal training in the first decade of the 1900s, Jung declared Toni a Jungian analyst, and at the peak of her career, she became the second-most prominent analyst, after Jung, in the Jungian community. Carl, Emma, and Toni created the Zürich Psychological Club in 1916, a club devoted to Jung's works. She created her own understanding of the feminine psyche and presented it to the club in 1934, where she remained president and teacher from 1928 to 1945. The C. G. Jung Institute of Zürich opened in 1948, and she taught training seminars. In the 1930s and 1940s, Toni served as a senior editor for Jung's works, editing, collating, reworking. She wanted to be personally responsible for his works to be presented correctly even though this goal stifled her own creativity (pp. 266–269).

Toni was a dinner guest at the Jung household, with Emma and his children for Sunday lunches, and had tea with Jung every Wednesday at Toni's mother's. Jung and Toni would retreat to the garden at Jung's home, or Toni's study in her home, often to discuss the psychological matters they were looking into. The Jung children didn't like her and considered her a disruption to their family life, yet they were supposed to call her Tante Toni (Clay, 2016, p. 242). Emma wouldn't let them be impolite to Aunt Toni. Jung vacationed frequently with only Toni, and sometimes she and Emma and Jung went to conferences in other countries.

Emma knew Jung would be a difficult husband. She was not easily intimidated and wrote Freud in 1911 when she was concerned about Jung's relationship with Freud not going well. She was a mother of five, an analyst in her own right, author of two books, and one of the richest women in Zürich. We are not privy to Emma's private thoughts, but she remained his wife for fifty-two years until her death in 1955, six years before Jung. She told Barbara Hannah, "You see, he never took anything from me to give Toni, but the more he gave her, the more he seemed able to give me" (Hannah, 1997, pp. 119–120). Hannah added, "Of course, this amazing insight was not reached easily or without suffering" (p. 120).

In the 1920s Toni pleaded with Jung to marry her. It took Toni years of insistence, desire, sadness, and despair until she realized he remained committed to the marriage with Emma. It seems that the greater her insistence, the less his interest in and projections onto her. Barbara Hannah recalls that Toni told her that this wish to marry Jung, "cost her more than anything in her life to learn that she must *not* give way to this almost universal feminine instinct" (Hannah, 1997, p. 120). Perhaps Toni lost her sense of self. Her heart was broken. Jung, powerful and charismatic, convinced her, at some level, that Toni's role must remain that of primary collaborator, lover, inspiration, intimate friend, but not maternal wife.

And Jung knew it was arduous and devastating for Toni. He confided to Barbara Hannah that he could never forget Toni's gift to him during his years with his confrontation with the unconscious: "She loved me—and it was nothing short of heroism. Such things stand forever, and I will be grateful for her to all eternity" (1997, p. 120). Even so, he was unable to publicly acknowledge her enormous work in their exploration together, with his *Psychology of the Unconscious* (1912/1916), later renamed as *Symbols of Transformation* (CW 5, 1956), or her enormous help with *The Transcendent Function* or *Psychological Types* and their mutual development of the technique of active imagination (see Healy, 2017, pp. 179–187). The most credit he offered her was in a footnote, with no credit given for her contribution to his primary and crucial theories. They remain a subjective confession.

Between the years of 1910 and 1916, as he was becoming more emotionally involved with Toni, Jung was torn, in conflict between individuality and convention (collectivity). Although he removed these sentences in a later printing, in 1912, in his essay "New Paths in Psychology," he wrote, "in the collective psyche, one's true individuality is lost" (1912/1953, CW 7, ¶478), and "loyalty to one's Self steers one toward the truest morality" (Healy, 2017, p. 73). Simply put, we experience his inner struggle between the *daimon* Eros, his erotic passion for Toni Wolff and her mind, and his conventional marriage, love for his wife, and position in the community. Jung's two personalities, One and Two, fit with his unconventional lifestyle. To simplify, Toni became part of Personality Two, the irrational, spiritual; and Emma, a sturdy wife, represented Personality One, Jung's traditional side (Saban, 2019, p. 121).

Jung's only son, Franz Jung, then 75, did acknowledge Toni's benefit to Jung when he confided that

Toni, "more or less" saved my father's life and sanity. She was his lover and "therapist"—he took his dreams (i.e., written into his "black books") to her, she did active imagination with him and then he later polished them, and wrote and drew them on better quality paper which eventually became the

Red Book. This was the period 1913–1919. They were … "co-therapists"—he worked with her dreams and she with his. She was his constant companion—not only the Wednesday lunches and evenings at her apartment, at his house, but also at Bollingen and travels to Ravenna in 1914 [immediately after the birth of his daughter, his fifth child, Helene], and again in 1933. I am concerned that Toni is not given sufficient credit for her major role in this amazing testament to the soul (*The Red Book*).

(Healy, 2017, p. 144)[7]

Many agree with Franz. James Kirsch, along with Barbara Hannah, both thought Jung "without Toni Wolff, would have perished in his effort during those years" (Hannah, 1997, p. 120). Aniela Jaffé determined Toni was Jung's *soror-mystica*, his mystical sister, other half, the alchemical adept's assistant. Toni and Jung's partnership modeled the *hieros gamos*, the union of the masculine with the sacred feminine, the image of the *coniunctio*, a royal, sacred, divine marriage. Hence, the image of the king and queen in the *Rosarium* drawings.

Toni's ego was more fragile than Sabina's or Maria's. She was less worldly, never moved away from her family home, and dined nightly with her mother, who died in 1940. In her very late years, she moved into an apartment on her family property. She tended to deny her own life and travel and promotion of her ideas in favor of Jung's. Toni deeply feared losing her connection to Jung and tried to remain his muse. But the more she committed herself to *his* exploration of the psyche, the more he ignored her and the lonelier she became. In 1944, Jung, age 69, was hospitalized for a medical crisis with his heart. Emma did not allow Toni to visit. The only person he was allowed to see was scholar, analyst, and author Marie-Louise von Franz, another researcher and collaborator. When he returned home from the hospital, he discontinued his Wednesday visits to Toni's home, and she was no longer invited to regular Sunday family meals at the Jungs. Perhaps her final blow came in 1948, with the founding of the C. G. Jung Institute in Zürich. Even after Toni's thirty-six years of devotion to the Psychology Club, Jung said he didn't want anyone too introverted on the board of the institute. She was crushed to be omitted. Prone to heavy drinking and smoking, damaged by arthritis and rheumatism, she died alone in her room in 1953, having given her life to Jung (Bair, 2004, p. 558).

Conclusion

I can only imagine Jung's impact on Sabina, Maria, and Toni. They were left without an analyst, bewildered, and disturbed by an incestuous lack of boundaries. I believe Jung's erotic relationship with these three patients should be taught to all candidates who will become Jungian analysts—candidates learn the Psychology of the Transference (Jung, 1946), but not what led Jung to it.

All candidates should be encouraged to have a critical, questioning eye on Jung's (or anyone's) theories. Do they work for the patient? Does the analyst understand how the theory impacts him/her personally and in her/his work? If Jung is correct, and all theories are a personal confession, should we know more about the person whose theory we are using? Students of Jung, even aging analysts, need to go beneath the theory to the creator of the theory, to understand as deeply as possible what we do and why.

Love is overwhelming and, with the enormity of erotic projections onto him, Jung handled it pretty well, I believe. Today he would have lost his medical license. But his involvement with love with his former patients is a major reason we today have rules about boundary violations. In the early history of psychoanalysis, several analysts had sex with their patients, often not understanding the power of the transference/countertransference. We have learned from their errors, and we thank them for their struggles. We have witnessed how human Jung was. We know he and his women suffered for years, and yet, we don't forget the existing vitality, Eros.

Notes

1

> In the opus alchymicum the erotic, sexual and incestuous features of the relationship between the king and the queen (or the sun and the moon) are outstanding characteristics which are only thinly veiled by the allegorical language of the adepts. In the transference, the erotic, sexual and incestuous elements never escape the attention of the analyst.
>
> (Fabricius, 1994, p. 32)

2 Jung also discussed the incest impulse as a wish for the return to childhood, a symbol of spiritual rebirth (1912/1953, CW 7). When the innate drive for wholeness appears, "it begins by disguising itself under the symbolism of incest" (1946/1954, CW 16, ¶471). "Jung's conception of incest is that of a *symbol*, revealing both the need to move on from mother, father and the family circle (the Incest taboo) and, at the same time, the opposite, the need to regress (the incest impulse)" (Samuels, 1985, pp. 166–167).

3 The classic paper on this is M. Williams, The indivisibility of the personal and collective unconscious, in M. Fordham, R. Gordon, J. Hubback, K. Lambert, & M. Williams (Eds.), *Analytical psychology: A modern science* (pp. 76–82), Academic Press, 1980.

4 Jung to Freud, October 1907,

> My veneration of you is ... the character of a "religious" crush. I still feel it is disgusting and ridiculous because of its undeniable erotic overtone. This abominable feeling comes from the fact that as a boy I was the victim of a sexual assault by a man I once worshipped.
>
> (McGuire, 1974, p. 95)

> John Beebe believes this occurred at about age eighteen, when he was seduced by a friend of his father's, a man of the cloth and then a spiritual mentor to Jung (personal communication). After Jung's confession to Freud, Freud was dismissive, joked, focused on a different part of Jung's letter, and did not mention the confession at all. An empathic failure! (Gasker, 1999, p. 87).

5 Katherine Olivetti, personal communication, February 2020.

6 The Roelli typescript is part of the Protocols, now housed at the Library of Congress. See C. G. Jung.
7 See also "Toni Wolff: Women around Carl Jung," *Jung Currents*, http://jungcurrents.com/women-and-carl-jung-toni-wolff

References

Bair, D. (2004). *Jung: A biography*. Brown.

Baynes Jensen, D. (2003). *Jung's apprentice: A biography of Helton Godwin Baynes*. Daimon Verlag.

Brooks, R. M. (2012). The ethical dimensions of life and analytic work through a Levinasian lens. *International Journal of Jungian Studies*, 5(1), 81–99. https://doi.org/10.1080/19409052.2012.728146

Clay, C. (2016). *Labyrinths: Emma Jung, her marriage to Carl, and the early years of psychoanalysis*. Harper Collins.

Covington, C., & Wharton, B. (2015). *Sabina Spielrein: Forgotten pioneer of psychoanalysis*. Routledge.

Douglas, C. (1990). *The woman in the mirror: Analytical psychology and the feminine*. Sigo Press.

Fabricius, J. (1994). *Alchemy: The medieval alchemists and their royal art*. Diamond Books.

Feldman, B. (1992). Jung's infancy and childhood and its influence on the development of analytical psychology. *Journal of Analytical Psychology*, 37(3), 255–274.

Gasker, J. A. (1999). Freud's therapeutic mistake with Jung's disclosure of childhood sexual abuse: Narrative lessons in the do's and don'ts of validation. *Journal of Poetry Therapy*, 13(2), 81–95.

Hannah, B. (1997). *Jung: His life and work*. Chiron Publications.

Healy, N. S. (2017). *Toni Wolff and C. G. Jung: A collaboration*. Tiberius Press.

Henderson, J. (1975). C. G. Jung: A reminiscent picture of his method. *Journal of Analytical Psychology*, 20(2), 114–121.

Henderson, J. (1982). *C. G. Jung, Emma Jung, and Toni Wolff: A collection of remembrances*. (F. Jensen, Ed.). The Analytical Psychology Club of San Francisco.

Jung, C. G. (1904–7, 1910/1973). The reaction-time ratio in the association experiment. In *The collected works of C. G. Jung: Experimental researches* (Vol. 2). Princeton University Press.

Jung, C. G. (1912/1953). New paths in psychology. *CW* 7.

Jung, C. G. (1913/1961). The theory of psychoanalysis. *CW* 4.

Jung, C. G. (1916/1989). Adaptation, individuation, collectivity. *CW* 18.

Jung, C. G. (1928/1964). The love problem of a student. *CW* 10.

Jung, C. G. (1929/1961). Freud and Jung: Contrasts. *CW* 4.

Jung, C. G. (1946/1954). The psychology of the transference. *CW* 16.

Jung, C. G. (1961). *Memories, dreams, reflections*. Pantheon Books.

Jung, C. G. (1989). *Analytical psychology: Notes on the seminar given in 1925*. Princeton University Press.

Keller, T. (2011). *The memoir of Tina Keller-Jenny: A Lifelong confrontation with the psychology of C. G. Jung* (W. K. Swan, Ed.). Spring Journal Books.

Kerr, J. (1993). *A most dangerous method: The story of Jung, Freud, and Sabina Spielrein*. Alfred A. Knopf.

Lothane, Z. (1999). Tender love and transference: Unpublished letters of C. G. Jung and Sabina Spielrein. *The International Journal of Psycho-Analysis*, 80, 1189–1204.

McGuire, W. (1974). *The Freud/Jung letters: The correspondence between Sigmund Freud and C. G. Jung*. Princeton University Press.

Owens, L. S. (2005). *Jung in love: The mysterium in liber novus*. Gnosis Archive Books.

Saban, M. (2019). *"Two souls alas": Jung's two personalities and the making of analytical psychology*. Chiron Publications.

Samuels, A. (1985). *Jung and the post Jungians*. Routledge and Kegan Paul.

Samuels, A. (2016). *The plural psyche: Personality, morality and the father*. Routledge.

Shamdasani, S. (1995). Memories, dreams, omissions. In (P. Bishop, Ed.). *Jung in contexts*. (pp. 33–50). Routledge.

Shamdasani, S. (1998). *Cult fictions: C.G. Jung and the founding of analytical psychology*. Routledge.

Tresan, D. (1992). The anima of the analyst: Its development. In (N. Schwartz Salant & M. Stein, Eds.). *Gender and soul in psychotherapy*. (pp. 73–110). Chiron Publications.

Introduction to "Jung, Groddeck, and Analytic Technique"

Georg Groddeck is best remembered for his notion, *das Es*, taken up by Freud and translated into English by Jones and then Strachey as the Id. This was unfortunate because Groddeck's term was much closer to Jung's concept of the self, and it obscured their shared philosophical roots in a line that runs from Paracelsus through Goethe to Carus. Given these roots and Groddeck's widespread influence in the psychoanalytic field, Balenci's chapter invites Jungians to celebrate these roots and, in effect, invites our post-Freudian colleagues back into this deeply rooted human science and post-Jungian field.

Chapter 13

Jung, Groddeck, and Analytic Technique

Marco Balenci

Introduction

Whereas studies concerning the philosophical foundations of analytic thinking usually discuss theoretical topics only, this chapter is focused on the therapeutic consequences of Carl Gustav Jung's and Georg Groddeck's cultural background. Groddeck is no longer well known, but he was an important figure in the psychoanalytic movement for having founded modern psychosomatic medicine and introducing the term *Es* albeit with a completely different meaning from that of Freud (Will, 1985).

Since they share the same philosophical influences, Jung's *Selbst* and Groddeck's *Es* are conceptually close, meaning the totality of the human being and "the god within us". These core notions—translated in English with the terms Self and It—mostly derive from Friedrich Nietzsche's thought, even if the works of Johann Wolfgang von Goethe and Carl Gustav Carus affected Groddeck and Jung's conceptions as a whole (Balenci, 2018). Previously, Groddeck (1909) had used Goethe's wording *Gottnatur* (God-nature): "Until 1913 Groddeck spoke occasionally and in a non-programmatic way of *das Es*. Since 1917 he refused *Gottnatur*'s existential speculative argument also linguistically; in its place the expression *Es* appears" (Will, 1985, p. 158).

Gottnatur is Goethe's term that Groddeck used for eight years. Although "nature" disappears in the sober term It, natural philosophy from Goethe and other German thinkers permeates the conceptions of both Groddeck and Jung. The latter indeed wrote: "the unconscious is the residue of unconquered nature in us, just as it is also the matrix of our unborn future" (Jung, 1923, para. 907). The ancient tradition of the philosophy of nature—which came to Paracelsus, Goethe, Carus, and Eduard von Hartmann—greatly influenced Jung, along with Nietzsche, Immanuel Kant, and Arthur Schopenhauer (Balenci, 2022). As Henri Ellenberger's (1970, p. 728) treatise points out: "Perhaps the most important of his [Jung's] sources are to be found in Romantic philosophy and in the Philosophy of Nature".

The holistic doctrine of the unity of God, soul, and nature is the fulcrum of the philosophy of nature, whose exponents are often mentioned in Jung's

DOI: 10.4324/9781032694603-17

works (Balenci, 2022). Friedrich Wilhelm Joseph von Schelling (1988) founded the Romantic philosophy of nature—known as *Naturphilosophie*—which represented the critical reaction of some German scholars to the emergence of physicochemical materialism during the 19th century, introducing a strong reductionism in philosophical and scientific thought. Like Paracelsus in the Renaissance, *Naturphilosophie*'s proponents advocated the principle of the unity of human being and nature.

Physician-Philosopher Carl Gustav Carus as a Precursor to Groddeck and Jung

Naturphilosoph C. G. Carus (1789–1869) was the connection between Goethe and von Hartmann because he had Goethe as his friendly guide and "was the source of von Hartmann and of the later philosophers of the unconscious" (Ellenberger, 1970, p. 208).

Carus was a comparative anatomist, university professor, and director of Dresden obstetrical clinic, physician of the King of Saxony, and also an appreciated landscape painter. He advocated medical care to be an art towards the human being as a totality—body and soul in a holistic view. Carus was the first systematic theorist of the unconscious (Bell, 2010, p. 156). His 1846 book *Psyche* opens with this sentence: "*The key to an understanding of the nature of the conscious life of the soul lies in the sphere of the unconscious*" (Carus, 2017, p. 17. Italics in original). Carus—using the word *unconscious* as a noun and not only as an adjective—gave it a full dignity towards consciousness, thereby creating a dialectical polarity between them. His holistic conception opposed Descartes's dualism, which equated mind with consciousness (Bell, 2010, p. 160), and the Illuminist view that the light of consciousness and rationality was the only positive aspect of the psyche. Conversely, dualism and the primacy of consciousness would remain unchanged along the entire evolution of Freud's theories.

Carus's model of the psyche is complex and does not attribute the central organizing role to consciousness. He wrote: "The unconscious is the *primordial source of life*. Its life is also most intimately merged with the life of the universe" (Carus, 2017, p. 83. Italics in original). Carus called *generalization* "the especially close connection of the unconscious with the non-individual, general world" (p. 78), so that the biological bases of the psyche belong to the totality of nature. Thereby, Carus attributed "nature's healing power" (p. 87) to the unconscious, whose energy he called *Lebenskraft*.

The psyche is divided into four parts in Carus's model, from an unindividuated *absolute unconscious* to partly individuated *relative unconscious* and *empirical consciousness* to an individuated *self-consciousness* (Bell, 2010, p. 166). We can see the progressive individuation of the psychic structures, from the biological bases of the absolute unconscious to the individual reflection of self-consciousness. Carus was also one of the first Germanic authors to use the term *Urbild*—primordial image (Shamdasani, 2003, p. 298)—introduced by Goethe.

Hence, it is possible to find the roots of Jung's concepts of *unus mundus*, libido, collective unconscious, archetype, and individuation in these ideas of Carus.

In 1946, Hans Schaer (1951, p. 33) wrote: "Comparing Freud's, Jung's, and Carus's teachings concerning the unconscious, one soon remarks that Jung is nearer to Carus than is Freud." In the same year, both James Hillman (1970, pp. 10–13) and Henri Ellenberger (1970, p. 729) recognized Carus as a precursor of Jung's ideas; as later Sonu Shamdasani (2003, pp. 164–167). Jung (2019, p. 32) himself stated in 1933: "Carus was the first to speak of the 'unconscious', and his writings comprise highly modern points of view on it." However, it was only in 1952 that Jung asserted: "My conceptions are much more like Carus than like Freud" (de Angulo, 1970, p. 207).[1] Similarly, "Groddeck's theory is essentially similar to that of Carus" (Alexander & Selesnick, 1966, p. 392). See also Ellenberger (1970, p. 844) and Bell (2010, p. 158).

Jung—along with Groddeck (Balenci, 2018)—followed Carus's "notion of an autonomous, creative, compensatory function of the unconscious" (Ellenberger, 1970, p. 208). Groddeck and Jung also shared the peculiar standpoints of refusing to set their discoveries in principles and of being critical towards scientificity (Martynkewicz, 1997; Shamdasani, 2003). However, unlike Jung, Groddeck was sceptical of knowledge and consciousness, even going so far as to write:

> There is no such thing as an I; it is a lie, a distortion, to say: 'I think, I live.' It should be: 'it thinks, it lives'. It, that is the great mystery of the universe. There is no I.
>
> (Groddeck, 1988a, p. 254. See Balenci, 2021, pp. 23–24)

Though Groddeck differed from Jung in downplaying the importance of consciousness, both he and Jung were pioneers who considered the unconscious as another intelligence and a spring of creativity; thereby deeply differentiating themselves from Freud. It should be emphasized that the way of theorizing the unconscious has significant consequences in clinical practice because it has direct effects on the method of conducting an analytically oriented psychotherapy. Groddeck's and Jung's main concepts It and Self were theoretical and clinical at the same time: hence, they represented reference points for a holistic approach in therapy. Indeed, It and Self constitute a third element superordinate to the ego-unconscious polarity which impacts the therapeutic approach. Groddeck (1988b, p. 113) proposed that the expression *the understanding of the It* should be used, since the manifestations of the It "are so similar to those of conscious reasoning, except that they are far superior to the latter". While according to Jung (1951/1952, p. 459), the Self

> is an image of the goal of life spontaneously produced by the unconscious, irrespective of the wishes and fears of the conscious mind. It stands for the goal of the total man, for the realization of his wholeness and individuality with or without the consent of his will.

The notions of It and Self therefore involve a focus on the totality of the individual and a therapeutic attitude of listening to a kind of understanding other than consciousness, which comes from the patient's unconscious. This orientation follows in the wake of Carus's theory and clearly differs from reductionist psychologies. Accordingly, the therapeutic goals of Groddeck and Jung contrasted with those of Freud, who had the rationality of consciousness as his point of reference.

Despite the closeness of their ideas, Groddeck and Jung did not know each other personally. However, both of them lectured at the School of Wisdom in Darmstadt, Germany. They met there once in 1927 thanks to the mediation of its organizer, *Naturphilosophie* scholar Count Hermann Graf Keyserling (Fuechtner, 2011, pp. 89, 94, 96; Balenci, 2022, p. 870).

The Collaboration between Georg Groddeck and Sándor Ferenczi

Groddeck came to psychoanalysis in 1917 after more than 20 years of practical medicine. From 1900 he had run a clinic in Baden-Baden, Germany—Sanitarium Marienhöhe—where the cure consisted of diets and physiotherapy techniques, following above all the teachings of Paracelsus and Ernst Schweninger (Grossman & Grossman, 1965; Martynkewicz, 1997). The latter, a naturopath, was the most important doctor in Germany at the time as a university professor and personal physician to the Imperial chancellor Otto von Bismarck. Groddeck's therapeutic method became a combination of psychotherapy and physical care: thereby he "contrasted sharply with Freud's technique of abstinence" (Rudnytsky, 1996, p. 8). Regardless, Groddeck healed many of his chronic patients, gaining the name of "wonder doctor" (Grossman & Grossman, 1965, p. 58; Will, 1987, p. 143). He refused the separation between psychological and physical diseases and believed that any illness could be cured by psychoanalysis, which he combined with all medical treatment. Thus, Groddeck had become an expert in the treatment of resistance, ambivalence, and of secondary morbid gain in the chronically ill.

In 1920, Groddeck met Sándor Ferenczi at The Hague psychoanalytic congress. They became friends, and letters were exchanged until Ferenczi's death in 1933. Ferenczi went every year to Groddeck's clinic for his physical disturbances. Along with friendship, a professional collaboration was created between them in which the influence of Groddeck on Ferenczi is apparent (see Ferenczi & Groddeck, 2002; Fortune, 2002, p. 86). Groddeck, unlike Freud, had no interest in competing with Ferenczi. In fact, their correspondence was based on openness, sincerity and mutual analysis (Poster, 2009). Groddeck had experienced this procedure during Miss G.'s long treatment, which he had begun in 1909 (Rudnytsky, 2002, p. 177). Miss G.'s "childlike attitude" towards Groddeck (1923, pp. 221–223) compelled him "to assume the mother's role", leaving his usual authoritative manner as a "father-doctor", which he had learned from Schweninger.

Hence, before writing to Freud for the first time on May 27, 1917, Groddeck had discovered the maternal transference and had outlined a dialectical idea of therapy. Freud would never have accepted such views. Regarding transference, Freud focused solely on the father-child tie, while Jung and Groddeck widened their attention to the maternal transference (Makari, 2008, p. 354). Ferenczi was influenced by Groddeck for many other therapeutic attitudes, as Herbert Will has shown: to encourage regression, to emphasize the importance of emotionality, to intensify the transference analysis, to adopt a natural and sincere attitude, to grant relaxation and freedom, to understand the language of the body in the symptom, to promote play as a form of therapeutic relationship, to discern the unconscious connection between analyst and patient, to encourage the patient to express his or her criticism of the analyst (Will, 1994, pp. 727–732).

Currently, not only is there evidence that Groddeck supported Ferenczi's clinical experiments—even against Freud's opinion—but it is also increasingly clear that Ferenczi developed the original psychoanalytic ideas which Groddeck sketched but did not carry out himself (Fortune, 2002; Poster, 2009; Hristeva & Poster, 2013). Actually, Groddeck was concerned primarily with therapeutic and not with theoretical issues (Schacht, 1988, p. 9). Consequently, "Groddeck had many original ideas related to his clinical practice. But he had no interest in formulating a theory or having disciples or a school" (Poster, Hristeva & Giefer, 2016, p. 171).

Groddeck and Jung as Therapists

Rudnytsky (2002) puts together Ferenczi, Groddeck, and Jung like those innovators who developed "alternatives to strictly Freudian models of therapy and technique" (pp. 179, 181). Although there are Jungian schools, and Ferenczi has had a strong "impact on contemporary clinicians" (p. 92), Groddeck has been neglected. The publication of his correspondence with Ferenczi has shown the necessity of reconsidering Groddeck's "role in generating original ideas within the psychoanalytic domain" (Fortune, 2002, p. 86). The influence of Groddeck on Ferenczi's clinical view was also acknowledged by Ferenczi (2002, pp. 122–123, Ferenczi & Groddeck, 2002, p. 49) himself. In the therapeutic field, Groddeck was a pioneer for his *dialectical conception* of the analytic relationship (Rudnytsky, 2002, p. 177); for his *maternal turn*, transforming the analytic attitude into "mothering" with a passive attitude (Hristeva & Poster, 2013, p. 233); and for his view of *countertransference* as a constructive concept (Poster, Hristeva & Giefer, 2016, p. 173). Each of these aspects is significantly close to Jung's conception of analytic therapy. Indeed, Jung (1935a, para. 2) wrote:

If I wish to treat another individual psychologically at all, I must for better or worst give up all pretensions to superior knowledge, all authority and desire to influence. I must perforce adopt a dialectical procedure consisting in a comparison of our mutual findings.

Jung did not write much on countertransference because he preferred to talk about two transferences. Accordingly, this was his view: "The countertransference is then just as useful and meaningful, or as much of a hindrance, as the transference of the patient" (Jung, 1916/1948, p. 273).[2]

The similarities between Groddeck and Jung also concern more general topics, such as a great relevance given to symbolization (Grotjahn, 1945; Balenci, 2022, p. 869) and the discovery of the pre-Oedipal period connected to the mother-child relationship (Hristeva & Poster, 2013). Jung (1917) dealt with these topics in *Psychology of the Unconscious*, the book that marked his separation from Freud. Groddeck was also an innovator in using play in the therapy of children (Hristeva & Poster, 2013, pp. 245–247) and prefigured the role of transitional phenomena in the transference, many years before Donald Winnicott (Rudnytsky, 2002, p. 188). For the relevance of the contribution provided by Groddeck, Balenci (2021, p. 28) attributed a name to the current of thought which has resulted from the collaboration of German Georg Groddeck and Hungarian Sándor Ferenczi: *Baden-Baden–Budapest branch of psychoanalysis*. Indeed, such a current of thought led to a paradigm shift in psychoanalysis (Poster, 2009), whose beginning up until recently had only been attributed to Ferenczi and the Hungarian school, whereas, it should be linked to "a dialectic rather than a dogmatic conception of therapy" due to Groddeck's It (Rudnytsky, 2002, p. 192). Wallerstein (1998) was the first to talk about paradigm shift: "a shift away from a natural science, positivistic model anchored in a one-person psychology … surveyed by an objective, neutral analyst, the privileged arbiter of the patient's reality … —to the ramifications of a two-person psychology" for an interpersonal, object-relational, intersubjective, and perspectivist approach (p. 1021).

Natural Healing

Groddeck's It and Jung's Self refer to the psychosomatic unity and totality of human being, as well as a holistic approach to health. As followers of the *Naturphilosophie*, Groddeck and Jung[3] endorsed natural healing—the core of the medical tradition of natural philosophy. Paracelsus (1988, p. 91) wrote: "Nature is the physician, not you. From her you must learn, not from yourself; she compounds the remedies, not you". And Carus (2017, p. 87) spoke of the unconscious life as "healing power of nature" and "physician in man". Odo Marquard (1987, p. 176) pointed out Jung's closeness to Carus regarding the healing power of the unconscious. According to the philosophy of nature, doctors can treat patients, but it is nature that heals them. The Latin sentence *Natura sanat, medicus curat* was used by Groddeck (1913) even as the title of one of his books. He saw awakening "the patient's will-to-health" as the aim of his treatments (Collins, 1951, p. 25). That is why, according to Groddeck (1988c, p. 218), "the fundamental task of all psychotherapy is the tracing and dissolving of resistance". Since the latter is mostly unconscious, Groddeck considered the analytic approach to be the best way to achieve this task. Jung (1911) also attributed a fundamental role to resistance: "What is characteristic of the diseased mind, therefore, is not the ambivalence but the resistance" as an effect caused by the feeling-tone complex (p. 199).

From Jung's perspective, it is necessary to understand what a neurosis means because it can only be removed when the false attitude of the ego has been changed: thus neurosis "is nature's attempt to heal" the patient. Jung (1940/1950, para. 234) regarded individuation as a form of "natural transformation". In his theoretical-clinical view, "This natural process of individuation served me both as a model and guiding principle for my method of treatment" (Jung, 1917/1926/1943, para. 187). Moreover, the analyst "must follow nature as a guide ... developing the creative possibilities latent in the patient himself" when the results are not satisfactory (Jung, 1931, para. 82). Unlike Freud's structural model, which implies a colonization of the Id by the Ego, both It and Self high-light the positive role of the unconscious as nature and lead to an analyst's attitude of humility. For Groddeck (1989, p. 126), the therapeutic process is conducted by the patient's It: "in the treatment itself it is not the doctor who is the essentially active partner, but the patient. The doctor's chief danger is Hybris". In parallel, Jung (1935a, para. 7) maintained that "the therapist is no longer the agent of treatment but a fellow participant in a process of individual development". Jung (1931, para. 81) too suggested an attitude of humility: the therapist "can hardly know better than the nature and will to live of the patient".

According to Wolfgang Hochheimer (1969, pp. 18–19), Jung's is a "spagyric psychotherapy", borrowing a Greek term coined by Paracelsus and relating to the philosophy of nature. The method which comes from this tradition implies that the therapist has the task of facilitating the restoration of balance with a work of analysis (*spao*) followed by a synthesis (*gyre*), letting nature exercise its healing power.[4]

Groddeck's Followers

In the same year, Groddeck (1923) expounded his ideas in one volume and Freud (1923) published *The Ego and the Id*. The second Freudian topography found its main counterweight precisely in Groddeck's *Book of the It* (Rudnytsky, 2002, p. 143), whereby, a "theoretical schism" (Poster, Hristeva & Giefer, 2016, p. 172) occurred between Freud's one-person paradigm of ego psychology and Groddeck's two-person paradigm of *das Es*.

For his alternative stance to Freud's, Groddeck had many opponents in the psychoanalytic movement—the strongest of whom was Ernest Jones. Nevertheless, a number of prominent psychoanalysts acknowledged the influence of Groddeck's writings on their own work: Franz Alexander, Michael Balint, Flanders Dunbar, Felix Deutsch, George Engel, and Smith Ely Jelliffe in the development of psychosomatic medicine (Poster, 2009, p. 203). Moreover, after The Hague congress in 1920, Groddeck gained the support of Frieda

Fromm-Reichmann, Karen Horney, Otto Rank, Ernst Simmel, along with Ferenczi (Grossman & Grossman, 1965, p. 97). Later supporters included Frances Deri, Elizabeth Federn, Erich Fromm, William Inman, Lou Andreas-Salomé, and Clara Thompson (Hristeva & Poster, 2013, p. 251).

Furthermore, Groddeck's clinic, Marienhöhe, became a model as a psycho-analytic hospital. Ernst Simmel started Sanitarium Schloss Tegel in Berlin in 1927 and was an inspiration for the psychoanalytic turn of the Menninger Clinic in Topeka, Kansas (Peck, 1966). Frieda Fromm-Reichmann became the director of Chestnut Lodge Hospital in Rockville, Maryland. Barbara Dionis Petratos (1990) points out that Fromm-Reichmann collaborated with Groddeck's clinic in 1934, learning from him the importance of early mother-ing and the idea of disease as a form of symbolic self-expression (see Groddeck, 1983; Grotjahn, 1945). At Chestnut Lodge, Fromm-Reichmann "referred to Groddeck in her lectures and assigned her students his work to study" (Dionis Petratos, 1990, p. 159). Whereby, Groddeck's thought influenced Harold Searles, a leading schizophrenia analyst. Searles widely developed Groddeck's therapeutic approach in his work with chronic psychotic patients, fully ques-tioning the analyst's countertransference feelings (Searles, 1979). He directly quotes Groddeck as a courageous pioneer for having described "the patient's functioning as therapist to the doctor" in *The Book of the It* (p. 446).

David Sedgwick (1993) compared Searles's and Jung's psychotherapeutic models for their similarities, which find their congruence with Groddeck's. In such models the analyst assumes a "natural, 'human' role" (p. 140), is spontane-ous (p. 123), nondirective (p. 126), and empathic—namely is able to have a "true identification with the client" (p. 128). These skills require that the therapist does not defend him or herself from the patient through the continuous work of self-analysis. "For Jung and Searles, it is the relationship between therapist and client that is the fundamental factor and mode of cure" (p. 74)—a relationship where the unconscious communications play a decisive role, as for Groddeck.

Jung's Fundamental Rule and Analytic Method

Jung began his psychiatric career in the Burghölzli hospital of Zurich in 1900, working assiduously to treat the mentally ill, including chronic ones. It was as a student of Eugen Bleuler and treating psychotics that Jung developed his psychotherapeutic style (Jung, 1948/1951). Before meeting Freud, Jung went to Paris to study Pierre Janet's psychological analysis for a semester in 1902. By 1900, Jung had already established a connection with the French-Swiss-English-American psychotherapeutic alliance through Théodore Flournoy of the University of Geneva, who was a close friend of William James (Taylor, 1991, 1996; Shamdasani, 1996). It is noteworthy that Flournoy was a pioneer in exploring the unconscious, highlighting features such as its tendency for dis-sociation, its compensatory function, its creative activity, and its mythopoetic function (Shamdasani, 1994, pp. xxiv–xxv). These characteristics of the unconscious, which are compatible with Carus's conception but not with Freud's, were shared by Jung and then taken up in analytical psychology.

The physicians Bleuler, Flournoy, and Janet had a psychological perspective. According to Ellenberger (1970), Bleuler's main concern was to understand the patients and to establish an affective rapport with them. He was the most successful psychiatrist in pioneering a psychological approach to psychosis from the early 1890s, introducing psychological understanding and treatment of the mentally ill. Developing this orientation in the Zurich University Hospital, Jung had used a psychological approach in psychiatry for five years before coming into contact with Freud. Therefore, Jung's way of relating to patients and his therapeutic method were established in the Burghölzli period, when he was affected by Bleuler, Janet, and Flournoy (McLynn, 1997, p. 67).[5] They are those whom Jung himself recognized as the teachers who above all influenced him (Shamdasani, 2003, p. 93).

Gaetano Benedetti (1973, p. 410) of Basel University, Switzerland, wrote that Jung was the first in the psychological treatment of psychosis, to the point that "before Jung a psychotherapy of schizophrenia, in the modern and scientific sense of the word, did not even exist" (p. 413). Nevertheless, Benedetti saw Jung's "absence of a technique" as an important limitation (p. 412).

It should be noted that such absence was a conscious and generalized orientation,[6] which Jung (1934) did not limit to schizophrenia treatments. Actually, the core of his therapeutic view was: "The fundamental rule for the psychotherapist should be to consider each case new and unique. That, probably, is the nearest we can get to the truth" (para. 358), for the characteristic of individuality is to be unique. Likewise, Groddeck's conviction was that "the personalized approach to each patient [is] an essential requirement" (Will, 1987, p. 141).[7] For this reason it is more correct to talk about therapeutic *method* for Jung and Groddeck, and not about technique.

According to Jung (1935a), "the therapist must abandon all his preconceptions and techniques and confine himself to a purely dialectical procedure, adopting the attitude that shuns all methods" (para. 6). Jung (1945, para. 198) believed that the only technical tool is the analyst's personality; his or her "human quality" is the crucial factor. Since the therapist is equally a part of the psychic process of treatment, Jung suggested that every analyst should submit him or herself to a training analysis before doing analytical work with patients (para. 166). The therapist's self-knowledge and criticism of his or her "personal equation" (Jung, 1934, para. 350) are intended to limit interference with the patient's process of individuation through a dialectical and spontaneous therapeutic relationship:

> I reject the idea of putting the patient upon a sofa and sitting behind him. I put my patients in front of me and talk to them as one natural human being to another, and I expose myself completely and react with no restriction.
> (1935b, para. 319)

The Couch Issue

Jung's anti-technique stance and his reluctance to form a school may have been reasons to seek technical tools elsewhere in many of his followers, who have turned to the Freudian technique and to the use of the couch. The latter was seen as an analyst's defense by Jung (1946, para. 358). Afterwards, communication scholars have regarded it as a physical setting in which the therapist's superior position is extreme (Haley, 1963, p. 72).

Freud first used the couch for the therapy of hysteria and later for the other neuroses, recommending a surgeon's cold attitude to analysts in his writings on technique, even though he himself was hearty and spontaneous with patients. Freud (1913, pp. 133–134) honestly recognized the defensive function that the couch performed towards his patients. From a sign of defensiveness, nonetheless, the couch has become the emblem itself of psychoanalytic therapy; a real "iconic status" (Friedberg & Linn, 2012). This fact may also explain the spread of its use among Jungians, whose analytical identity has been lacking—like they are *Jung's unwanted children*.[8] Michael Fordham—also rejected as an analysand (Bair, 2003, pp. 471–472)—theorized the advantages of the couch, well aware of going against Jung's position (Fordham, 1978, pp. 65–70). Actually, the couch is a foreign body in Jung's way of understanding analytic process. Groddeck also did not use the couch, nor the white coat when he was working as a physician in his clinic. Fordham defended the couch as "a manifest indication that the analysand is different from the analyst" (p. 67) and adopted the subject-object technique of psychoanalysis, a closed-system model.[9] This represents the opposite of Jung's and Groddeck's conceptions, which considered analytic therapy as a real dialectical process, ushering in an open-system approach.

It appears comprehensible to find a strong criticism of the couch as the "most striking" psychoanalytic ritual by one of Groddeck's followers, Erich Fromm (1959, pp. 107–108). Frieda Fromm-Reichmann also treated patients face-to-face, like other neo-Freudians of the Interpersonal School of Psychoanalysis. Among them, Searles (1979, p. 227), who showed the important role of the therapist's face as a mirror in the process of the patient's ego-integration, as it happens in early childhood with the mother's face. On the same line, discussing the reasons to adopt face-to-face arrangement, Jung (1935b, para. 319) maintained that it is the analyst's "duty to accept the emotions of the patient and to mirror them."

The role of mirroring is important for any analytical therapy, because it performs a fundamental function in empathy and also in maturational identifications. Research carried out at the University of Parma, Italy, has identified the physiological basis of empathic processes in a mirror neuron system. These studies have explained the neurologic basis of nonverbal intersubjective communication (Gallese, 2003; Iacoboni, 2009), and with recent infant and psychotherapy research (Schore, 2016), they have provided evidence that the couch is a depriving factor for the patient, who would have a therapeutic benefit from visual exchange (Connolly, 2015; Lingiardi & De Bei, 2011). Today there is, thus, a scientific support for Groddeck's and Jung's face-to-face arrangement, which is capable of allowing a higher relational information for both the analyst and the patient.

Analytical Psychology and the Baden-Baden–Budapest Branch of Psychoanalysis

The time span of Jung's and Groddeck's collaboration with Freud was similar, about six and a half years: from 1906 to 1913 for Jung; from 1917 to 1923 for Groddeck. Today there is solid evidence that both Groddeck and Jung had their own system before entering the psychoanalytic movement and they kept it also afterwards: Groddeck as an outsider in that movement; Jung leaving Vienna psychoanalysis. Despite—as already noted by Roustang (1976, pp. 59, 165)—neither of them remained psychologically independent of Freud, their ideas did.

Although both Jung and Groddeck had considerable influence, neither of them were interested in creating a school. However, Jung was forced to do it, and some of Groddeck's followers formed an independent group in the United States. This group was led by Clara Thompson and became the American Academy of Psychoanalysis in 1956. Groddeck's influence came to Britain through Ferenczi's analysands, Michael Balint and Melanie Klein. They were the first British object-relations theorists, followed by Ronald Fairbairn, Harry Guntrip, and Donald Winnicott. Other psychoanalysts referable to the Baden-Baden–Budapest branch were John Rickman, Sándor Radó, Geza Roheim, Harry Stack Sullivan, Margaret Mahler, John Rosen, John Bowlby, René Spitz, and Heinz Kohut.[10]

Among these psychoanalysts there are authors much studied by Jungians for their relational orientation, mainly Klein, Winnicott, and Kohut. This can be explained by the common origin of analytical psychology and the Baden-Baden–Budapest branch of psychoanalysis. The different evolutions of these two veins of depth psychology depended on their founders' interests: Jung was mostly a researcher, while Groddeck focused on therapy. Apart from this divergence, they shared fundamental aspects of the analytic process.

Freud's therapeutic aim was to find a compromise between the patient's instinctual drives and social demands, whereas, both Groddeck and Jung would have agreed on the motto that Groddeck had taken from Nietzsche: "Become who you are!" (Will, 1987, p. 170).

In his writings, Jung has repeatedly contrasted his constructive-synthetic method with Freud's reductive method. Homans (1995, pp. 162–173) highlighted that, even in his mature years, Jung consistently sought to determine Freud's thought in relation to his own, presenting "his theories as a fulfillment of Freud's views" (p. 163). Jung's papers on psychotherapy also are more concerned with criticizing Freud's therapy than with specifying his own. Hence, we can argue that Jung maintained an indirect dialogue with Freud, being unable to fully process the mourning of detachment. Jung thus contributed to the narrative that he was a mere pupil of Freud and then a dissident of the psychoanalytic movement. On the contrary, when Jung became interested in psychoanalysis he had already discovered complexes and was the deputy director of the most prominent psychiatric hospital in Europe. In addition, as we have seen previously, he was part of the French-Swiss-English-American psychotherapeutic alliance. We must be especially grateful for Ellenberger's (1970) and Shamdasani's (2003, 2005) research which detached Jung from a "Freudocentric" perspective.

The *Freudian legend* (Borch-Jacobsen & Shamdasani, 2012; Ellenberger, 1970, p. 547; Sulloway, 1979) has determined "the complete mislocation of Jung and analytical psychology in the intellectual history of the twentieth century" (Shamdasani, 2003, p. 13). Although Jung's sources have been numerous and varied, his psychology should be placed in the current of psychodynamic thought to which we have seen it historically belongs: Carus's theory of the psyche. This is the same theory that shaped Groddeck's work, which gave rise to the Baden-Baden–Budapest branch of psychoanalysis.

Currently, the two-person paradigm has supplanted Freud's one-person psychology even in the psychoanalytic field (Rudnytsky, 2002, p. 143). Hence, Jung's and Groddeck's relational approach turned out to be a better therapeutic conception than Freud's. Even if these are alternative models, post-Jungians have often used psychoanalytic theories and techniques. Moreover, both post-Jungians and the psychoanalysts of the Baden-Baden–Budapest branch[11] have mixed the holistic approach derived from *Naturphilosophie* with the reductionism of Freud's drive theory, without carrying out epistemological feasibility studies.

These facts await insights on a cultural and clinical level.

Notes

1 This delay could be due to Jung's desire to avoid a comparison between his theory and that of Carus (Balenci, 2022, p. 867). Jung (1945, para. 204) eventually wrote that Carus's medical philosophy had been an anticipation of "modern psychotherapy".
2 About the analyst's passivity, see Jung (1935a, para. 7).
3 On the relationship between analytical psychology and *Naturphilosophie*, see Thomas Arzt (2008), who claims that Jung must be placed entirely within the philosophy of nature.
4 The English version of Hochheimer's book was edited by the C. G. Jung Foundation for Analytical Psychology in New York with a favourable Introduction by Edward Whitmont. Moreover, Marie-Louise von Franz (1975, p. 66, note 45) considered this book excellent in describing Jungian analysis as a "non-technical approach".
5 Jung began teaching psychotherapy at Zurich University from 1906 (Ellenberger, 1970, p. 668; see also Lewis, 1957).

6 Not even Jung's 12 papers in *The Practice of Psychotherapy*, volume 16 of his *Collected Works*, provide practical guidance for analytic technique, as Jung expounded only general principles.
7 Jung's and Groddeck's personalized approaches bear a great resemblance to Carl Rogers's (1951) *client-centered therapy*, which is close also in terms of the therapist's request for authenticity. According to Wolfgang Hochheimer (1969, p. 79), Jung and Rogers are similar in other respects: the scarce importance attributed to the diagnosis of the patient and the approach without technique.
8 This difficult lineage has produced effects that are still little studied. See Samuels (1985) and Kirsch (2000).
9 Fordham's (1993) theoretical-clinical synthesis is called "Jung-Klein hybrid". It is a medical model where the patient must agree to lie down on the couch and become an object of observation in the context of an "asymmetrical and non-reciprocal" relationship (Zinkin, 1989, p. 51).
10 About Kohut's self as a return of Groddeck's ideas, see Balenci (2018, pp. 57–58).
11 In the Baden-Baden–Budapest branch there are the psychoanalysts that Andrew Samuels (1985, pp. 9–11) called *unknowing Jungians*: Michael Balint, Wilfred Bion, John Bowlby, Ronald Fairbairn, Harry Guntrip, Melanie Klein, Heinz Kohut, Margaret Little, Heinrich Racker, Harold Searles, René Spitz, Donald Winnicott, and others.

References

Alexander, F. G., & Selesnick, S. T. (1966). *The history of psychiatry: An evaluation of psychiatric thought and practice from prehistoric times to the present*. Harper & Row.
de Angulo, X. (1970). Comments on a doctoral thesis. In W. McGuire & R. F. C. Hull (Eds.), *C. G. Jung speaking: Interviews and encounters* (pp. 205–18). Princeton University Press (Original work from 1952).
Arzt, T. (2008). Analytische Psychologie und Naturphilosophie. In D. Klein & H. Weyerstrass (Eds.), *Jung heute* (pp. 14–28). Dieterklein.com Verlag.
Bair, D. (2003). *Jung: A biography*. Little, Brown & Company.
Balenci, M. (2018). Totality in Groddeck's and Jung's conception: Es and Selbst. *International Journal of Jungian Studies*. Hard version 2019: 11(1), 44–64. https://doi.org/10.1080/19409052.2018.1474127
Balenci, M. (2021). Jung's and Groddeck's analytic practice: Alternative methods that have prevailed over Freud's psychoanalysis. *International Journal of Jungian Studies*. Hard version 2022: 14(1), 20–46. https://doi.org/10.1163/19409060-bja10010
Balenci M. (2022). The analytic methods of Groddeck and Jung in light of the philosophy of nature. *Journal of Analytical Psychology*, 67(3), 860–883. https://doi.org/10.1111/1468-5922.12822
Bell, M. (2010). Carl Gustav Carus and the science of the unconscious. In A. Nicholls & M. Liebscher (Eds.), *Thinking the unconscious: Nineteenth-century German thought* (pp. 156–172). Cambridge University Press.
Benedetti, G. (1973). Jung e la schizofrenia. *Rivista di Psicologia Analitica*, 4(2), 399–413.
Borch-Jacobsen, M., & Shamdasani, S. (2012). *The Freud files: An inquiry into the history of psychoanalysis*. Cambridge University Press.
Carus, C. G. (2017). *On the development of the soul. Part 1: The unconscious*. Spring Publications (Original work published 1846/1851).

Collins, V. M. E. (1951). Translator's preface. In G. Groddeck, *The unknown self* (pp. 13–29). Vision Press.

Connolly, A. (2015). On Murray Jackson's 1961 'Chair, couch and countertransference'. *Journal of Analytical Psychology*, 60(4), 449–461.

Dionis Petratos, B. (1990). The European teachers of Dr. Frieda Fromm-Reichmann. *Journal of American Academy of Psychoanalysis*, 18(1), 152–166.

Ellenberger, H. F. (1970). *The discovery of the unconscious*. Fontana Press, 1994.

Ferenczi, S. (2002). The principle of relaxation and neocatharsis. In *Final contributions to the problems and methods of psycho-analysis*, M. Balint (Ed.), (pp. 108–125). Karnac Books (Original work published 1930).

Ferenczi, S., & Groddeck, G. (2002). *Correspondence 1921-1933*, C. Fortune (Ed.). Open Gate Press.

Fordham, M. (1978). *Jungian psychotherapy: A study in analytical psychology*. John Wiley & Sons.

Fordham, M. (1993). The Jung-Klein hybrid. *Free Associations*, 3(4), 631–641.

Fortune, C. (2002). Georg Groddeck's influence on Sandor Ferenczi's clinical practice as reflected in their correspondence 1921-1933. *Psychoanalysis and History*, 4(1), 85–94.

von Franz, M. L. (1975). *C. G. Jung: His myth in our time*. Hodder & Stoughton (Original work published 1972).

Freud, S. (1913). On beginning the treatment (Further recommendations on the technique of psycho-analysis I). In *Standard edition*, J. Strachey, A. Freud, A. Strachey, & A. Tyson (Eds.), vol. 12 (pp. 121–144). Hogarth Press.

Freud, S. (1923). *The ego and the Id*. In *Standard edition*, J. Strachey, A. Freud, A. Strachey, & A. Tyson (Eds.),vol. 19 (pp. 12–59). Hogarth Press.

Friedberg, A., & Linn, L. (2012). The couch as icon. *Psychoanalytic Review*, 99(1), 35–62.

Fromm, E. (1959). *Sigmund Freud's mission: An analysis of his personality and influence*. Harper & Brothers Publishers.

Fuechtner, V. (2011). *Berlin psychoanalytic: Psychoanalysis and culture in Weimar Republic Germany and beyond*. University of California Press.

Gallese, V. (2003). The roots of empathy: The shared manifold hypothesis and the neural basis of intersubjectivity. *Psychopathology*, 36(4), 171–180.

Groddeck, G. (1909). *Hin Zu Gottnatur*. S. Hirzel Verlag.

Groddeck, G. (1913). *Nasamecu. Natura sanat, medicus curat. Der gesunde und der kranke Mensch gemeinverständlich dargestellt*. S. Hirzel Verlag.

Groddeck, G. (1923). *The book of the it*. Martino Publishing, 2015.

Groddeck, G. (1983). *Krankheit als Symbol. Schriften zur Psychosomatik*, H. Seifert (Ed.). Fischer Taschenbuch Verlag (Original work from 1889-1934).

Groddeck, G. (1988a). Language. 3rd ed. In L. Schacht (Ed.), *The meaning of illness. Selected psychoanalytic writings by Georg Groddeck* (pp. 248–264). Karnac Books (Original work published 1912).

Groddeck, G. (1988b). Psychic conditioning and the psychoanalytic treatment of organic disorders. In L. Schacht (Ed.), *The meaning of illness. Selected psychoanalytic writings by Georg Groddeck* (pp. 109–131). Karnac Books (Original work published 1917).

Groddeck, G. (1988c). Some fundamental thoughts on psychotherapy. In L. Schacht (Ed.), *The meaning of illness. Selected psychoanalytic writings by Georg Groddeck* (pp. 211–234). Karnac Books (Original work published 1928).

Groddeck, G. (1989). Headaches. In *The unknown self* (pp. 119–130). Vision Press (Original work published 1926).

Grossman, C. M., & Grossman, S. (1965). *The wild analyst. The life and work of Georg Groddeck*. George Braziller.

Grotjahn, M. (1945). Georg Groddeck and his teachings about man's innate need for symbolization. A contribution to the history of early psychoanalytic psychosomatic medicine. *Psychoanalytic Review*, 32, 9–24.

Haley, J. (1963). *Strategies of psychotherapy*. Grune & Stratton.

Hillman, J. (1970). Introductory note: Carus and Jung. In C. G. Carus (1846/1851). *On the development of the soul. Part 1: The unconscious* (pp. 5–13). Spring Publications, 2017.

Hochheimer, W. (1969). *The psychotherapy of C. G. Jung*. G. P. Putnam's Sons for the C. G. Jung Foundation for Analytical Psychology (Original work published 1966).

Homans, P. (1995). *Jung in context. Modernity and the making of a psychology* (2nd ed.). University of Chicago Press.

Hristeva, G., & Poster, M. F. (2013). Georg Groddeck's maternal turn: Its evolution and influence on early psychoanalysts. *American Journal of Psychoanalysis*, 73(3), 228–253.

Iacoboni, M. (2009). *Mirroring people. The science of empathy and how we connect with others*. Picador.

Jung, C. G. (1911). A criticism of Bleuler's theory of schizophrenic negativism. In *Collected works*, H. Read, M. Fordham, G. Adler, & W. McGuire (Eds.), vol. 3 (pp. 197–202). Princeton University Press.

Jung, C. G. (1916/1948). General aspects of dream psychology. In *Collected works*, H. Read, M. Fordham, G. Adler, & W. McGuire (Eds.), vol. 8 (pp. 237–280). Princeton University Press.

Jung, C. G. (1917). *Psychology of the unconscious. A study of the transformations and symbolisms of the libido. A contribution to the history of the evolution of thought*. Moffat, Yard & Company (Original work published 1911–1912).

Jung, C. G. (1917/1926/1943). On the psychology of the unconscious. In *Collected works*, H. Read, M. Fordham, G. Adler, & W. McGuire (Eds.), vol. 7 (pp. 1–119). Princeton University Press.

Jung, C. G. (1923). Psychological types. In *Collected works*, H. Read, M. Fordham, G. Adler, & W. McGuire (Eds.), vol. 6 (pp. 510–523). Princeton University Press.

Jung, C. G. (1931). The aims of psychotherapy. In *Collected works*, H. Read, M. Fordham, G. Adler, & W. McGuire (Eds.), vol. 16 (pp. 36–52). Princeton University Press.

Jung, C. G. (1934). The state of psychotherapy today. In *Collected works*, H. Read, M. Fordham, G. Adler, & W. McGuire (Eds.), vol. 10 (pp. 157–173). Princeton University Press.

Jung, C. G. (1935a). Principles of practical psychotherapy. In *Collected works*, H. Read, M. Fordham, G. Adler, & W. McGuire (Eds.), vol. 16 (pp. 3–20). Princeton University Press.

Jung, C. G. (1935b). The Tavistock lectures. In *Collected works*, H. Read, M. Fordham, G. Adler, & W. McGuire (Eds.), vol. 18 (pp. 1–182). Princeton University Press.

Jung, C. G. (1940/1950). Concerning rebirth. In *Collected works*, H. Read, M. Fordham, G. Adler, & W. McGuire (Eds.), vol. 9i (pp. 113–147). Princeton University Press.

Jung, C. G. (1945). Medicine and psychotherapy. In *Collected works*, H. Read, M. Fordham, G. Adler, & W. McGuire (Eds.), vol. 16 (pp. 84–93). Princeton University Press.

Jung, C. G. (1946). Psychology of the transference. In *Collected works*, H. Read, M. Fordham, G. Adler, & W. McGuire (Eds.), vol. 16 (pp. 163–321). Princeton University Press.

Jung, C. G. (1948/1951). Depth psychology. In *Collected works*, H. Read, M. Fordham, G. Adler, & W. McGuire (Eds.), vol. 18 (pp. 477–486). Princeton University Press.

Jung, C. G. (1951/1952). Answer to Job. In *Collected works*, H. Read, M. Fordham, G. Adler, & W. McGuire (Eds.), vol. 11 (pp. 355–470). Princeton University Press.

Jung, C. G. (2019). *History of modern psychology: Lectures delivered at ETH Zurich*. Vol. I, 1933–1934, E. Falzeder (Ed.). Princeton University Press.

Kirsch, T. B. (2000). *The Jungians: A comparative and historical perspective*. Routledge.

Lewis, A. (1957). Jung's early work. *Journal of Analytical Psychology*, 2(2), 119–136.

Lingiardi, V., & De Bei, F. (2011). Questioning the couch: Historical and clinical perspectives. *Psychoanalytic Psychology*, 28(3), 389–404.

Makari, G. (2008). *Revolution in mind: The creation of psychoanalysis*. Duckworth Overlook.

Marquard, O. (1987). *Transzendentaler Idealismus, Romantische Naturphilosophie, Psychoanalyse*. Verlag für Philosophie Jürgen Dinter.

Martynkewicz, W. (1997). *Georg Groddeck: Eine Biographie*. Fischer.

McLynn, F. (1997). *Carl Gustav Jung*. Black Swan.

Paracelsus (1988). *Selected writings*, J. Jacobi (Ed.). Princeton University Press (Original work published 1942).

Peck, J. S. (1966). Ernst Simmel (1882–1947): Psychoanalytic pioneering in California. In F. Alexander, S. Eisenstein & M. Grotjahn (Eds.), *Psychoanalytic pioneers* (pp. 373–383). Basic Books.

Poster, M. F. (2009). Ferenczi and Groddeck: Simpatico: Roots of a paradigm shift in psychoanalysis. *American Journal of Psychoanalysis*, 69(3), 195–206.

Poster, M. F., Hristeva, G., & Giefer, M. (2016). Georg Groddeck: "The pinch of pepper" of psychoanalysis. *American Journal of Psychoanalysis*, 76(2), 161–182.

Rogers, C. R. (1951). *Client centered therapy*. Houghton Mifflin Company.

Roustang, F. (1976). *Un destin si funeste*. Éditions de Minuit.

Rudnytsky, P. L. (1996). Introduction: Ferenczi's turn in psychoanalysis. In P. L. Rudnytsky, A. Bókay, & P. Giampieri-Deutsch (Eds.), *Ferenczi's turn in psychoanalysis* (pp. 1–22). New York University Press.

Rudnytsky, P. L. (2002). *Reading psychoanalysis: Freud, Rank, Ferenczi, Groddeck*. Cornell University Press.

Samuels, A. (1985). *Jung and the post-Jungians*. Routledge & Kegan Paul.

Schacht, L. (1988). Introduction. In L. Schacht (Ed.), *The meaning of illness. Selected psychoanalytic writings by Georg Groddeck* (pp. 1–30). Karnac Books.

Schaer, H. (1951). *Religion and the cure of souls in Jung's psychology*. Routledge & Kegan Paul (Original work published 1946).

von Schelling, F. W. J. (1988). *Ideas for a philosophy of nature as introduction to the study of this science*. Cambridge University Press (Original work published 1797/1803).

Schore, A. N. (2016). *Affect regulation and the origin of the self: The neurobiology of emotional development*. Routledge.

Searles, H. F. (1979). *Countertransference and related subjects*. International Universities Press.

Sedgwick, D. (1993). *Jung and Searles: A comparative study*. Routledge.

Shamdasani, S. (1994). Encountering Hélène: Théodore Flournoy and the genesis of subliminal psychology. In S. Shamdasani (Ed.), *From India to the planet Mars: A case of multiple personality with imaginary languages* by Théodore Flournoy (pp. xi–li). Princeton University Press (Original work published 1899).

Shamdasani, S. (1996). From Geneva to Zurich: Jung and French Switzerland. *Journal of Analytical Psychology*, 43(1), 115–126.

Shamdasani, S. (2003). *Jung and the making of modern psychology. The dream of a science*. Cambridge University Press.

Shamdasani, S. (2005). *Jung stripped bare by his biographers, even*. Karnac Books.

Sulloway, F. J. (1979). *Freud, biologist of the mind: Beyond the psychoanalytic legend*. Basic Books.

Taylor, E. (1991). C. G. Jung and the Boston Psychopathologists, 1902-1912. In K. Gibson, D. Lathrop, & E. M. Stern (Eds.), *Carl Jung and soul psychology* (pp. 131–144). Routledge (Original work published 1986).

Taylor, E. (1996). The new Jung scholarship. *Psychoanalytic Review*, 83(4), 547–568.

Wallerstein, R. S. (1998). The new American psychoanalysis: A commentary. *Journal of the American Psychoanalytic Association*, 46(4), 1021–1043.

Will, H. (1985). Freud, Groddeck und die Geschichte des "Es". *Psyche*, 39(2), 150–169.

Will, H. (1987). *Georg Groddeck: Die Geburt der Psychosomatik*. Deutscher Taschenbuch Verlag.

Will, H. (1994). Ferenczi und Groddeck. Eine Freundschaft. *Psyche—Zeitschrift für Psychoanalyse*, 48(8), 720–737.

Zinkin, L. (1989). Flexibility in analytic technique. In M. Fordham, R. Gordon, J. Hubback, & K. Lambert (Eds.), *Technique in Jungian analysis* (pp. 45–61). Karnac Books (Original work published 1969).

Introduction to "Jung and Kristeva: The Looking Glass between Self and Other"

Susan Schwartz brings together Jungian and French psychoanalytic traditions in her analysis of autoimmune disease as a psychosomatic response to unspeakable and complex trauma. She uses a composite case to ground her theoretical thinking regarding autoimmune disease and psychosomatics generally, and to outline the analytic conditions and processes of healing. Her central project is to integrate Jung's concept of the shadow with the more fully developed notion of the abject in the writings of Kristeva. Especially notable is how Schwartz does not follow common conceptual practice separating body and psyche in dissociative states. She shows, rather, that dissociation is between a traumatized psyche buried in the relative opacity of the lived body and an impoverished, anxious mental life. We might say that the embodied psyche is the abject shadow. Readers will also appreciate Schwartz's noting the emergence of the transcendent function through the transference in her patient's healing.

Chapter 14

Jung and Kristeva
The Looking Glass between Self and Other

Susan E. Schwartz

Introduction

The development of personality sometimes occurs from the throes of the disintegration, despair, confusion, and dissociation of body and psyche. Here are aligned the diverse yet coincident perspectives of Julia Kristeva, French Lacanian psychoanalyst, and Jungian analytical psychology. Both acknowledge the border between self and other, describing the defenses of the self, hindering and/or enhancing the personality. Linking these perspectives bridges psychological and cultural shadows. In this instance these authors elucidate the self-division in both psyche and soma manifesting in autoimmune disease.

To explicate the theories is the composite clinical example of an accomplished professional Middle Eastern woman we shall name Shirin, living in the United States for many years. She developed an autoimmune illness, lupus, affecting body and soul and sending her into Jungian analytical therapy. She portrayed psychologically, physically, and culturally what Julia Kristeva described as the abject and Jung described as the shadow. These issues apply to many who have lost connection between body and psyche, becoming the self-attack of autoimmune diseases. The Jungian concept of the transcendent function is explored with its effect on restoring balance to the psyche. Dreams and other symbolic representations reveal the process of individuation developing through the analytical relationship and its transferences.

The Example

We live in an era of uncertainty, including alienation from the body. This is reflected in the rise in autoimmune disease with 78.8% affected being women (Fairweather, 2004, p. 3). This statistic raises the question of why more women are affected and what that says about the personal and cultural issues concerning the feminine and female body. Tracing autoimmune disease reveals the body turned against itself, lost from its central connections to self due in part to past traumas buried and held within. The constructed ego is cut off from the

DOI: 10.4324/9781032694603-18

wider self, including the body and her world. Jacques Derrida described, "Autoimmunity is an illness that affects the 'self'... where a body's immune defenses—that supposedly protect an organism from harm ... suicidally destroy its self through the very act of defending its self" (Derrida, 2005, p. 123).

Shirin is an example of many who suffered and verbalized feeling unloved, abandoned, emotionally paralyzed, displaced. Although not phrased as such, the body and the psyche have become abject, distanced into the shadows. Through the autoimmune illness of lupus the psyche/soma exposes Shirin's fragility, the cracked and dissociated parts, and unmet narcissistic needs.

Embedded in the body are experiences extending from past to present. The personal and collective story is sequestered in bodily memory as it reminds us again and again about the losses and events unrecalled solely through verbal narration. The body discloses openings to these silent, but loudly resonating memories. This includes repressed depression and anxiety, longing and suffering, the loss of meaning and connection occurring on conscious and unconscious levels.

Autoimmunity can be described as unforgotten material living in the system, reproducing the very thing it seeks to get rid of. Personal and transgenerational trauma and emotional conflict sedimented because they are formerly denied. In addition, many women are at war with their body and inflict punitive requirements of unattainable perfection. They feel disembodied, dislike or hate their shape, and go to dire lengths to change them. Integration occurs through encountering these dissociations, despair, and depression, the "as if" and the real, the shadow and the stranger. Then the body can be a catalyst for deeper reflection, investigation, analysis, and imagination.

Those who develop autoimmune disease face the difficult assimilation of the unaccepted abject and shadow elements as one is confronted with internal and external alienation. They describe an absence, a vacuum at the center with feelings of loneliness and solitude—a sense of absence in the presence of the other (Modell, 1996, p. 78). The absence of a stable self is narrated in autoimmunity, yet it also demonstrates a double movement of protection and destruction, threat and opportunity. This is not just a poison threatening to destroy the system, but a possible medicine that, when made conscious, opens to opportunities and hope.

The Abject

The work of Julia Kristeva includes the body linked to the psychological, notably through her concept of the abject. Kristeva described the abject as a potentially harmful entity that cannot or will not be assimilated. This is an important theoretical contribution to understanding trauma as the breakthrough of the dissociated material, the preverbal and unsymbolized aspects of the trauma itself. The abject is what is put outside, made separate and as such disturbs identity. It is conceived as something that betrays, defiles, stigmatizes, and is associated with what destabilizes our sense of certainty, compromising the existence of the self and abjection ascribed to what is felt as dangerous (Kristeva, 1982, p. 10).

The abject brings one to the distinction between self and other in the realization of one's existence. Ignoring the abject is a violence against nature because it is an inner expression calling to be understood. Kristeva commented that the secret and unknown wound can drive one to wander (Kristeva, 1992, p. 267). The abject signifies the foreigner within referring to a person's sense of being. Kristeva contended that what is foreign to oneself is part of oneself but has been excluded and marginalized. This happened as those with autoimmune disease learned to reject or deny themself, wandering from any caring attention.

Finding herself without security or a sense of belonging, Shirin felt excluded, on the outside, in a liminal state. She did not fit where she once did and felt rejected in the United States not only for being Middle Eastern, but for being a woman and older. Illustrating this she related a dream,

> *I am lost. I find myself on a street with many openings but no help anywhere. I wander around increasingly disorganized. I am so upset and panicky. I remind myself things will work out. It seems I must go up and down some stairs. Now I remember I was here before and this time I will find the exit.*

This dream looks both backward and forward, to the past and toward the future she needs to explore. The dream illustrates the delays, hesitations, and the questions on her psychological journey. Without a sense of direction, she is rudderless, lacking support or connection. However, the dream ends with the determination to find the way out.

Shirin was raised in a country of political turmoil where there was little safety. As she grew, she became politically active and was even imprisoned for a time with her very existence at stake. It seemed, in the words of Kristeva, "the disintegration of her self was a thanatic, death dealing reaction to a threat that was itself thanatic" (Kristeva, 1992, p. 18). Shirin had to turn from these horrors, repress her fears to survive and make it out. She focused only on her intellect and prolific professional achievements, negating attention to her physical and emotional life. She paid little attention to her body as it always seemed in the way.

Kristeva describes the abject as something both terrifying and intriguing. Abjection is the phenomenon of tossing away what are felt to be the undesirable elements of life accompanied by affective responses of disgust. Abjection is activated when the person feels unable to incorporate experiences or symbolize them. One has unconsciously lost the self connection from the earlier terrifying experiences. Kristeva calls this the abject, representing a breakdown that "disturbs identity, system and order" (1982, p. 4).

Abjection is simultaneously a "sickness at one's own body, at the body beyond the 'clean and proper' thing" (Kristeva, 1982, p. 78). The abject betrays, defiles, stigmatizes, and is associated with what destabilizes certainty; the bodies that leak, the chaos of illness and disease. The resultant sorrow constitutes a substitute object to which one clings, cultivating and cherishing it, for lack of any other. The recovery of loss occurs through a return to this latent sadness lodged in the body.

In relation to this, Kristeva conceptualized the complex arena of the abject as pushing the margins beyond what is known and predictable. She described abjection as a place acknowledging something awful has happened, something grand has descended into nothing and decayed to its basic self. The abject heightens awareness of the materiality of existence and the need to make conscious the past and present traumatic events impacting our lives. Kristeva named this melancholia and the noncommunicable grief about feeling off and uncomfortable with others (Kristeva, 1992, pp. 12–13). Here is Shirin with her world crashed, slowly realizing the old defenses work no longer and leaving her open to what has yet to evolve. Kristeva noted analysis is a journey into the strangeness of the other and oneself (Kristeva, 1994, p. 182).

The Shadow

There is a stranger within us whom we do not know. Jung referred to this as the shadow in its personal and collective aspects, reaching into the depths of the unconscious. The multicultural and plural nature of the psyche includes the strange and the stranger; arising from worlds we cannot yet imagine. Jung commented, "Don't run away and make yourself unconscious of bodily facts, for they keep you in real life and help you not to lose your real way in the world of mere possibilities where you are simply blindfolded" (Jarrett, 1998, p. 66). But now with the onset of lupus, Shirin reached what marathon runners describe as hitting the wall and was quite overcome with exhaustion and bewildered. She found herself running on empty, typical of many with autoimmune diseases. Developing lupus pushed her into therapeutic work to rediscover her ability to survive and find meaning.

The descent into the shadow is part of gaining consciousness and involves a fundamental shift to a distinct state of consciousness. This turn can reveal something about the nature of consciousness itself. Jung commented, "to the degree a person does not admit the validity of the other she/he denies the 'other' within the right to exist—and vice versa" (Jung, 1960, para. 187). Problems accumulate when the body and the shadow are fused and undifferentiated.

For Shirin, a lifelong attitude of distance from her body and a denial of its needs has become her defensive structure. Locked in internal combat, she engaged in vicious self-attacks, leaving her into what she called the blown-apart place. Another way of saying this is that the self-disappearance and disinvolvement, self-contempt, destructive withdrawal, and self-depreciation have a predominantly masochistic quality (Green, 1986, p. 644).

These were enacted in her mental and physical lack of care with defeatist and persecutory self-talk. Amid it all she was emotionally numb and did not know if she cared to come alive. This was juxtaposed with the vulnerability shown by the tears shed in therapy even though they embarrassed her. Yet, to hide all this, Shirin was adept at mimicking her adopted culture, taking on the popular mannerisms, slang, and dress. There is both danger and attraction to the persona adaptation. It can serve as pretense, devoid of real connection or integration, attempting to hide the shadow elements. These masked the blown-apart place marked by destructive, obsessive drives and self-persecutory impulses such as overeating and the oppressive weight of mindless television.

Shirin lived in a solitary confinement of the self ... There was fear of opening to another at the risk of psychological annihilation (Solomon, 1998, p. 228). The traumas suffered as an adult most probably replicated events in childhood but were disremembered. One cannot erase the attitudes, actions, affects, assumptions, rituals, and culture from early life (Singer and Kimbles, 2004, p. 200). The trauma complex expressing itself in moods and repetitive behaviors lives on in the psyche as unassimilated material. Nothing really goes away, but there comes a time when the old defenses become unbearable, unchanging, and no longer controllable (Singer and Kimbles, 2004, p. 85). This psychological process stimulates the seemingly sudden onset of the autoimmune disease.

Shirin experienced impoverishment of the self from the early attachment experiences with a longed-for other. Such lacks in parental devotion affect development. The unfolding of the self meets a blank, hostile, or inappropriate environment and feels unseen and/or noxiously related to (Solomon, 1998, p. 198).

Trauma

Trauma occurs when reality overwhelms with a brutality and speed exceeding the capacity to experience. Trauma is the story of a wound crying out to tell a reality not otherwise available. The word *traumatic* is from the Greek, referring to a piercing of the skin, a breaking of the bodily envelope. It is a foreign element destabilizing the former security and status quo. Trauma breaks through the protecting body and psychological shield, overwhelming the existing defenses confirming their need from the systemic threat.

Shirin dreamt about a baby she was trying to revive and was not sure she could. The dream illustrates hope for a rebirth but sadly expresses her lack of confidence this can happen.

Trauma experiences can divide one psychologically, leaving a wake of pain covered with denial and suppression. Life can become desiccated from the past traumas, with lingering memories stored in the psyche and body emerging years later. The rift in identity marked a split between what could be described as a demonic persecuting double and an invisible, disappearing, ghost-like self. These are the perils that enslave psychologically and disallow both self-acceptance and love.

This becomes apparent in autoimmune disease as the body, the embodied psyche, is a symbolic communicator of the traumas and dissociations and conveying these messages from the unconscious. Kristeva described trauma as: "I hate it, because I love it, and in order not to use it, I imbed it in myself; but because I hate it, that other within myself is a bad self, I am bad" (Kristeva & Oliver, 2002, p. 186).

In autoimmune illness the differentiation between destructive cells and those able to self-protect are enacted as self-hatred and self-refusal arising from and exacerbating the lost connection to self. The cells turn against from the traumas and lose their supportive connection. Reflecting a pattern of body betrayal, autoimmune illness also denotes the return of the repressed with the undercurrent of melancholia, the internalized trauma indicating the previously unmet needs and desires.

Unconscious contents lurk in the body, and the violation of its natural order becomes hidden behind façades and illusions. Although Shirin had much professional success, she was wracked by self-despair. The stress and crises combined with dissociation between her body and mental life became apparent with the development of the auto-immune disease. The psyche is now embodied only and present in the physical symptoms. The psychological descent propelled by the autoimmune illness is like analchemical dissolution, the *massa confusa* necessary for the old patterns to fall away and then to re-form. This replicates the alchemical process beginning with a painful loss of bearings. Called the *Negredo*, it depicts the time when life is unpleasant, full of confusion and bewilderment, disorientation, sickness of spirit. It brings forth confrontation with the shadow or the undeveloped and hidden elements of the personality. This coincides with immersion into the unknown and unfamiliar, becoming separated, facing the unfamiliar compositions of identity, the disconnected and estranged.

The consciously held values and former self-image are outmoded. Old habits do not guide any longer. One is at a crossroads, confused and torn. Essentially, ego-consciousness has yet to work out a new relationship with the unconscious. Jungian psychology attends to the paradoxes, the warring parts, and the cross-cultural aspects of the personality through accessing the collective unconscious, the symbolic, imagistic, archetypal, and psychological layers.

The autoimmune illness indicates the other within has been separated, as if a stranger, the early wounds that were put into the shadows. Jung paradoxically said, "The secret is that only that which can destroy itself is truly alive" (1944/1968, para. 93). Although the psyche seeks equilibrium, the ego consciousness will do much to avoid discomfort and ignore the rejected, uncomfortable material. Jung addressed the dissociation originating from traumatic experiences showing up physically and psychologically in what he called the complex. About this he stated, "The essential factor is the dissociation of the psyche and how to integrate the dissociation ... by living the traumatic situation over again, once or repeatedly" (Jung, 1966, para. 366).

If the information is not integrated consciously, it manifests in increasingly difficult symptoms so the issues can be known and resolved. In trauma situations the psyche shatters. One is sent to the bottom, the alchemical *nigredo*, and the foundational core. The defense, as traumatizing as the original trauma, focuses on survival. The system becomes reactive and defensive with these effects lasting long after the initial threat, as the realizations of harm linger over time. The protective defensive mechanisms preserve rather than permit the fearful ego to be annihilated. About this reaction British Jungian analyst Michael Fordham said,

> There is a need for defenses against what is not-self as essential to health ... little or no inner world can develop; the self-integrate becomes rigid and persists. ... Directed against foreign bodies, ie. those coming from sources external to the self and internally as auto-immune reactions.
>
> (Fordham, 2003, p. 167)

This leads to the accumulation of violence and hostility focused inward and split from any loving communication.

Shirin was facing the emotions and material she formerly could not decode. The situations of alienation remained untranslatable from the past but continued residing as foreign bodies in her psychic reality. Alchemically, she had descended into a dark abyss, detached from life, and had become strange to herself. This meant encountering the melancholia, the internal conflict while the self felt incomplete, flawed, deficient.

For Kristeva the abject resides in the psyche and body, where meaning collapses in the psyche and body. Kristeva further described the abject as falling to pieces. Kristeva depicted this as "caused either by drive-related nonintegration impeding the cohesion of the self, or by a disintegration accompanied by anxieties and provoking schizoid splitting" (Kristeva, 1992, p. 18). Developing lupus marked the instability accumulating from years without sufficient internal security, lack of body connection, distance from the maternal, and the body eventually becoming a battleground. Psyche is disconnected from mental life, with little imagination, impoverished sense of self, drives diminished.

Autoimmune disease symbolizes the psyche folding in on itself and the instability of a self, insulated and excluding. The former and now present traumatic memories were commanding much energy and one can no longer maintain the self-deception from denying her emotional needs. Kristeva called this a lost mirage of the past, leaving in its wake absence, ennui, and self-loathing (Kristeva, 1994, p. 271). Kristeva noted the effect of the other as the catalyst for the return of repressed otherness or the abject, the human part in the self formerly turned from with disgust. In Jungian parlance this is the recognition and acceptance of one's shadow, or one's hidden and denied aspects, physically and psychologically.

An outsider, Kristeva was sensitive to those who were marginalized and oppressed. Shirin likewise represents the predicaments of many in the twenty-first century, the dislocation, alienation, and internal divisions. These are the personal, cultural, and historical processes appearing in clinical practice (Singer and Kimbles, 2004, p. 201).

Over time, sometimes after a long time, we become more conscious of the emotional and physical losses and subsequent grief suffered from the beginning. These affect the imaginary realm and the symbolic entry so early a child cannot name what it has lost nor what it mourns. "The more extreme traumatically engendered condition is that in which any capacity to represent self-experience is ruptured: a state of paralysis in which even the blank impress is lost within a void" (Connolly, 2011, p. 5).

For Shirin the occurrence of lupus re-created the memories of childhood isolation, abandonment, and lack of the maternal care. She described a mother poorly attuned to her, unable to empathize accurately with her internal experiences. From the disappointment and longing to get close or feel securely accepted, she did not know how to mother herself or be soothing or comforting. The division from within is based on the psyche's rigid defenses deemed necessary early in life for protecting the self from dissolution (Solomon, 1998, p. 229). Distanced from the maternal and the body, Shirin learned to rely on her intellect and work. As a child she was favored by her father for her mind, but also envied and beaten by her brother. Because she told no one, the many emotions stored in her body and psyche became unassimilated material, compensated by her competent mind.

And now Shirin, formerly in love with words and the mind, had lost her intellect as she struggled to even speak. She tentatively and brokenly described psychologically and physically the former resources exhausted. One of the major casualties of this disintegration is the capacity to think (Cavalli, 2012, p. 597). Part of her personality seems cast off and the inner spaces filled with emptiness and blankness of mind. Jung cautioned about one-sidedness, "We should not pretend to understand the world only by the intellect; we apprehend it just as much by feeling" (Jung, 1960, para. 657).

For Shirin, shadows were cast early in life, repressing the vulnerabilities and wounds. This reminds of Jung's comment on the shadow, "assimilating the thing a person has no wish to be" (Jung, 1954, para. 470). The unconscious memories created an estranged and melancholic language in the body and now were a crucible for mourning. The illness marked the instability of a secure, safe, immune self, representing the body and mind in conflict. Jung commented, "The spirit is the life of the body seen from within, and the body the outward manifestation of the life of the spirit—the two being really one" (Jung, 1970, para. 195). Shirin was at a loss about how to unite body and mind and fill the absence and dissociation.

Shirin dreamt she was up high and eating a zebra with a knife and fork. Other people are around and watching. She is upset in the dream because zebras are showy and cannot easily hide. They are black and white, and she wants to be gray. Perhaps that is why she needs to eat the zebra. She must regain self-definition and internal differentiation previously lost. To comprehend the psychological includes exploring differences, lack of belonging, the loneliness and isolation (Singer and Kimbles, 2004, p. 125). In the dream she is too high up, removed. Also, zebras are not native to her country of origin or to the United States, nor are they eaten, so she is ingesting the unknown and unusual. As Jung noted the analytical work creates an "*opus contra naturam*" as it is against nature (Jung, 1968, para. 256).

The development of lupus led Shirin to therapy as she felt controlled by a strange and alien part of her personality. She became afraid to drive and lacked confidence with others, feelings not experienced previously. She felt guilt and shame and was devoid of self-acceptance or love. She tried to keep up the façade of a functioning persona to hide the increasing desperation, ineffectiveness, and malaise. Kristeva (1992, p. 17) described psychoanalysis as an apprenticeship in living beyond despair. It offers not a manic defense, but rather receptivity and a way of endowing despair with meaning. In Jungian terminology it provides a place for the alchemical mixture of conscious and unconscious and the analytical relationship to transform the destructive elements.

Transcendent Function and the Symbolic

The transcendent function presents the dynamics for healing composed of a counterposition from the unconscious. Analysis initiates one to free the psyche, readjusting and re-creating psychological contents. Their symbolic constructions open a bridge to the fuller self.

The analytical process entails the capacity for growth, development, and creative agency. It is dependent upon existing in the mind, eyes, and gaze of the other in a dance of attuned, rhythmic, and imperfect resonance. It is confronting the gaps between the subject and her outline in the mirror, the symbol and the symbolized, the abject and the shadows.

A task of therapy balancing and self-regulating to harmonize the person both phsycially and psychologically. A principle of synthesis dominates as psyche and nature seek to re-establish balance. An axiom of Jungian psychology is that each complex contains within itself how it can be healed. This perspective supports self-discovery and soul repair through opening to the imaginary and symbolic realms, assisting the connection between self and other, body and mind.

The tension of the opposites within brings forward the third or the transcendent, the unknown emerging through the therapeutic relationship—and then into the culture. The transition from one psychic condition to another moves the psyche from oppositional defensive states to coming together through symbol formation. The confrontation with the unconscious, the shadow and the abject, brings about a relative dissolution of the ego and a reconstruction in which both conscious and unconscious play integral parts. Bridging the gap between conscious and unconscious, the transcendent function involves conflict and collaboration mediated by the emergence of symbols.

The transcendent function breaks the impasse obstructing personality differentiation, containing a new level of complexity described as representational space for emergent meaning. "The psyche accomplishes its transformation through the creation of symbols which are capable of bringing together opposing aspects of the self" (Solomon, 1998, p. 227). Symbols are the impersonal metaphors, sharing meaning from convention, myth, and cultural artifacts in mediums of communication revealing our inherent intersubjectivity. They connect past memory wrenched from time with associations emerging from the shadows. Interpreting the unconscious reverberates with the movement of the analytical relationship for personality growth.

Shirin decided to write her social and cultural experiences, transforming the private events into public reflection. She would put into words the unbearable nature of these events and her survival in her original language used with family, but not professionally. This might free her from the intellectual and professional strictures by expressing the heart and emotions, love and losses put away years ago.

Although now the traumas are now experienced at a distance, writing them as French psychoanalyst Andre Green said, "presuppose a wound and a loss, a work of mourning, of which the text is the transformation" (Green, 1986, p. 322). In the analysis Shirin was bringing together past and present, multiple cultures, old ways, and newly evolving ones. The old traumas and the newly felt shock of lupus were working together in the alchemy of her psyche and could lead to physical and psychological creation or destruction.

There is an innate longing for acceptance and belonging. Without it we feel lonely, depersonalized, on the outside, abject, in the shadows. We may withdraw, yet remain raw, sensitive, caught in a void and numb. Shirin expressed: "Inside me is silence / Who and what am I? / I feel only inner pain and panic." Linking the unfamiliar with the familiar, the memories and connections with now and then, the interconnectedness of transferences, Shirin noticed a tree in the yard of my office, reminiscent of her homeland. "The symbolic capacity signifies the possibility for integration and the symbolic life through the holding together of the opposites and the creation thereby of a third thing" (Solomon, 2007, p. 159). This is the transcendent function knitting the unconscious and conscious relationships of both difference and similarity seeking to repair the cracks in the personality.

However, therapists can become blocked without awareness of the systemic social and personal traumas affecting clients. Theory can be used as a defense to assume recognition or slot the information of the client into something familiar to the therapist, at the detriment to both. Replicating the fear and us-them feelings like in autoimmunity, Shirin questioned in therapy if she would be met with denigration or misunderstanding due to her Middle Eastern background. The anticipation of estrangement and discrimination were mirroring the inclusion/exclusion divide she now acutely registered.

Both therapist and client were in the cultural and personal shadows, attempting to open the subjective material and find the expressive symbols. Both participants were witness to the complex objects and situations resurrected as layer after layer of the neglected emotions became unwrapped. Shirin continued to express feeling foreign and displaced. Analytical sessions included descriptions of her lack of fulfillment, her daily fears and felt lack of security, and anxieties over being lovable to others or, alternatively, being toxic to them. Kristeva referred to the notion of alienation or splitting of the self as the result of the repressed material. She described when instincts turn self-destructive, the ego, from early in life, lacks cohesion (Kristeva, 1994, p. 19). The injury of separation from her country still in turmoil, loved ones remaining there, and professional advancement compromised were addressed in dreams, the transference, and our analytic conversations.

The psychological bridges culture and time, creating the links for self and other in the analytic relationship. As the personality seeks self-regulation, the analytic process collects the dissociated fragments and brings them into relationship. Shirin wrote in her journal: "This morning I once again glanced over what I had written a few years ago and it made me shiver. I feel it may open some venues to the discovery of my own self-selves." As Jung said, "And if such a person wants to be cured it is necessary to find a way in which his conscious personality and his shadow can live together" (Jung, 1969, para. 132).

Traumatic knowledge is clandestine and not only haunts, but also strikes back to shatter the fictions and façades of Shirin negating and rejecting parts of herself. Kristeva speaks about the notion of the stranger, the foreigner, the outsider who feels alien in a society not their own—as well as the notion of strangeness within the self, or a person's core sense of being. She suggests we touch this otherness, escape its hatred and burden through accepting the differences it implies (Kristeva, 1994, p. 3).

As therapy proceeded, another symbol occurred when Shirin noticed a tree in the yard outside the therapy office with one branch reaching out and leaning on another, giving it support like analyst to analysand. She then mentioned sitting outside my office looking at a monk image in the mountain, reminding her of the hallucinations from the fevers she had as a child. But it also reminded her of when she was imprisoned as an activist years earlier, and seeing a similar mountain outside. The trees meant life and the maternal as trees reach out to protect the new shoots. The mountain was an image of attainment and strength. As we discussed these images, the past and the present became contiguous and meaning started a return to Shirin.

The capacity for growth, development, creative agency, and love is dependent upon existing in the mind, eyes, and gaze of the other in a dance of attuned, rhythmic, and imperfect but sufficient resonance. Shirin dreamt we were working on putting two wooden objects together. It was a gradual process not accomplished with her former quickness of mind but nonetheless forming, taking shape.

The analytic process aims for psychological regulation. In relation to this, Jean Knox, British Jungian analyst, discussed the reflective function for focus on the subjective, intuitive, poetic, and symbolic narrative emerging. This requires the analyst's capacity to link experiences in a meaningful way, resonating with the multiple and sometimes contradictory threads of the patient's narrative in the co-construction of a symbolic space (Knox, 2004, p. 13). From an ill-functioning self that learned to destroy, integration includes the abject, the shadows within both therapist and client as generators for psychic processes.

Summary

The process of individuation means working with the foreign, repressed, and projected material formerly separating self from other, body from mind. For Shirin, the initial despair gave way to dialogue between her mental life and her body, where her psyche had been abjected and imprisoned, making meaning from the autoimmune disease of lupus. The transcendent function emerging through the analytical relationship brought dreams and their symbols accompanied by formerly repressed emotions and traumatic memories. The ruptures eventually led to expansion and growth, opening Shirin to a quieter yet fuller life.

Engagement with the other, abject, and the shadow brings recognition of the self. Kristeva's abject offers to Jungian analysis and trauma studies additional perspective on the recognition of the unwanted but necessary human aspects defining the self. Jung commented, "Relationship to the self is at once relationship to our fellow man, and no one can be related to the latter until he is related to himself" (Jung, 1946/1966, para. 445).

References

Cavalli, A. (2012). Transgenerational transmission of indigestible facts: From trauma, deadly ghosts and mental voids to meaning-making interpretation. *Journal of Analytical Psychology, 57*(5), 597–614.

Connolly, A. (2011). Healing the wounds of our fathers; intergenerational trauma, memory, symbolization and narrative. *Journal of Analytical Psychology, 56*(5), 607–626.

Derrida, J. (2005). *The rogues: Two essays on reason.* Stanford University Press.

Fairweather, D. L. (2004). Women and autoimmune diseases. *Emerg Infect Disease.* Nov. 10(11). doi: 10.3201/eid1011.040367

Fordham, M. (2003). *Explorations into the self.* Karnac Books.

Green, A. (1986). *On private madness*. The Hogarth Press.

Jarrett, J. (Ed). (1998). *Jung's seminar on Nietzsche's Zarathustra*. Princeton University Press.

Jung, C. G. (1916/1969). *The structure and dynamics of the psyche. CW 8*. Princeton University Press.

Jung, C. G. (1928/1970). *Civilization in Transition. CW 10*. Princeton University Press.

Jung, C. G. (1934/1968, 1940/1968). *The archetypes of the collective unconscious. CW 9i*. Princeton University Press.

Jung, C. G. (1944/1968). *Psychology and alchemy. CW 12*. Princeton University Press.

Jung, C. G. (1960), *The Structure and Dynamics of the Psyche. CW 8*. Princeton University Press

Jung, C. G. (1966). *The practice of psychotherapy. CW 16*. Princeton University Press.

Jung, C.G. (1969). *Psychology and religion. CW 11*. Princeton University Press.

Knox, J. (2004). From archetypes to reflective function. *Journal of Analytical Psychology* 49, 1.p. 1–19.

Kristeva, J. (1982). *Powers of horror: An essay on abjection*. Columbia University Press.

Kristeva, J. (1994). *Strangers to Ourselves*. Columbia University Press.

Kristeva, J. (1992*)*. *Black Sun*. Columbia University Press.

Kristeva, J. and Oliver, K. (2002). *The portable kristeva*.: Columbia University Press.

Modell, A. (1996). *The private self*. Harvard University Press.

Singer, T. & Kimbles, S. (2004). *The cultural complex: Contemporary Jungian perspectives on psyche and society*. Routledge.

Solomon, H. (1998). "The self in transformation: The passage from a two- to a three-dimensional internal world", *Journal of Analytical Psychology*, *43*(2), 225–238.

Solomon, H. (2007). *The self in transformation*. Karnac Books.

Introduction to "*Ressentiment*: Its Phenomenology and Clinical Significance"

John White's chapter is the only one to address the question of psychological types. He approaches Jung's notion of the feeling function, which at its heart is about our capacity to differentiate values, through a phenomenological explication of Nietzsche's discussion of ressentiment, as taken up and developed by an early pioneer in phenomenology, Max Scheler. *Ressentiment* is an organizing mood obscured by feelings such as rage or envy, but its hallmarks are impotence, the desire for revenge, loss of any meaningful object relatedness, and an inversion of values. White develops his phenomenology of *ressentiment* in terms of deficit in the feeling function. Because ressentiment is so diffuse, organizing, and often paranoid in its structure, he indicates why it tends to be prominent in personality disorders. He then suggests how the Jungian psychotherapist might be of help, although therapeutic goals may remain more aspirational than met. What is especially interesting is the development of a dynamic understanding of this fateful phenomenon together with therapeutic recommendations based on working with the feeling function.

Chapter 15

Ressentiment

Its Phenomenology and Clinical Significance

John White

Introduction

One of Friedrich Nietzsche's most interesting contributions to philosophy and, I would suggest, to psychology is his description of the nature of *ressentiment*. By *ressentiment*, Nietzsche refers to a specific psychological and emotional phenomenon: an intense, partially unconscious, and in some sense "structural" resentment, one which can become so potent and so definitive an emotional force in the human psyche that it produces substantial deceptions, deceptions both about oneself and about the world. According to Nietzsche, *ressentiment* is "creative," in that it produces false moralities by means of an inversion or transvaluation of values, while simultaneously deforming one's emotional experiences to the point that that value inversion is experienced in some respects as if it is authentic and valid (Nietzsche, 2009).

In this chapter, I will suggest that *ressentiment* is an important and wide-spread clinical phenomenon, that what clinicians often describe simply as "anger" or "rage" is often better understood as *ressentiment*, and that this fact has potentially important clinical and technical consequences. I will begin by describing *ressentiment*, with the help of phenomenologist Max Scheler. Though Nietzsche's descriptions of *ressentiment* are emotionally potent, Scheler better articulates the nature of *ressentiment* phenomenologically and his analyses are far more useful both philosophically and clinically. Second, I will relate Scheler's phenomenological descriptions specifically to Carl Jung's understanding of the "feeling function," since the latter, I will suggest, is particularly afflicted when a person suffers from *ressentiment*. Finally, I will illustrate some clinical issues associated with *ressentiment* through a few fictional but realistic clinical vignettes.

The Phenomenology of *Ressentiment*

Our first step is to describe *ressentiment* according to some general and essential features, which I draw largely from Scheler. Scheler's phenomenological and schematic definition of *ressentiment* is as follows:

DOI: 10.4324/9781032694603-19

Ressentiment is a self-poisoning of the mind which has quite definite causes and consequences. It is a lasting mental attitude, caused by the systematic repression of certain emotions and affects which, as such, are normal components of human nature. Their repression [however] leads to the constant tendency to indulge in certain kinds of value delusions and corresponding value judgments. The emotions and affects primarily concerned are revenge, hatred, malice, envy, the impulse to detract, and spite.

(Scheler, 1998, p. 29)

Thus *ressentiment*, on Scheler's account, is in some way similar to highly charged emotions like anger, rage, fury, and the like. For like those latter feelings, *ressentiment* is generally born of intense emotional energy which, once repressed, may take any number of other emotional forms, often including value delusions and distorted value feelings, both conscious and unconscious. How often a torrent of exaggerated value feelings and judgments flows from our lips when we are in the grip of *ressentiment*! However, *ressentiment* is further defined by certain other distinctive features.

Thirst for revenge, according to Scheler, is the most important source of *ressentiment*, due to the specific nature of revenge. Revenge is characterized first of all as a reaction to being attacked or injured by someone. Nonetheless, reacting to an attack, though essential to revenge, is insufficient to define it: for example, self-defense can also be a reaction to an attack, but it is not revenge. Revenge is, in contrast, characterized by two further features: (1) first, in revenge, the immediate impulse to return the attack is internally checked; (2) Second, this checking of the immediate impulse is motivated by the feeling that one might not succeed, that is., that following through with this aggressive impulse might result in defeat (Scheler, 1998).

This checking of the emotionally charged and often aggressive reaction also gives a distinctive emotional cast to *ressentiment*. For, according to Scheler, the feelings of anger and rage thereby become associated with feelings of incapacity or of impotence, born of the sense that one may not succeed in retaliating, at least in the current moment. Consequently, what might at a conscious and intellectual level be experienced as that kind of "prudence which is the better part of valor," at an affective and partially unconscious level includes an emotional tone of impotence and powerlessness – and, we might add, the potentially devastating blow to self-esteem which can accompany those latter feelings. The affective charge and the acute inrush of energy associated with retaliation is therefore intentionally blocked, the dammed-up energy, over time, becoming the "self-poisoning" to which Scheler refers in his definitional statement.

Scheler sees *ressentiment* as the natural endpoint of a relatively typical emotional process, a series running from desire for revenge, to rancor, then envy, the impulse to detract, spite, and until finally genuine *ressentiment* arises. Each of these emotional contents, on Scheler's account, moves in the direction of *ressentiment* if one does not deal with them psychologically and/or morally and, once that trajectory begins, these feelings often include sufficient emotional force to take over substantial parts of a personality, at least at times. Particularly important here is the part of this series of experiences mentioned above in this paragraph, beginning with the impulse to detract.

Scheler notes that the thirst for revenge typically has a definite object – the person who attacked us – and thus the impulse to vengeance disappears once it is achieved; revenge does not outlast its motives. In contrast, the impulse to detract, as is also true of spite and of *ressentiment* itself, is an attitude which has in some measure become *disconnected from its original motivational objects*: it has freed itself, as it were, from its experiential moorings and thus exists apart from the original motivating object. Since it does not have definite objects, it therefore cannot be satisfied or relieved by this or that expression of detraction. On the contrary

> [the impulse to detract] *seeks* those objects, those aspects of men and things, from which it can draw gratification. It likes to disparage and to smash pedestals, to dwell on the negative aspects of excellent men and things, exulting in the fact that such faults are more perceptible through their contrast with the strongly positive qualities.
>
> (Scheler, 1998, p. 30)

Generally speaking, when intense emotional reactions of this kind gain ground in our personality, we either cannot see the positive in someone or cannot do so without being provoked to envy, detraction, spite, or resentment and therefore tend to underline what is negative about them, ignoring or distorting the positive sides. In the case of full-blown *ressentiment*, the negative impulses often appear unmotivated because the person on whom one vents one's spleen may be totally unrelated to the resentful person – just someone heard about in passing or a character in a movie or a distant celebrity. We all know people, I imagine, who spend their time detracting others, who can't hear about any person or situation which includes positive value qualities without denigrating that person or situation by cynically underlining whatever is negative about them or by devaluing those positive value qualities by extolling others in comparison. In many cases, on Scheler's account, this state of affairs is the result of *ressentiment* and its accompanying feelings of inner scarcity, in contrast to the perceived abundance in others.

In some cases, these feelings can become so large and intense and become so disconnected from definite objects that they virtually *cannot be satisfied by any given situation*; they have, so to speak, become too large and too disconnected from their sources and objects for any specific expression of the *ressentiment* to achieve satisfaction or comprehensive release. Hence the feelings often become a vague "rage against the collective," not so much because the person is concerned about, say, social justice or about someone "undermining the American way of life," but because the *ressentiment* is so large and object-free, that only a virtually indeterminate collective of some sort feels as if it can contain the experience.

This generally vague and vaguely general quality is one of the decisive characteristics of *ressentiment*: *ressentiment*, though originally born of definite experiences of resentment toward definite objects, can grow internally like a psychological infection, a spiritual pus, constantly expanding both in its own magnitude and in the range of real or imagined objects. *Ressentiment* is not a straightforward resentment about this or that event or toward this or that person; such resentments have definite object relationships in both the psychoanalytic and the phenomenological senses and so can be dealt with through straightforward psychological and/or moral effort. They transform into *ressentiment* proper only after a process whereby those feelings lose their motivational moorings and become instead a vaguely general yet potent feeling with no definite object but rather encompassing any or even all possible objects of experience which remind the person of the *ressentiment*. Thus, if unchecked, *ressentiment* can become the general and essential form of a person's emotional life, the dominant feeling tone dominating all other feeling tones, since its undifferentiated nature includes no inner principle of limit.

Value Inversion

The most defining feature of *ressentiment*, however, extends beyond these delineated characteristics, which can in some measure be shared with other emotional reactions such as spite and malice, namely, that *ressentiment* includes an "inversion or transvaluation of values."

Now in English-language philosophies and thinkers, the term "value" tends to have a strongly subjective cast, due, on the one hand, to the influence of Empiricism and Positivism on most philosophical and social science disciplines and, on the other, the fact that consumer capitalism appears to be a stronger cultural dominant in many English-language cultures than it is, say, in Continental European settings. Consequently, "value" often more or less correlates to subjective preferences in English-language thought (White, 2023a). But the German-speaking intellectual world in which both Scheler and Carl Jung wrote about value was deeply imbued, in both its philosophical and sociological assumptions, with a quite different view of value. For each assumed that there is such a thing as *intrinsic values*, that is, values which, as it were, form a part of the furniture of world, and are not merely subjective evaluations and preferences, and which may even form a system of ideal value relationships. This more objective and intrinsic concept of value was already implicit in Nietzsche – a major influence on Jung – and was relatively common in the intellectual milieu in which Jung wrote in the 1920s. By way of example, both phenomenological and Neo-Kantian philosophical traditions and the Southwest German School of social science affirmed such conceptions of value, despite their disparate theoretical articulations of the nature of value. Often, the prototypical examples of value were beauty and moral values of various kinds. When I am touched by the beauty of the starry sky or moved by a noble act of forgiveness or outraged by a callous injustice, it seems somewhat far-fetched to call such experiences mere "subjective preferences." Rather, such experiences seem to transcend my preferences: if anything, they break through my encrusted subjectivity, demanding I rise to the occasion of acknowledging them on their own terms. Value, on this model, is both too objective in its demands and too universal in its impact to be validly reduced to individual personal subjectivity (Scheler, 1973; Von Hildebrand, 2020).

As a way of describing this phenomenon theoretically, we might – following Scheler – posit a general hierarchy or rank-order of value types, such that values come in kinds or categories, united according to certain thematic connections (Scheler, 1973). Scheler, for example, differentiates values of utility, pleasures values, vital values, cultural and political values, and spiritual and religious values, each a categorial type and each category differentiated each from the others. Further, according to Scheler, these categories taken together form a system of connections, such that any given category may be intrinsically higher or lower than another category. For example, Scheler considers pleasure values, that is, values associated with physical pleasure and displeasure, to be a category of values all its own. A different category of value would be what Scheler terms "vital values," those values associated with organic life, for example, with health, physical well-being, psychological flourishing, and so forth. Though each of these categories forms a thematically unified set of values, they also stand in a hierarchical relationship in that, all things being equal, vital values are of a higher order than pleasure values, a point with both psychological and ethical implications. Scheler would argue, by way of example, that pleasure values are legitimate pursuits – ethically legitimate – *insofar as* they do not violate higher categories of value, such as vital values around health and well-being. Yet to pursue pleasure values, let's say the pleasure of smoking, to the extent that it actually *harms* the higher values of life and health, would be, for Scheler, questionable from an ethical standpoint. A cigar here and there is one thing; consistent smoking of such would be another. Such a hierarchical conception also has implications for collectives: by a similar logic, to pursue excessive and unnecessary consumption as a society – usually pursuits of both the utility and the pleasure types of value – to the extent of long-term damage to the environment, a set of higher, vital values, would be ethically questionable (White, 2012).

Whether or not one accepts this theory in all its details, Scheler's idea of a ranking of value types can help us understand *ressentiment*. For if value types have an inherent ranking, it would follow that understanding that ranking could aid us in understanding a relatively healthy feeling function, for the latter is the function, as we will see, associated with the experience of value. Indeed, for Scheler, our moral substance as persons can in part be evaluated by the extent to which we experience, understand, and live according to values in a way that approximates this value hierarchy. But then it also follows that, if there can be distortions in the realm of feeling – feeling being the function by which we experience value – those distortions can in principle result in experiencing value according to a different order, that is, as a value inversion, just what Scheler and Nietzsche posit about *ressentiment*.

Jung and the Feeling Function

Jung's articulation of the feeling function assumes just this sort of analysis of value and, once that is recognized, we can better understand what he asserts about both feelings and values and further what that tells us about the essence of *ressentiment*. When Nietzsche and Scheler refer to an "inversion of values," they each suppose there is something like a rank order among values and that that hierarchical order is significant both emotionally or psychologically and also ethically. They also assume that a person's experiences and perceptions of such values can be modified and distorted, through certain kinds of emotional experiences, such as *ressentiment*. The clinical significance of this latter point hinges in part on the nature of the feeling function, the function through which one experiences values.

What is the feeling function? Jung claims, based on his own empirical observations, that there are four basic functions to the psyche: thinking, feeling, intuition, and sensation, a generally well-known thesis due to the popularity of the Myers-Briggs personality test, though the latter perhaps conceives the functions somewhat differently from what Jung originally had in mind. For there is a discernible tendency to understand these functions as something like "personality traits" rather than the more dynamic range of possible adaptive relationships to one's environment, which Jung understands them to be (Jung, 1971a; Jung 1971b). In clinical experience, one often finds that one's clients have one dominant function, one or two secondary functions, and one or more functions which Jung would describe as an "inferior function," a function significantly less developed than the others. Much of classical Jungian analysis is predicated on recognizing concrete deficits in healthy adaptation due to inferior functioning and consists in aiding one's patient in developing the inferior function (Jung, 1972; White, 2023). Generally speaking, the lesser used a function is, the more unconscious it is, because the psychic energy and structural orientation are therefore latent and not readily available to the ego and conscious psyche.

The feeling function is contrasted to the other functions primarily according to (1) its primary object and (2) the quality of its functional experiences. Regarding the first point, Jung defines the feeling function in part through its having reference to values (Jung, 1971a, para 723 ff.). Jung in fact differentiates the thinking and the feeling functions by, on the one hand, noting that each is "rational" in its orientation – that is to say, they connect directly to the world

– but that whereas thinking relates to the *nature* of things, feeling relates to the *values* of things, an idea suggesting or at least parallel to Scheler's conception of value being an actual part of the world, not a mere placeholder for subjective evaluations. The psychic qualities associated with the feeling function are of course feelings, a specific sort of psychic experiencing comprising distinctively emotional characteristics, clearly differentiated from the kind of experiencing characteristic of thinking, sensing, or intuiting, and presumably further differentiated according to nature and kind, such as love, hate, gratitude, revenge, and so forth. Jung also distinguishes *affect*, which is typically an excess of emotional energy – "excess" here implying that affect does *not* correlate to value and to the value-charged situation – from feeling proper, the latter correlating or being in some sense "appropriate to" the value to which it has reference (Jung, 1971a; White, 2023).

Jung says little about the nature of value and value experience directly, other than to insist that values correlate to feelings and thus to the feeling mode of adaptation, though he does claim that value is experienced in terms of greater or lesser *intensity of feeling*, evidently a way of describing that values are higher or lower in rank while simultaneously using interior, quantitative, and energic terms (greater or lesser intensity). In favor of Jung's usage here is the tendency to speak of "having strong feelings about" something, a phrase suggesting that something is experienced as extremely important or, in other words, ranking very high in value or being a disvalue very much in opposition to a value ranked high.

If this is a sufficient description of the feeling function according to Jung, it aids our understanding of *ressentiment*. For it would suggest that *ressentiment* is not so much a "feeling" in Jung's technical sense of an emotional experiencing correlating to a value as a case of extreme *affect*, and not just the usual affect associated with an activated complex but a kind of affect running amok in a person's emotional life. Rather than correlating to definite values, as a simple case of resentment would, it is rather a kind of affective infection which in essence overwhelms and derails the natural mode of the feeling function, even overlaying healthy value experience to the point that the feeling function itself becomes disengaged from values and value hierarchies and distorts its own experience. We would expect the person whose feeling function has been either partially or totally colonized by *ressentiment* simultaneously to experience just enough of genuine value in the Other to produce, for example, envy, rancor, spite, and resentment but also to *deform* and *overwhelm* that value experience through *ressentiment*, either comparing those good qualities negatively in comparison to someone else's purported values or highlighting purported negative and shadow qualities in the resented person, even if those supposed negative and shadow qualities are actually due to the positive values implicitly perceived but explicitly denied: a straightforward value inversion.

Furthermore, we would expect such a person to live out sets of emotional contradictions due to the predominance of *ressentiment*, such as occasions of a generally sound feeling function alternating with other occasions where their conscious psychological and ethical compass is partially or entirely thrown off amid inexplicable feelings of rage, leading for example to caustic words aimed at a loved one, volcanic and destructive affect around relatively insignificant issues, emotional abuse toward those significant others apparently without provocation, even to the point of possible violence to oneself or others. This latter can occur due to a combination of, on the one hand, the emotional intensity of *ressentiment* having no specific or definite outlet which can satisfy it as well as no inner principle of limitation and, on the other, there being little moral compass to inhibit it, because one's relationship to value and value hierarchies – the basis of one's moral compass and ethical life – is exactly what the experience derails. Consequently, once *ressentiment* is activated, it can be a wide-open question what behaviors will follow.

Clinical Vignettes

I hope this sketch is sufficient to establish the point that *ressentiment* is not just any sort of anger or rage and that it is simultaneously more structural to the feeling function yet less determinate with respect to objects than most emotional experiences – a challenging clinical problem. It is also challenging because, as Scheler points out, collectives often produce *ressentiment*, especially capitalism, which almost inevitably promises more than it delivers, leaving many of those living under its burden feeling impotent to improve their lives significantly – a fertile field for the growth of *ressentiment* (Scheler, 1998; White, 2023a).

The treatment of *ressentiment* is in my experience a tricky business, depending on how deeply rooted the *ressentiment* is. Since feelings of impotence are structural to *ressentiment*, standard psychodynamic procedures looking at the sources of feelings of impotence as well as standard Jungian approaches to the negative parental complexes are often a part of the treatment. However, I find there is a good deal of amnesia around definite historical events which might have engendered *ressentiment* and, more often, only a vague general tenor about its early sources.

Because of the vague generality associated with *ressentiment*, it is often necessary to aid a client to differentiate some particular feeling of resentment which has some definite object, from the general feeling of *ressentiment*. This is not always an easy task, because, depending on its intensity, each single example feels to the patient like a mere confirmation of the larger experience of *ressentiment*. Also, as with all conflicts and ambivalences around the feeling function, it can be a help to clarify the values to which the feelings refer. If capable, showing patients how they are simultaneously recognizing and denigrating the same values can allow the values to become something like an anchor as the client works through the ebbs and flows of feeling conflicts. When the client tends to oscillate between the healthier aspects of the feeling function and the other *ressentiment*-based experiences, it can be important to ally with the healthier place and remind the client of that part of themselves, once *ressentiment* is activated.

The endpoint of treatment of *ressentiment*, in my experience, consists in two generally difficult attitudes for such a person to attain: (1) self-acceptance without self-denigration or self-loathing; (2) forgiveness toward those who may have in fact wounded or betrayed them originally. In the end, it may not be forgiveness proper but a *forgiving attitude*, one which does not let others off the hook for what they are truly responsible for yet one that is willing to feel enough solidarity with them as fellow human beings that one can at least understand their actions. In my experience, these goals are generally more of an ideal to work toward than a certain outcome.

Let me offer some fictional if realistic clinical vignettes in the hopes of adding more clarity to my exposition.

Process example. It is easy to imagine cases in which one sees the process Scheler describes leading to *ressentiment*. Joseph is the newly selected chair of a religious studies department, in which he is the youngest member. Joseph is moderately published (primarily in ethics), a successful teacher, and is a more than adequate department chair, but he has a youthful style which at times provokes some of his older male colleagues to talk and act toward him as if he is younger and more inexperienced than he is. Though Joseph dislikes this situation, these same older male colleagues also treat him as a kind of favored son and golden boy of the department, something he enjoys since he always played second fiddle to his older brother in his family of origin. Joseph is very much a "company man" for his department and his university, and he has some ambitions to become a higher administrator.

However, one older male colleague, Paul, treats Joseph neither as an inexperienced young man nor as a "golden boy," but simply as the department chair and is not invested in the latter's personality. Though active in the department, Paul generally keeps to himself, living an hour away from campus and from his colleagues. While Paul's different style at first did not bother Joseph, he begins to have a growing anger, malice, and finally *ressentiment* toward Paul. Though it is difficult to trace the beginning of these feelings, Paul's not being effusive about Joseph like the rest of his older male colleagues produces some doubt in Joseph. Once Joseph is chair, he sees Paul's class evaluations and begins to envy the latter's popularity. When Joseph reveals that he seeks higher administrative positions, most of his older male colleagues excitedly encourage him as if Joseph is a younger brother, while Paul simply wishes him well. Joseph is enraged and speaks of this to his therapist, who wonders why Paul "only" wishing Joseph well feels like an affront, to which Joseph replies he just "knows" that Paul is thumbing his nose at him. At a later point, Joseph discovers Paul is working simultaneously in another, non-liberal arts discipline, something "not done" in his department, which Joseph angrily interprets to his therapist as a "slap in the face" to him as chair of the department and takes personally. When his therapist questions whether Paul's actions were aimed at Joseph, the latter rages that his therapist "just doesn't understand." His therapist does some "anger management" exercises with Joseph, but though that helps Joseph control some of his behavior, it does not impact the anger itself. Finally, Joseph decides to get his revenge, claiming on Paul's annual evaluation that the latter is doing insufficient work for the department by working in other disciplines. In response, Paul invokes the faculty handbook, which encourages cross-disciplinary work. The situation is brought before the dean, leaving Joseph furious since he wants to become associate dean: he interprets Paul's defense as insubordination and his invocation of the faculty handbook as an attempt to thwart Joseph's hopes at promotion.

In the end, Joseph loses when Paul's case is brought before the dean. When his term is over as chair, Joseph no longer seeks any further administrative positions, saying to his therapist that the university "doesn't deserve his service." Joseph becomes a bitter critic of the university, though speaking only behind the scenes.

While there are many clinical issues here, this is also a typical illustration of the development of *ressentiment*. At the beginning, feelings of envy and rancor develop toward Paul, though it seems doubtful that Paul's actions are intended to harm Joseph at all. Our imagined therapist cannot understand either the intensity of the affect or the exaggerated certainties in Joseph's attitudes, in part because he does not recognize the core feelings of impotence. The intensity of the anger and the questionable interpretation of Paul's activities suggest feelings not correlated to the object – it is an inversion of values – and the disconnect between intense affect and object leaves Joseph too certain about the meaning of the situation. By the time the process is over, Joseph is subject to full-blown *ressentiment*, including finding his *ressentiment* to be too large just for despising Paul and requiring the larger institution of the university to be the vague object of his gigantic rage.

Whereas anger is often an overlay of hurt or disappointment or betrayal, *ressentiment* is more closely associated with feelings of impotence due to having been deprived of something – real or imagined. In fact, it is often easy to miss *ressentiment* in a case like Joseph because he is in a position of power, from which one can wrongly infer that the anger is not born of feeling impotent. Yet his position in practice increases his sense of impotence, because Paul did not bend to Joseph's will. By the time the anger had gone beyond mere envy, the early impulses to *ressentiment* were already doing their "creative" work, producing false moralities – to the point that anything Paul would do would be interpreted through its distorting lens. Though Joseph specialized in ethics, he could not recognize how his own psychological infection was blinding him to his own self-righteousness and to the possibility of a straightforward conversation with Paul and possible forgiveness, the kind of moral work that could have had positive psychological consequences.

Comorbid case. A different case is when *ressentiment* accompanies other specific clinical conditions and diagnoses. Maureen is studying to become a social worker at a Christian college. Maureen had a difficult and abusive family background, having had a father who was judgmental, arbitrary, and critical toward her, and a mother who did little to defend her from her father's ways. Maureen seems something of an anomaly to her friends who have seen both the lighthearted, charming, and generous side that appreciates her Christian faith and her goal of being a social worker but also a different, often furious, aggressive, and critical side that can tear down the very things she otherwise treats as good. Maureen has significant self-esteem issues, can be histrionic around anything negative which happens to her, and can be excessively negative toward the college, finding extreme fault with it in moments of rage. When she is in a rage, people sometimes ask Maureen why she remains at that college if she finds it so bad, to which she responds contemptuously that probably all Christian colleges are that bad, so what's the use of moving on?

As her therapist works with Maureen, she discovers that Maureen's feelings tend to go well beyond what individual events merit, to larger institutions and collectives. If, for example, she is very angry at something happening at the college, her mind quickly goes to criticizing all colleges for being corrupt, or to the entire educational system, or to American culture as a whole. Maureen's feelings seem unduly negative and often overly personalized in that even broad collective forces are interpreted as if some definite person, institution, or organization is intentionally doing things to Maureen, provoking a rage one might expect from a direct and personal affront.

With Maureen, we can see specifically the way in which *ressentiment* both grows beyond the phenomenological proportions of simple anger and becomes so disengaged from objects that its general vagueness and vague generality are among its most decisive characteristics. In my work with patients of this kind, I refer to this as the tendency to "go macro," that is, the rage around the feelings of impotence as well as the distance from the original experiences – in this case of rage toward her father – are so great that every alleged affront is ultimately attributed to larger organizations or even to society in general, often with more than a tinge of paranoia, because the feelings are too large for any immediate object to explain. Many people who suffer from histrionic and borderline sorts of conditions seem particularly susceptible to *ressentiment*, in part because the inner feelings of scarcity lead them to project an extraordinary amount of power and fullness on the objects of their *ressentiment*. Yet the inversion of values is also present here in that Maureen oscillates between valuing her faith and educational ambitions and yet, when *ressentiment* flares up, her experience undermines and exaggerates whatever negatives or disvalues might also be present there.

Case based on collective attitudes. There can also be forms of *ressentiment* that have less to do with personal experiences than absorption in a collective and its values. Robert is a baby-boomer who "made it" as a high-level corporate lawyer and is quite proud and satisfied with his own achievements, considering himself to have "pulled himself up by his bootstraps." As a young man, growing up in the late '50s and early '60s, and beginning law school in the early'70s, Robert had tended to be politically liberal. Yet following the movements to the Right in the Democratic Party of the late '70s and then later influenced by Ronald Reagan, he found himself moving consistently to the Right as well, even as he succeeded more and more in his profession. Religiously, Robert is a Roman Catholic and has become more devout the older he has become.

Now that he is in his late sixties, Robert's wife asked him to go to therapy because he frequently flies off the handle over seemingly unimportant things. When Robert watches the news, he gets uncontrollably furious at government programs for the poor "misusing *his* tax money"; he rages at Catholics who disagree with Church teaching, for example, on the use of birth control, and thus "get away" with doing things that he never allowed himself to do; he seems to be angry at younger legal colleagues simply for being younger and for "having it easier" than he did.

Robert represents, among other things, a widespread form of *ressentiment* often found currently in older and more successful Americans. *Ressentiment* of the old toward the young is not an unusual phenomenon (Scheler, 1998) but is often not a clinically important or intense feeling. However, especially important in Robert's case are the feelings of scarcity and impotence, which turn into *ressentiment* toward others, even toward those who have no apparent connection to Robert's life (Scheler, 1998; White, 2023a). Robert's attitude toward Catholic moral teaching for example suggests *ressentiment*, because he appears more concerned that others are "getting away with things" than any purported value in the moral teaching itself, a clear mark of inner feelings of scarcity. Robert's political trajectory mirrors shifts in the American collective from the '60s to the '80s rooted in collective *ressentiment*, with the idea that tax money is "your" money, rather than a way one is responsible to the collective and the common good, thus evoking a sense of personal affront around its "objectionable" use. Personalization of collective *ressentiment* is something often met with clinically. The inversion of values emerges in him both knowing and being proud that he can count himself successful and yet, when acting from *ressentiment*, he manages to experience himself not as a success but as a victim of the needs of or responsibilities to others.

Conclusion

Ressentiment is, I believe, a widespread clinical phenomenon, one which can appear simply to be some sort of anger or rage, but which has a more definite structure and also more definite indications. Indeed, it may even merit being considered its own syndrome. More often than not, *ressentiment* is seen in (1) implicit feelings of impotence; (2) intense anger, rage, and thirst for revenge becoming progressively more disengaged from definite objects; (3) general vagueness regarding who or what the anger and rage are about; (4) profound feelings of inner scarcity; (5) the experienced inversion of values. Once understood, the therapist should expect that the client's condition will require (as a minimum) (1) recognizing the dynamics of *ressentiment*, (2) allying with the healthier aspects of the feeling function, and (3) clarifying the values which evoke both positive and negative feelings. The ideals of self-acceptance and of a forgiving as well as self-forgiving attitude are also goals of treatment, but often remain only ideals throughout.

References

Jung, C. G. (1971a) *Psychological types. Psychological types. Collected works*, vol. 6. (R. F. C. Hull, Trans.). Princeton University Press.

Jung, C. G. (1971b) Psychological types. In *Psychological types, collected works*, vol. 6, Trans. R. F. C. Hull, (Princeton University Press).

Jung, C. G. (1972) On psychic energy. In (R. F. C. Hull, Trans.). *The structure and dynamics of the psyche. Collected works*, Vol. 8. Princeton University Press.

Nietzsche, F. (2009). *On the genealogy of morality: A polemic*. (M. Clarke & A. Swensen, Trans). Hackett Pub. Co.

Scheler, M. (1973). *Formalism in ethics and non-formal ethics of values: A new attempt toward the foundation of an ethical personalism*. (M. S. Frings & R. L. Funk, Trans. & Eds.). Northwestern University Press.

Scheler, M. (1998) *Ressentiment*. (M. S. Frings, Trans. & Ed.). Marquette University Press.

Von Hildebrand, Dietrich. (2020). *Ethics*. Ed. J. Crosby. Hildebrand Press.

White, J. (2012). "Person and environment. Vital sympathy and the roots of environmental ethics". In (M. Sanders & J. J. Wisnewski, Eds.). *Phenomenology and ethics*. (pp. 221–240). Lexington Books.

White, J. (2023). *Adaptation and psychotherapy. Langs and analytical psychology*. Rowman & Littlefield.

White, J. (2023a). Colonizing the American psyche. Virtue and the problem of consumer capitalism. In *Critical theory and psychoanalysis. From the Frankfurt School to contemporary critique*. Ed. Jon Mills and Daniel Burston (pp. 211–230). Routledge.

Introduction to "From Grievous to Grief"

Questions of personal, institutional, and structural racism, ancestral memory, and the weight of history have become increasingly present over the past several years. After George Floyd was murdered in Minneapolis in May 2020, Black Lives Matter marches sprung up not only in the United States but around the world. The legacy of racism and slavery has emerged as subject matter for psychoanalytic enquiry as well. Object relations are ancestral relations, since our epigenetically inherited and internalized parents ("objects") are themselves relational and historical in the structure of their identities, and so with their parents, stretching back through generations. Racial complexes reach through personal and collective levels of unconsciousness. It must be admitted we all share them too, since we swim in the same linguistic and imaginal sea. Fanny Brewster, one of the few African American Jungian psychoanalysts, draws from her own experience, with its history, to reach through layers of justifiable grievance, with its self-preservative and, yes, defensive intent, to a grief that might finally be healing and liberating. She finds in grief an open heart, an opening to the soul, through which we can meet each other in the fullness of our humanity. Of special note in this chapter is Dr. Brewster's seamless integration of (Jungian) psychology, cultural anthropology, and sociopolitical history in the way she thinks about analytic work.

Chapter 16

From Grievous to Grief*

Fanny Brewster

Wade in the Water

I think it would be safe to say that we are living during a time of racial psychological turbulence. Stormy weather. It has taken centuries to arrive at this place
of opportunity for deepening conversations without a physical war between
opposing parties. This time it appears that we can face one an(Other) with
more openness and willingness to see. We are "woke."

The willingness to be open and speak the truth of our racial and cultural
divide within the society has taken centuries. It is longer than one hundred
years since the end of the American Civil War. It is also one hundred years
since C. G. Jung came to America, visiting with William Alanson White as well
as what the latter considered to be dream research with fifteen Black men at St.
Elizabeths Hospital in Washington, D.C. This study according to Jung proved
the basis for his theory of the Collective Unconscious.

Modern Psychology is to have given us a different way of considering ourselves as human beings. It was to have moved us beyond just seeing the surface
needs of our lives but offered us a journey to the depths of our understanding.
A travel to the Unconscious. Freud's work and later Jung's and the other men
of those early days of beginning psychological studies were based in social and
cultural traditions of Europe. These roots formed the foundations of American
psychology. Freud visited America only once, in 1909. He vowed never to
return. During that trip C. G. Jung, a close colleague, was also invited to attend
the twentieth anniversary celebration of Clark University. Unlike Freud, Jung
returned to America on three later occasions. One of these times was for the
month-long visit to Washington, D.C.

Jung was curious about psychology and the culture of others in a way that
Freud never ventured into the waters to explore. The former was intrigued by
the oceanic waves and psychological undertow of the Unconscious. This was a
place that Freud saw as dangerous and in need of having its contents repressed.

* Segments previously published in Courage and Fear: Weathering the Collective Racial Storm.
  The Psychoanalytic Review, 109(1), March 2022. Reprinted with permission of Guilford Press.

DOI: 10.4324/9781032694603-20

Jung wanted to go there. To explore the depths of this place as much as he could, and because of it we have his own confrontation with the unconscious written about in his autobiography and developed further in *The Red Book*.

As Jung chose to develop his working theories, it became more powerful and engaged with by Europeans and eventually Americans. The most obvious lack of engagement of these theories extended to people of Africanist origin. The ocean waters that brought millions of Africans to the American shores of North and South America also brought the tears and grief of this African Holocaust—Middle Passage. All that followed, up until today, some of it addressed and much still hidden in the American psyche Shadow, haunts us in the form of racism. This is of course not only reflected in Jung's theories but is what we have come to understand as American institutional racism. As we try to catch our breath from the last two years of near-social drowning caused by the murder of George Floyd, Breanna Taylor, Ahmaud Arbery, we are trying to learn more about our racial relations. American Jungian psychology can share some of what it knows to support our heterogenous society but yet must recognize and define its applicability to individuals of color. The Eurocentric focus of Modern Psychology works in some ways for Africanist people but has culturally failed for the most part.

The history of psychiatry and psychology has been inundated with the institutional racism of all other American institutions. The most recent apology by the American Psychological Association directly addresses how embedded racism was within the structure of its own organization.

This is not to accuse it of intentional racism but rather an unconscious racism that just "is," that just lives because it always has and will not be eradicated until we can speak about it and feel the pain and grief of what it has caused to our American society. We must wade in the water of our unconsciously racialized self, moving toward a shoreline that holds equity as an attribute of our ethnically diversified society. We are not in the nineteenth century, at the beginning stages of colonization and the thinking of a *colonial psychosis* that remained in existence past the days of the Middle Passage. Our twenty-first century societal vision for how we can be better in terms of diversity, equity, and inclusion continues to emerge. And there is cultural pushback. I consider this an aspect of white culturalism with its embeddedness of racist ideas that has always for the most part refused to accept that Africanist culture is worthy of value. This lack of cultural value entered and survived within psychological theory and practice (mostly because Africanist people did not go for white medical care). In this moment of what has become confrontational on the political stage it has also become more into our wake state consciousness that we cannot continue to be asleep in the waters of an unconsciousness that supports color blindness, valued ethnic differences and racist actions against BIPOC citizens.

I believe that we are seeing more into Jung's perspective of not only the archetypal power of the unconscious but also the psychological complexes of the personal unconscious that drives us emotionally. These complexes can be parental, guilt, money – and, as I have proposed, racial (Brewster 2020).

Jung, in the early stages of development of the Word Association Experiment, that later has become the Word Association Test, noted personality traits that he later defined as psychological complexes. The specific complex in which he described a racialized complex that he called a "color complex" only indicated for Africanist people that they wanted to be white.

They wanted to negate their skin color. This was basically his reference to African Americans and this particular complex. In my own work I have attempted to deepen Jung's idea regarding the racial complex. This was significant to his theoretical approach – to make the unconscious conscious, to increase conscious awareness. This he suggested was a true path to healing us of our neurotic compulsions brought on by psychological complexes. These compulsions are combined with archetypal energies and emotions that cannot be predicted and oftentimes cast the individual into a "blind" space as to their behaviors. We can be taken over by our complexes and have moments of amnesia. Sometimes we say, "I don't even remember saying that or doing such and such." These are moments where the complex dominates ego consciousness. I suggest that these moments can happen collectively and with groups that form and are led unconsciously by philosophical ideas. When these ideas are driven by a racial complex then within the collective we must bear witness to the physical harm and even death of another.

Dr. Martin Luther King once said that we may all have arrived on different ships, but we are all in the same boat now. This is especially true for this significant moment as we re-visit racial relations in America. This is also relevant because we are not only political beings but are psychological first and foremost. We have ego needs and a consciousness as well as those forces that we swim in from unconscious waters.

We are at a moment when we can become stronger swimmers or collectively drown, once again, in our inability to see the possibilities of racial justice and equity that await us on the shores. We must all be free, or none will survive and have peace.

Letting My Heart be Broken: Tears of Grief

What does it truly mean to be a person? To be part of a cultural group that you call your own, where they can claim *your* person? What is it to have grievous as a part of this personhood?

In the Foreword to Dr. Robert D. Romanyshyn's book *The Soul in Grief*, Thomas Moore says this: "How important our mourning is, and how blind our ways of desperately seeking distance from our melancholy!" (Romanyshyn, 1999, p. XX).

My first impulse when considering grievousness is to be in that defensive place, to take a stand against something – to have my psychological complexes satisfied with the release of an emotion. Disappointment perhaps, frustration, but not melancholy. I have come to believe that which is grievous, which holds the beginning words of grief, must also *contain* grief. They reflect upon one another and seem to need one another. I think this more recent understanding allows me to breathe, at least in this moment. I *can* take a breath. I can fall more softly and readily into the grief of that which is grievous. The expectations of an Other is not here – only my reverberating memories of something that might have happened back in my history that was a grievous offense to my personhood. However, I wish I could rest comfortably on this threshold. Discussions of raciality – this reference to identity – always cause discomfort, within our persons.

There is an Other who watches, waits to see how the language flows, the ideas, the energy in the field. This is one of the definitions of being an Other in the American psyche. Always bearing witness. Then there is learning how to be comfortable in the discomfort.

Yes, this *is* something to be grievous about. White privilege does not have to consider this place of the grievous in terms of most things because belonging and owning can be a natural part of personhood.

Even when the privilege of "whiteness" is not acknowledged due to a strong sense of social justice, intently desirous of fairness for the Other – the person of color, I do not think we can remove ourselves from the attractive pull of the imaginal. Perhaps it is not being in the present moment, the "lived" moment, but rather the fantasy of what we have come to know of the Other through centuries of "living" together and creating false narratives.

How do we embrace the Africanist personhood that is us, as the individual, when society's oppression has said this is disallowed? Even American psychology, and its inheritance of Jungian psychology, says that we, those of African descent, will be together because of *participation mystique*. In this constructed language, the grouping of Africans, the ancestors, there is no space for the individual. None for individuation. The meaning of being a person, within a village of other kin and family, translated into Eurocentric psychology, meant a decrease in human consciousness. A fall into unconsciousness, without a possibility for redemption due to ethnicity, unless you were white, only then you *could* individuate. *Participation mystique*.

How does personhood live within an Africanist consciousness? Without reference to a white Other?

Thinking about the formulation of a lived moment, knowing that it will encompass all that I can possibly speak of, my beingness in that moment, where does my identity go, what are the boundaries of the phenomenological field? What reflects back to me?

Franz Fanon (1965) says the following when describing Muslim women freed from the veil:

> Without the veil she has an impression of her body being cut up into bits, put adrift; the limbs seem to lengthen indefinitely … The unveiled body seems to escape, to dissolve. She has an impression of being improperly

dressed, even of being naked. She experiences a sense of incompleteness with great intensity. She has the anxious feeling that something is unfinished, and along with this a frightful sensation of disintegrating.

(Fanon 1965, p. 59)

The loss and re-gaining of self, personhood, is a repetitive experience being in and of a black body. My skin color is a part of this personhood that does not have the privilege of forgetfulness born of being white. What makes me human to another Africanist individual, a person, is not only our shared cultural lineage but also the personal and personalized ways in which we have come to know one another. This happens because we have spoken together. We have shared not only the cultural experience, the ancestral DNA of cultural trauma. We have shared a single moment or two or ten, even more, of looking into each other's eyes and being naked. We have let fall our defense because we can see each other's personhood without fear of being cast into a role that only sees skin culture, and the tortuous signifier of *all* that means in the American psyche. The gaze of being in that one-to-one lived moment can search and find a place to rest that is not usually given, freely available in the eyes of an Other, when there are ethnic differences. Here, trust cannot be felt. It cannot be seen, and so what falls into space and time is the distrust born of all the centuries following slavery. The lived moment cannot exist without the psychological deadness of former lost lives appearing like apparitions, blocking the view. Blocking a vision for whatever may become possible in a future lived moment.

Can an Africanist person have a truly lived moment of trust with someone of a different ethnicity and *without* the consciousness of racialized pain?

One deeply personal task for the person of color, the person of interest of whom I speak, is finding the birthright of humanness that comes as freely as taking a breath. This is also the challenge. It matters that the centuries of slavery and the years past have spoken and taken so *much to heart* the bestiality of how we were made to appear.

The twenty-first century, right now, demands that we re-visit the painful past of Africanist persons made into beasts of labor. To not acknowledge this history keeps us in a moment of history, locked into lies. It will not promote healing, truth, or trust. Stories of African ancestors who worked from before dawn to sunset have yet to be fully told. Should there be no honoring of these individuals for all that they lost over the centuries? Do we not *honor* them by acknowledging their pain experienced *through* the centuries?

When we consider how to emerge from the shadow of an imposed *participation mystique* and claim personhood, Africanist people will consider the layering of our ethnic history.

The amount of time, the words, the actions, the economics of slave labor, the whip. These and more, unfortunately, and horribly, demand recognition. But this demand is also of the ancestors, the ones before us who truly paid the price for us, their twenty-first century descendants.

Jung in listing the four necessary requirements for good psychological work, I believe of the *soul's work* to proceed, spoke first of confession. Some are just now in our societies beginning to see confession as a necessary means to a societal racial healing. Justice is served first by *seeing* and acknowledging that which has caused suffering and injury. This I believe is to be in this moment, to feel into *this* moment and to endure the lived moments of those who have been injured.

We do not even have to go back to 1840 or 1953, any of those times with lynching or discrimination against American black soldiers fighting wars of freedom over there and returning to none over here. We can be in this moment – the times demand it, to be here, living through this experience. Black lives do *still* matter.

How does each person of color bear witness to their humanity, the continuous alchemical exchange of grievousness to grief?

I believe there are those moments of quiet intimacy with oneself that a white Other may not even believe can exist. Negative racialized narratives may have hidden the truth for the entire lifetime. It seems that we could not know each other through the centuries because the biased stories kept us apart. Apartheid, medical apartheid, Jim Crow. All the centuries when we could have been looking into each other's eyes instead of having to cast our Africanist eyes down and walk in the gutters. This reality of suffering cannot be ignored and yet it is not all there is because each of us is also bound by an interiority of soul. This cannot be taken away or cast aside even by the individual as suffering occurs. It is the deeper movement into the grief and suffering that allows soulfulness to escape. That allows for the purity of grief to be free.

This is the true dance, a dance of love, self-forgiveness, and worthiness that takes place inside and eventually seeks an outward direction. Dr. Robert D. Romanyshyn in his book *The Soul in Grief* says the following:

Grief and mourning are not only psychological conditions. They are also cosmological opportunities. When out of lament we praise the world, we release those things that we praise into their larger domain and with their release we win our own, as well as the release of the one who has died. Why is it that the soul in grief can eventually begin to sing the praises of the world? Why is it that the soul in grief can feel an expansion of love which reaches to the stars? These are the mysteries to me.

(Romanyshyn, 1999, p. 109)

I want to allow for these mysteries. I was birthed into this world, my human self, brought forth and held by my midwife grandmother's hands. My soul entered and was joined by that of my mother and my grandmothers and all of my foremothers. My soul sought something else with which to join in addition to my human family. It found itself years later circling a myth of Icarus because of my human desire to create reveries of life as a writer. Romanyshyn again in the *Soul in Grief*:

> Reverie is a surrender of the desire to know things so that we might once again, at least for a moment, be with them. A knowing which springs solely out of utility always needs and wants to do something with what it knows. Reverie is a way of being present to the world which wants nothing and needs nothing from things. In this respect, it is so much like the world of grief, when I wanted nothing because I was nothing.
>
> (p. XX)

Most often when I write poetry it feels to be a space very similar to, if not exactly like, a state of reverie. When I think about courage and fear, feeling into my own, I know that these aspects of my emotional body also reflect an archetypal DNA. Writing can also come from that place.

The following poem was inspired by the celebrated Nigerian poet Remi Raji.

Poem

We have just survived (following Remi Raji's "My Country is Bereaved")

Those of us descendants of Yemanjá
Her waters bear us through the depths of waves,
Carry us on wooden planks,
Stand us on the boards of auctions,
while white voices rattle our worth in a foreign tongue.
We have just survived
the days of dirt, hoed and raked
through the fields of cotton whiteness
bearing us forward one day,
one hundred days
one hundred years
another hundred years.

We have just survived
the bullwhip
the rope
the gun
as our eyes look back
always to our Motherland.

The last drop of us Diaspora
we are washed,
beyond imagination,
into our blackness.
We take breath now
from the howling winds
sent across the ocean waters.
                    (Fanny Brewster)

References

Brewster, F. (2020). *The Racial Complex: A Jungian perspective on culture and race.* London: Routledge Publishers.

Fanon, F. (1965). *The wretched of the Earth.* New York: Grove Press.

Romanyshyn, R. (1999). *The soul in grief: Love, death and transformation.* Berkeley: North Atlantic Books.

Index

Pages in *italics* refer to figures and pages followed by 'n' refer to notes.

For Product Safety Concerns and Information please contact our EU
representative GPSR@taylorandfrancis.com
Taylor & Francis Verlag GmbH, Kaufingerstraße 24, 80331 München, Germany

www.ingramcontent.com/pod-product-compliance
Lightning Source LLC
Chambersburg PA
CBHW050638280326
41932CB00015B/2691

9 781032 694993